"Frank's investment in future generations
of architects is his greatest asset—his legacy,
monumental body of work, and philosophies
to educate, inspire, and influence."

—Robert Tannen

This book accompanies the exhibition

Frank Gehry and Robert Tannen: Art, Architecture, & Ideas
at the Ohr-O'Keefe Museum of Art, Biloxi, Mississippi

April 13 - July 6, 2024

Designed by Virginia Walcott

Museum photography by Bobby R. Harrison
Museum photography assistant Robert C. Harrison
Tannen residence photography by Virginia Walcott

ISBN: 9798991223447

Library of Congress Control Number: 2025936954

Printed in China

This publication is supported by The Ohr-O'Keefe Museum of Art
and funded in part by the Community Foundation of Alabama.

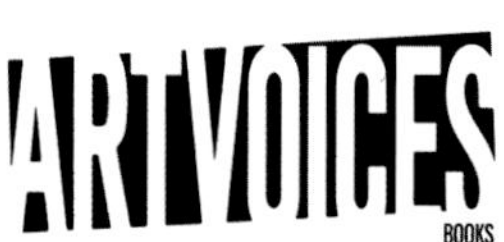

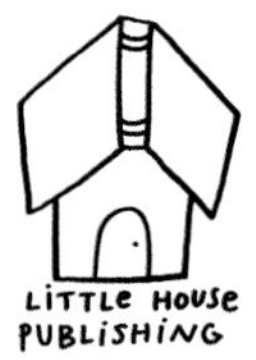

www.artvoicesbooks.com www.littlehousepub.com

Frank Gehry & Robert Tannen: Art, Architecture, & Ideas

Ohr-O'Keefe Museum of Art | April 13 - July 6, 2024

This exhibition was organized by Gehry Partners, LLC
and the Ohr-O'Keefe Museum of Art

Curators: Samuel Gehry and David Houston

Texts by

D. Eric Bookhardt
Frank Gehry
David Houston
Robert Ivy
Shawn Kennedy
Susan Lengen Henning
Kristine McKenna
Jeanne Nathan
Adolfo Nodal
Terrence Sanders-Smith
Robert Tannen

Designed by Virginia Walcott
Museum photography by Bobby R. Harrison
Museum photography assistant Robert C. Harrison
Tannen residence photography by Virginia Walcott

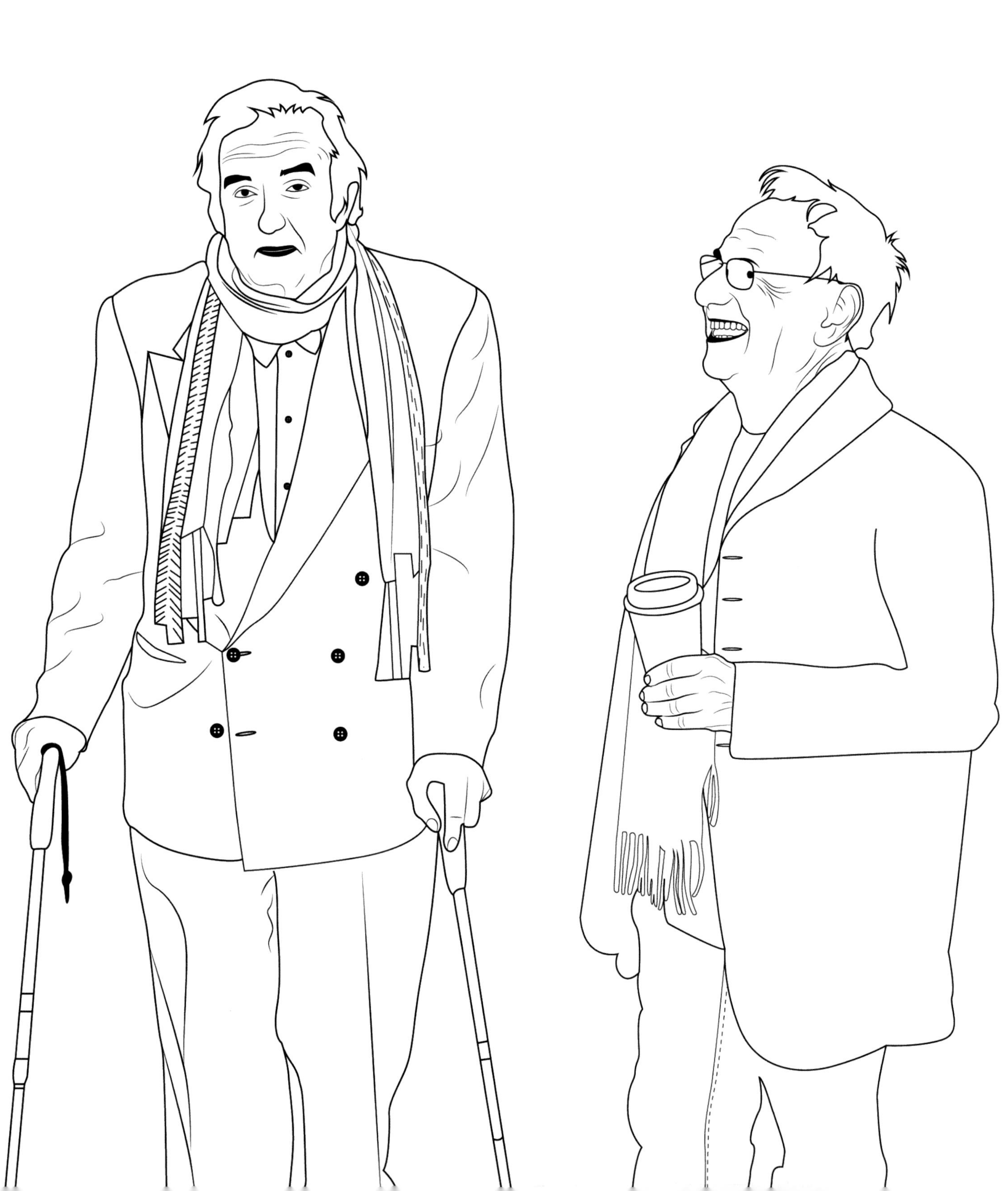

Frank Gehry & Robert Tannen:
Art, Architecture, & Ideas

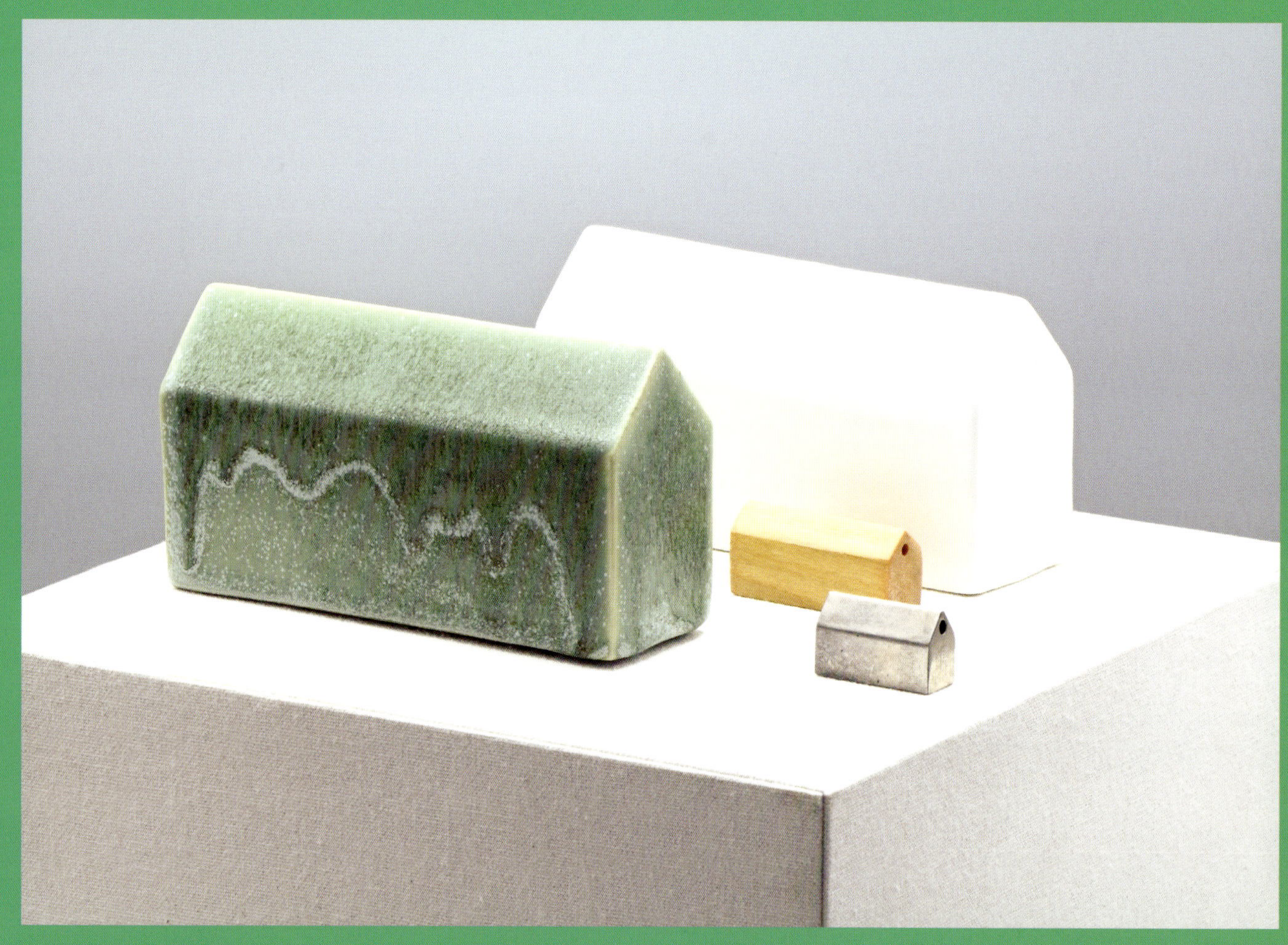

SHOTGUN HOUSES AND JEWELRY DESIGNED BY ROBERT TANNEN
HOUSES MADE BY JOHN HODGE, JEWELRY MADE BY MIGNON FAGET

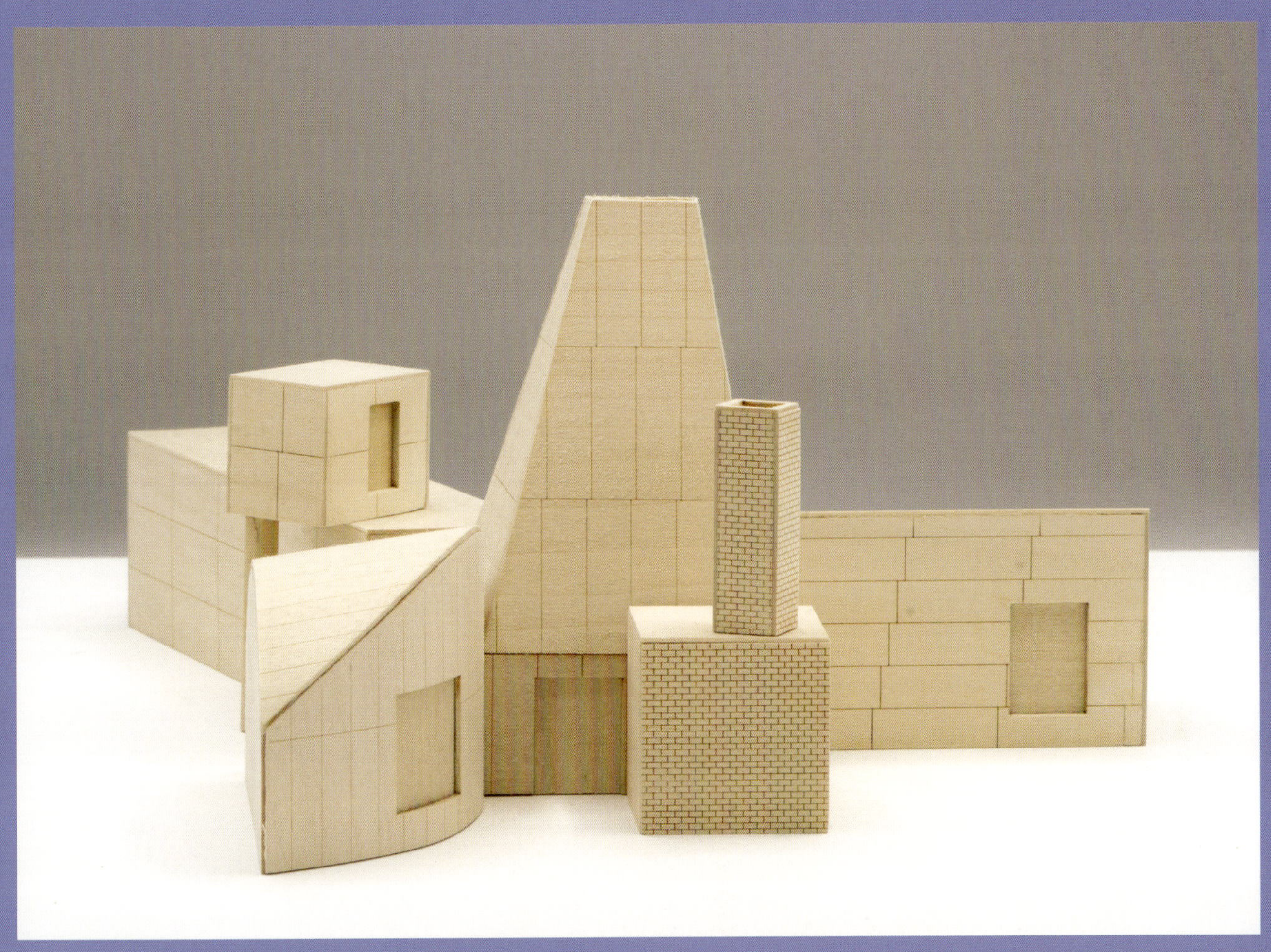

WINTON GUEST HOUSE (1982)
FRANK GEHRY

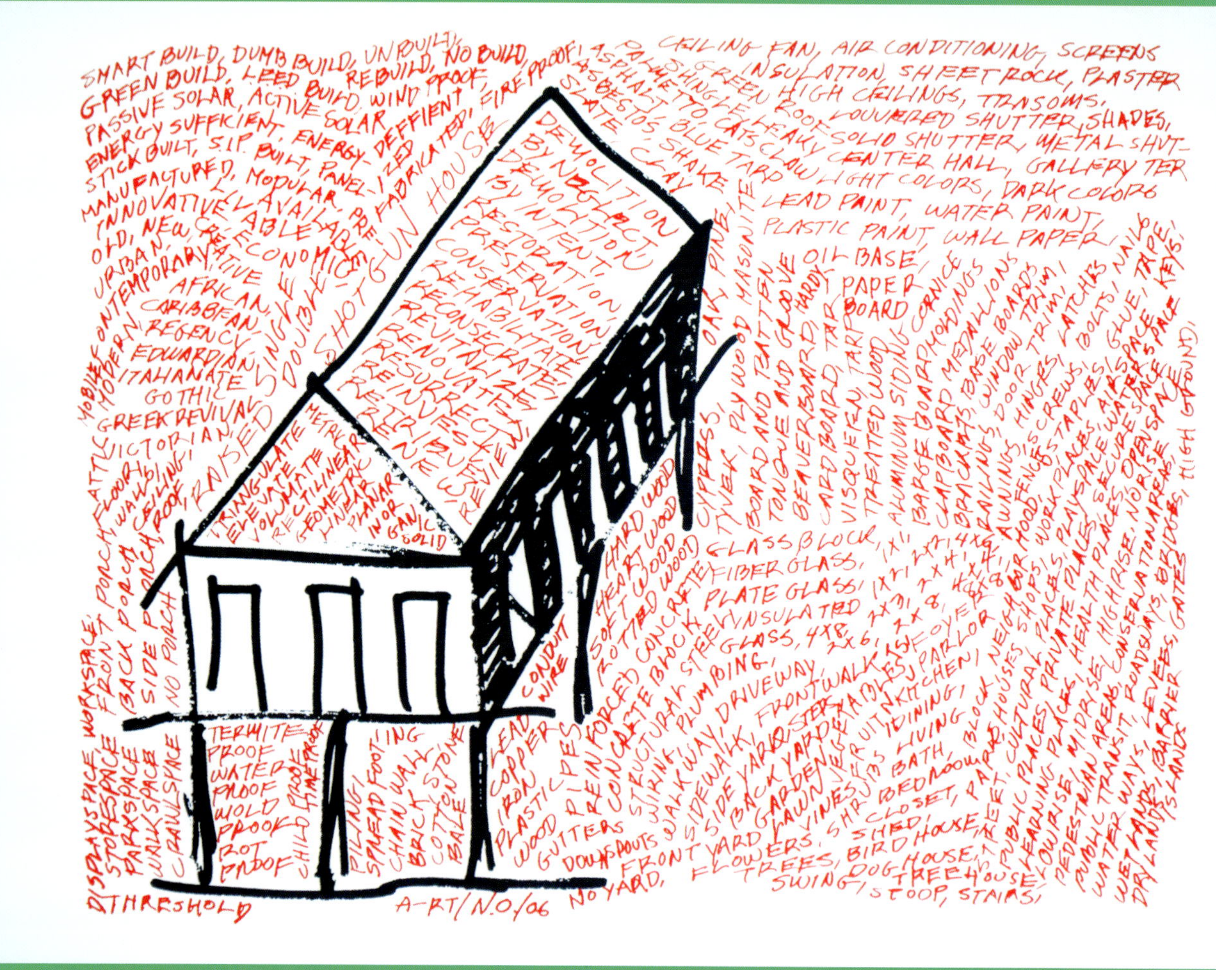

POST-HURRICANE KATRINA RAISED SHOTGUN PRINT & PROPOSAL (2006)
ROBERT TANNEN

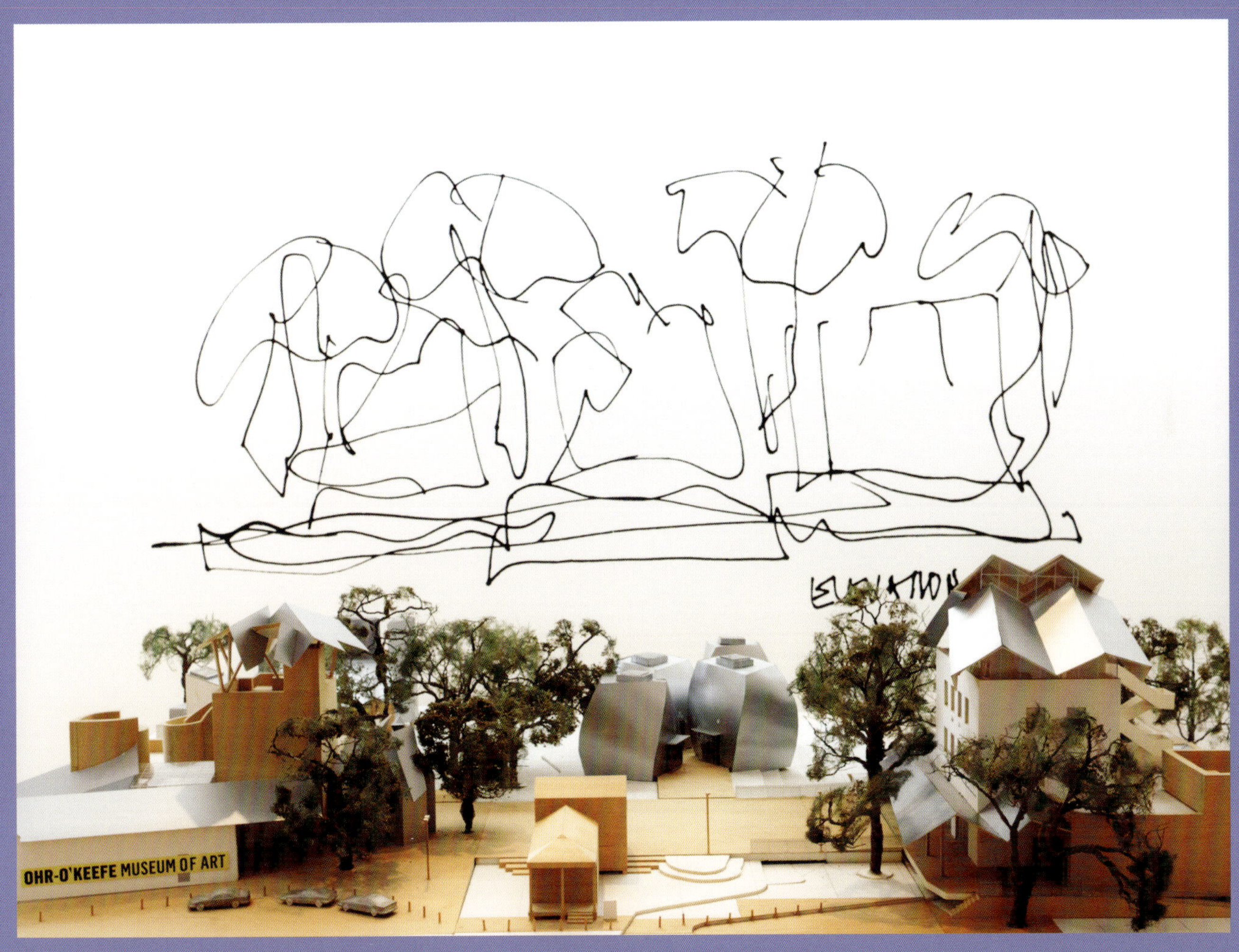

THE OHR-O'KEEFE MUSEUM OF ART
FRANK GEHRY

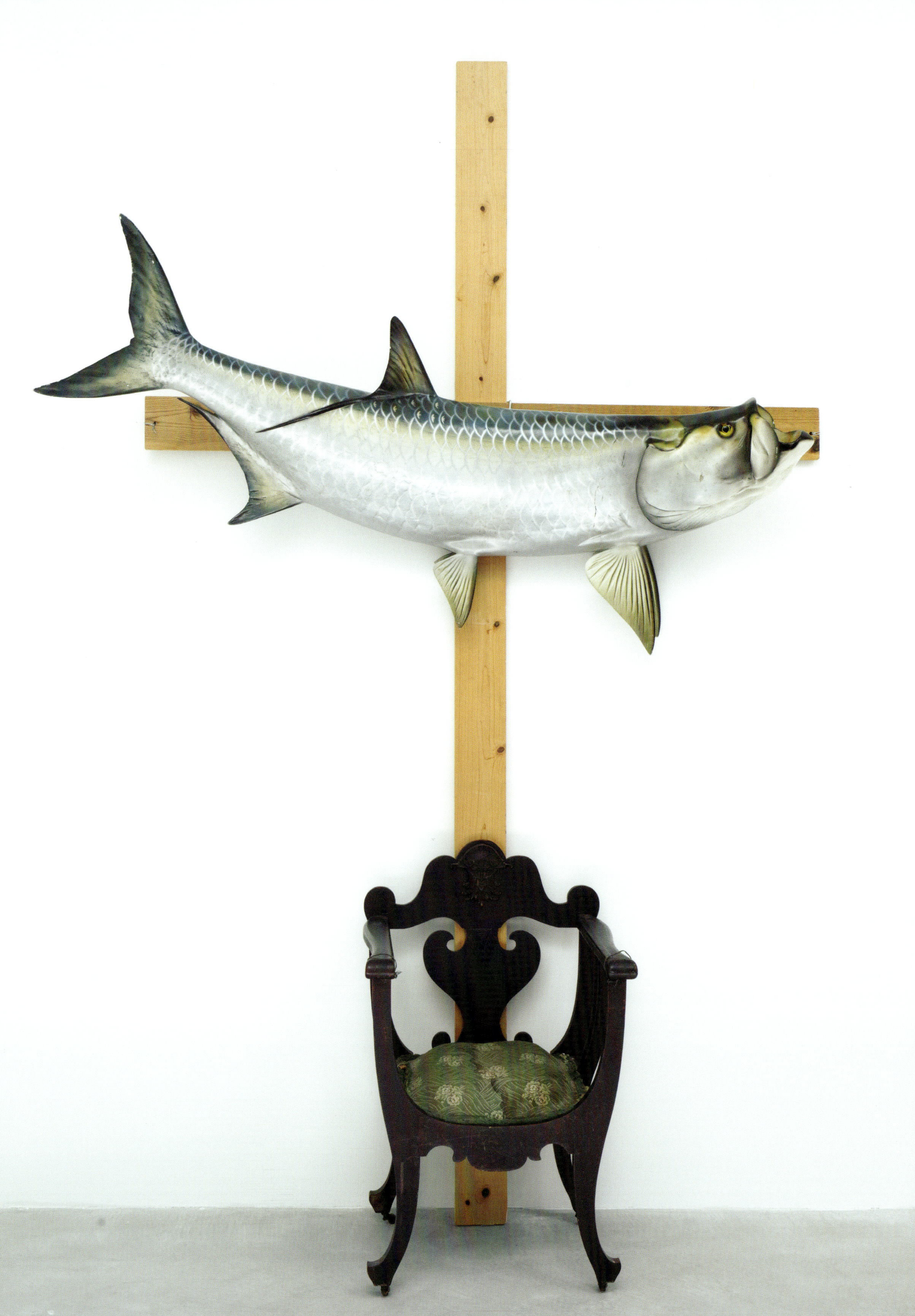

Table of Contents

LEFT: *CRUCIFISH*, ROBERT TANNEN (1975)

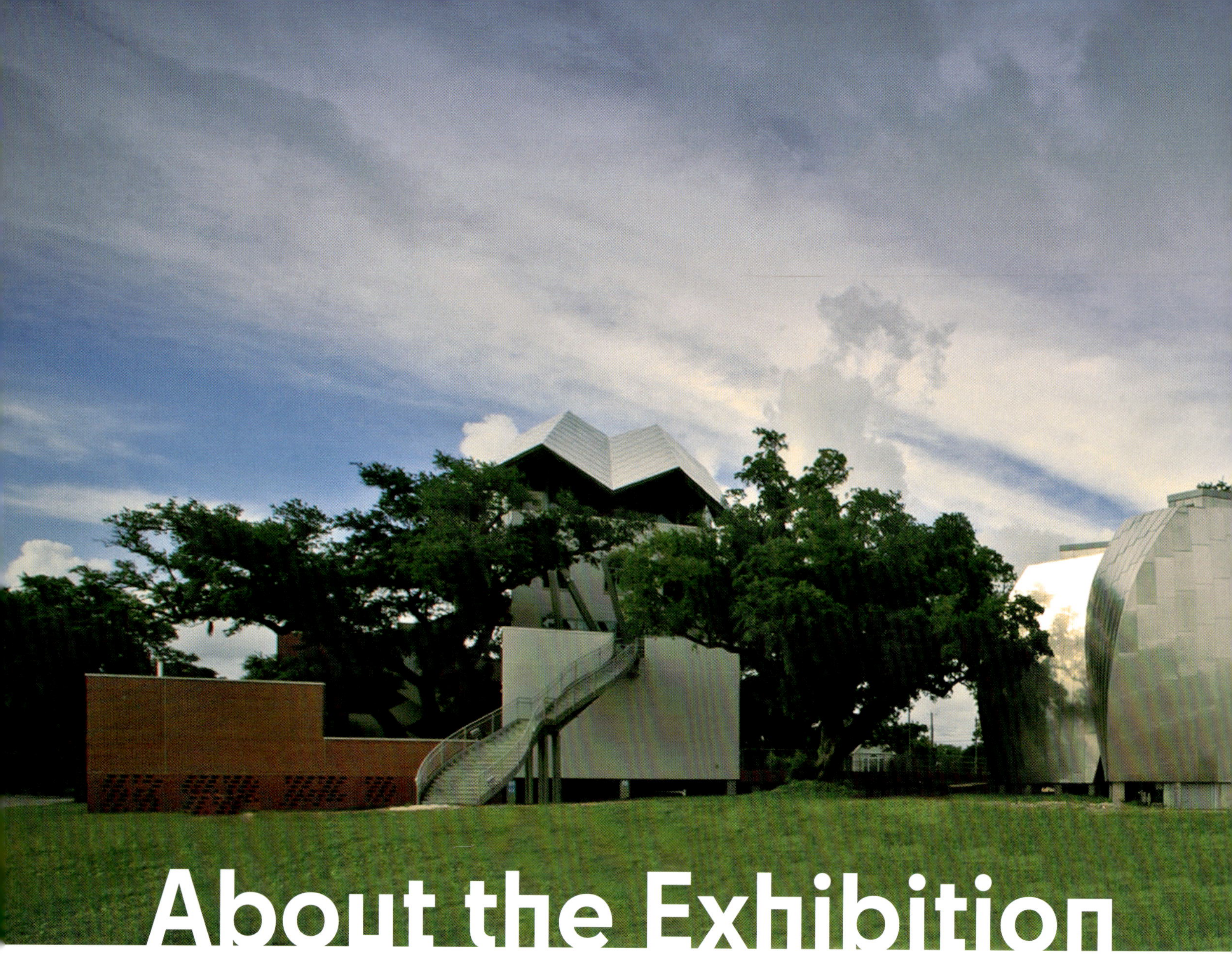

About the Exhibition

Text by David Houston
Executive Director, Ohr-O'Keefe Museum of Art

Art, Architecture, & Ideas: Frank Gehry and Robert Tannen

brings together over five decades of work in a range of media, including architectural models, sculpture, painting, printmaking, urban planning, and product design. Recognized as the defining architect of our times, Frank Gehry changed the cultural landscape with his designs for the Walt Disney Concert Hall in Los Angeles and the Guggenheim Museum in Bilbao, Spain. At ninety-six years old, his architectural and art practices continue to evolve through the exploration of energy and dynamic movement.

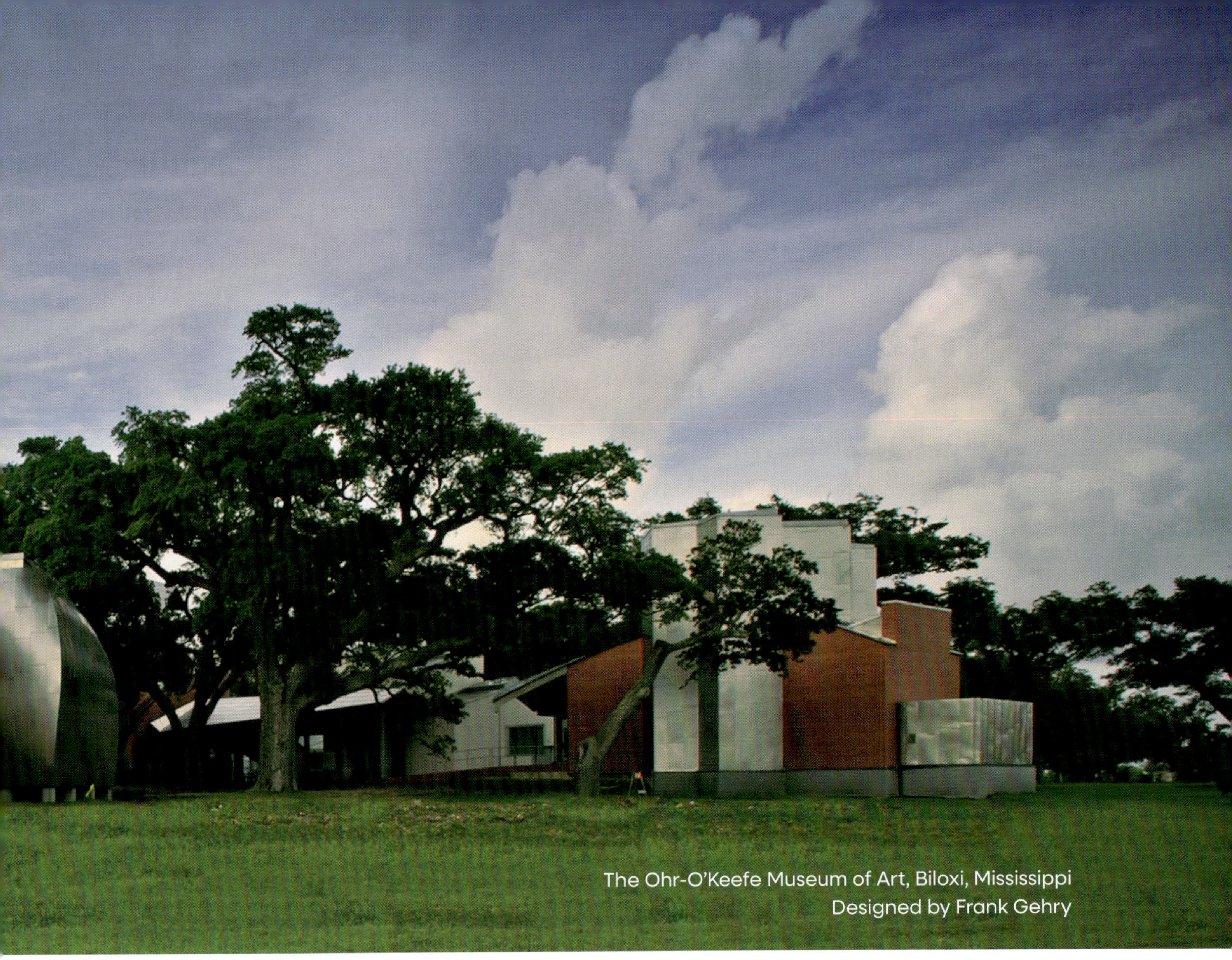

The Ohr-O'Keefe Museum of Art, Biloxi, Mississippi
Designed by Frank Gehry

Robert Tannen's career includes sculpture, painting, conceptual art, and urban planning. After coming to Biloxi, Mississippi to create a masterplan for the Gulf Coast post-Hurricane Camille, he relocated to New Orleans where he master planned the second span of the Mississippi River Bridge, was a founder of the Contemporary Arts Center, and continues his distinctive practice of urbanism, art, and community activism.

Frank Gehry and Robert Tannen's work have intersected with major projects, built and unbuilt, in New Orleans, the Biomuseo in Panama, and the Freeman house in Pass Christian, Mississippi. Tannen, and his partner, Jeanne Nathan, were also instrumental in the choice of Frank Gehry as the architect of the Ohr-O'Keefe Museum in Biloxi, Mississippi, Gehry's only museum in the Southeast.

My friend, Frank

INTERVIEW BY TERRENCE SANDERS-SMITH (2025)

TERRENCE SANDERS-SMITH: After your first meeting with Frank Gehry in New Orleans, what professional and personal characteristics did you find endearing about him as you two became closer friends?

ROBERT TANNEN: Frank and I shared the same philosophy of thinking and making things. That invention and innovation, as opposed to repeating ideas that others had created, was important. That there was no orthodoxy for architecture or regional planning. It was important to find a way of dealing with the issues, whether the issue is a client who wants a building, or a regional plan for an area. We both begin with our own ideas. Frank and I found a common place where his work and my work were understandable to each other and appreciated.

SMITH: Looking back with hindsight being 20/20, what's the connective tissue that keeps you both invested in each other over the decades?

TANNEN: We both look for common interests and opportunities. We usually begin with a conversation about issues in the world, or the place where we're focusing on. For example, he wanted to do a museum in Panama where his wife is from, but he didn't want to get involved in the politics of Panama. So, he hired my wife, Jeanne, and me to go to Panama to work with the Panamanian government. Frank wanted to use one of the military facilities that had been returned to Panama by the United States. He wanted to build an ecological museum and wanted us to convince the Panamanian government of the benefits of such a museum. In the case of Panama, it was a strategy to have a specific tourist attraction which would present the ecological history of Panama to its visitors, residents, and citizens. We worked with several governmental agencies, local architects and engineers. Jeanne and I wanted to find a way to make the museum happen so that it would be funded by the people and the government of Panama, as opposed to a US-run institution. We were successful working with the government of Panama through several administrations. The result of our collective efforts is that there is an ecological museum in Panama.

SMITH: Is there a particular project or design by Frank that you are the most impressed by that exhibits his genius?

TANNEN: There are two. One was his home where he used traditional materials. He had a Los Angeles cottage that he turned into a three-dimensional sculpture using materials that were not necessarily meant for residential structures. For example, he renovated the kitchen with a floor that was made of asphalt as opposed to being wood or tile. That's just one example. He used unconventional materials and ideas to create this dwelling that he and his family would occupy. He began with a traditional Los Angeles home and turned it into a new kind of place to live in and occupy, which is an example of what I said earlier: he reinterprets the idea of a house by approaching it not as a traditional idea of a house, but as a new kind of structure that still functions as a residence or as a home. Also, the Guggenheim Museum Bilbao he designed

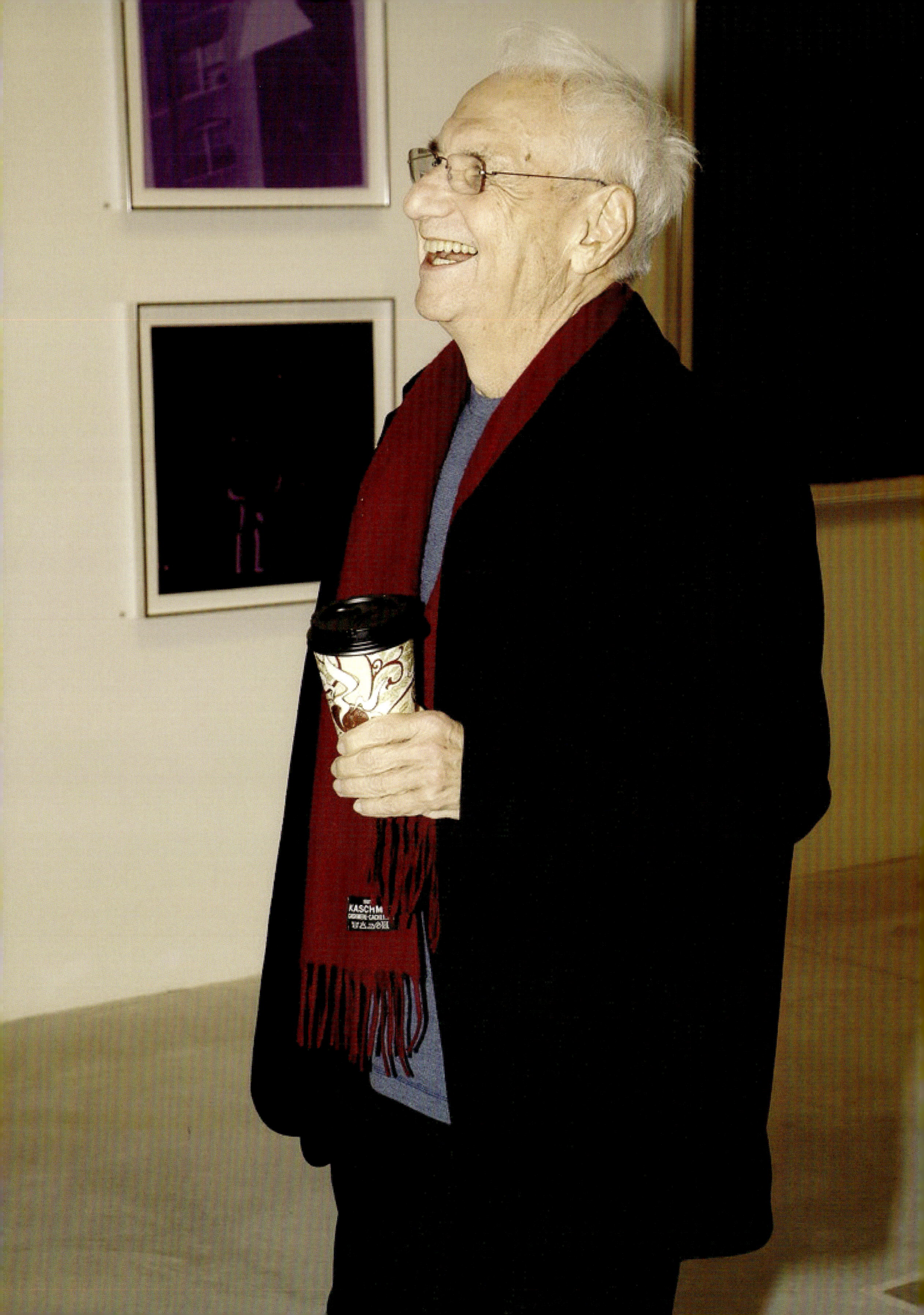

in Spain, which was a totally new kind of building. The client was the Guggenheim Foundation. Bilbao was just a secondary port city in Spain, and the design for the museum created a new way of thinking about Bilbao, not only by having a major museum but by turning the city into a place where the arts become accessible through that building. Prior to the Guggenheim Museum in Bilbao, the arts were usually just part of the environment that you find in so many cities and countries and places, whereas the museum focused on how to present creative work in this city. Another design, the third, would be the amphitheatre in New Orleans that didn't come to fruition. In my opinion, these are the three projects that are Frank's greatest achievements.

SMITH: Has Frank influenced or inspired you in any of your projects?

TANNEN: Frank and I influence each other in ways that are maybe not too obvious. It begins with a conversation. It's Socratic. We use a Socratic dialogue without thinking it is a Socratic dialogue. When we're talking about a project or a potential issue, we discuss it from a variety of positions. His ideas and my ideas tend to work off each other. In some cases, his ideas become dominant; in other cases, mine. It is always a shared belief that the foundation of our thinking is similar. Therefore we trust and encourage each other to advance the ideas of the project under discussion.

SMITH: I believe you both see the world through the lens as artists. Do you identify as an artist or an architect? How do you interpret the relationship between art and architecture in the twenty-first century, and what advice would you give the next generation who want to break the mold?

TANNEN: We both believe that innovation and invention allow us to think outside traditional norms for art, architecture, and regional planning. I plan with people rather than imposing my will and determinations. I listen to the people of the place where I'm conducting the planning, and the voice of the people who occupy that landscape is very important. In Frank's case, I think he presents ideas that are non-traditional to a client, so that the building represents his thinking and his client. We both have clients that believe what we are doing is important. My advice is that non-traditional ideas and the Socratic dialogue to find solutions are more important than imposing a decision, independent of the situation.

SMITH: When working together on a project, how do you and Frank complement each other?

TANNEN: We both bring something to the discussion that's different. We use this dialogue to support what we hope will be a positive outcome and a project that will be appreciated by the public and the client.

SMITH: As a friend, colleague, and sometimes collaborator what do you believe to be Frank's greatest asset?

TANNEN: Frank is a visiting professor at the Yale School of Architecture. He likes to share his thinking about architecture with students. I believe Frank's investment in the future generations of architects is his greatest asset. His legacy is a monumental body of work and philosophies to educate, inspire, and influence.

SMITH: How would you describe Frank's commitment, passion, and contributions as an architect, and his value to the world?

TANNEN: Frank has been fortunate to have clients who appreciate the way he thinks, and what his buildings are all about. He has had many clients who encompassed opportunities to utilize the way he thinks about architecture.

SMITH: My final question... if Frank were in the room with you today, at this moment, and this was the last time you were to see him, what would be your last words to him to define your relationship?

TANNEN: I love you, Frank, for what you do and how you think. I think he may share a similar sentiment in my case.

SMITH: Thank you, Bob, for your countless contributions and for being an influence to so many creatives who were fortunate to be in your presence.

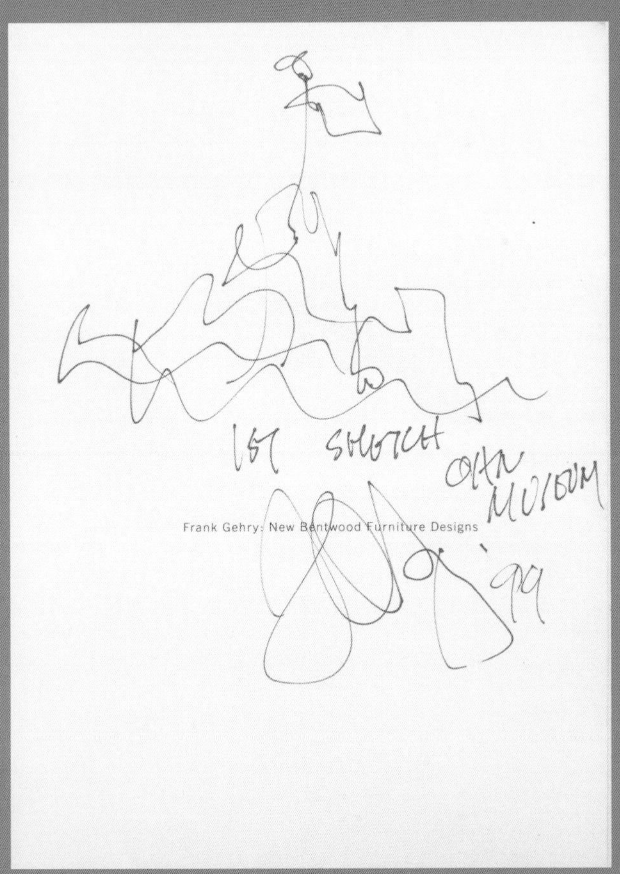

Initial sketch of the Ohr-O'Keefe Museum of Art during the first meeting between Robert Tannen, Jeanne Nathan, and Frank Gehry, as they discussed a new museum for George E. Ohr.

FRANK GEHRY (1999), BILOXI, MISSISSIPPI

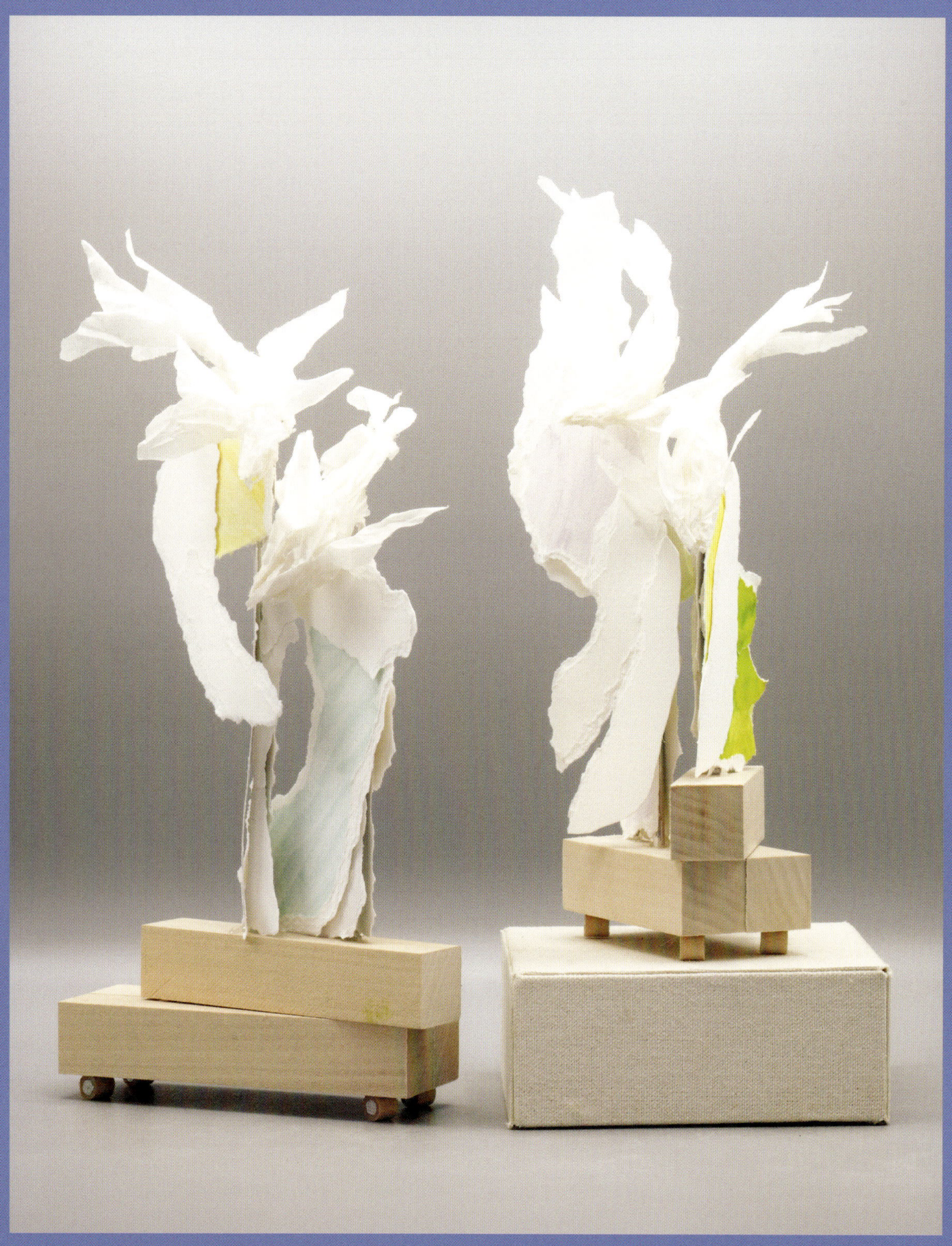

FISH SCULPUTRES
FRANK GEHRY

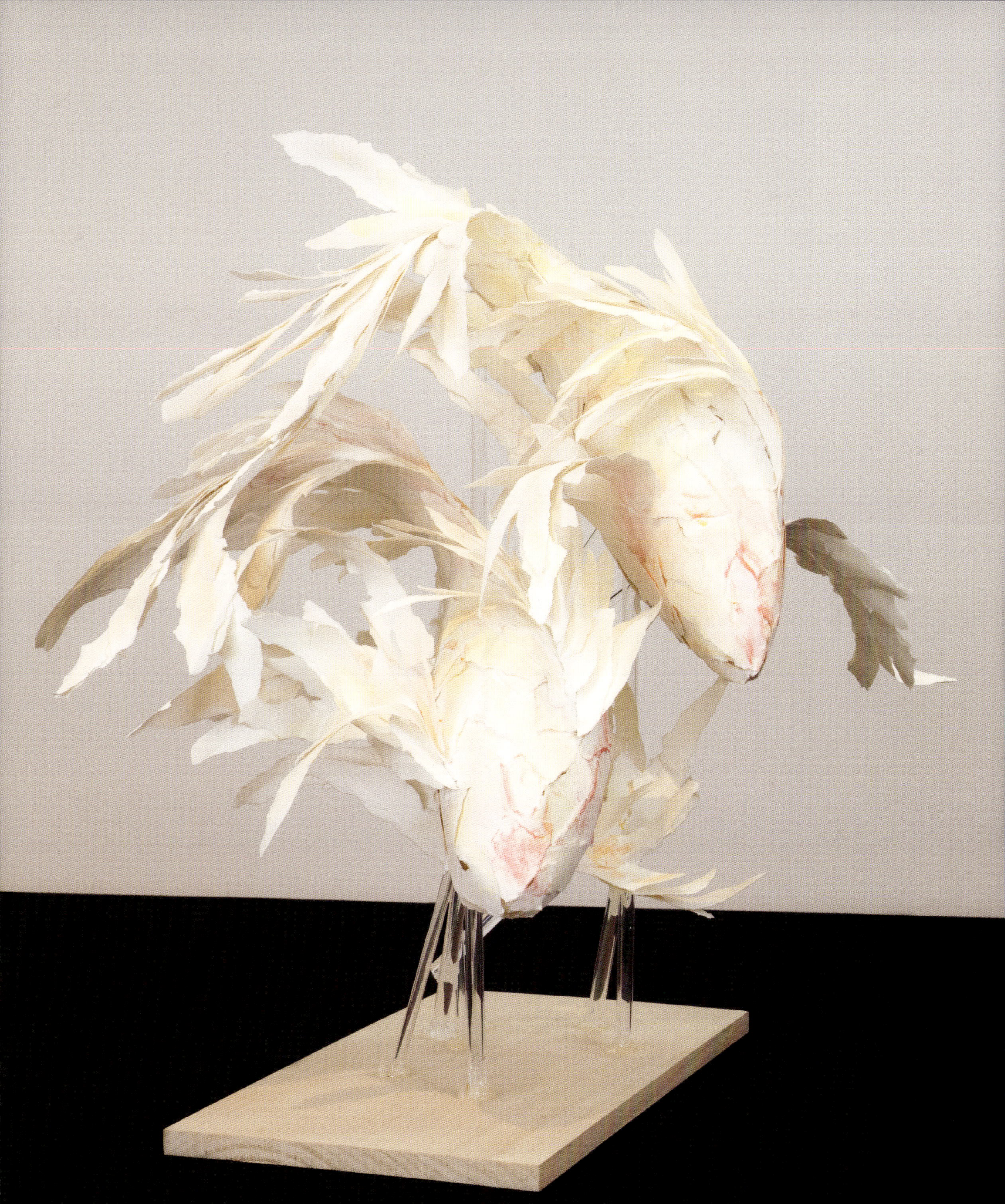

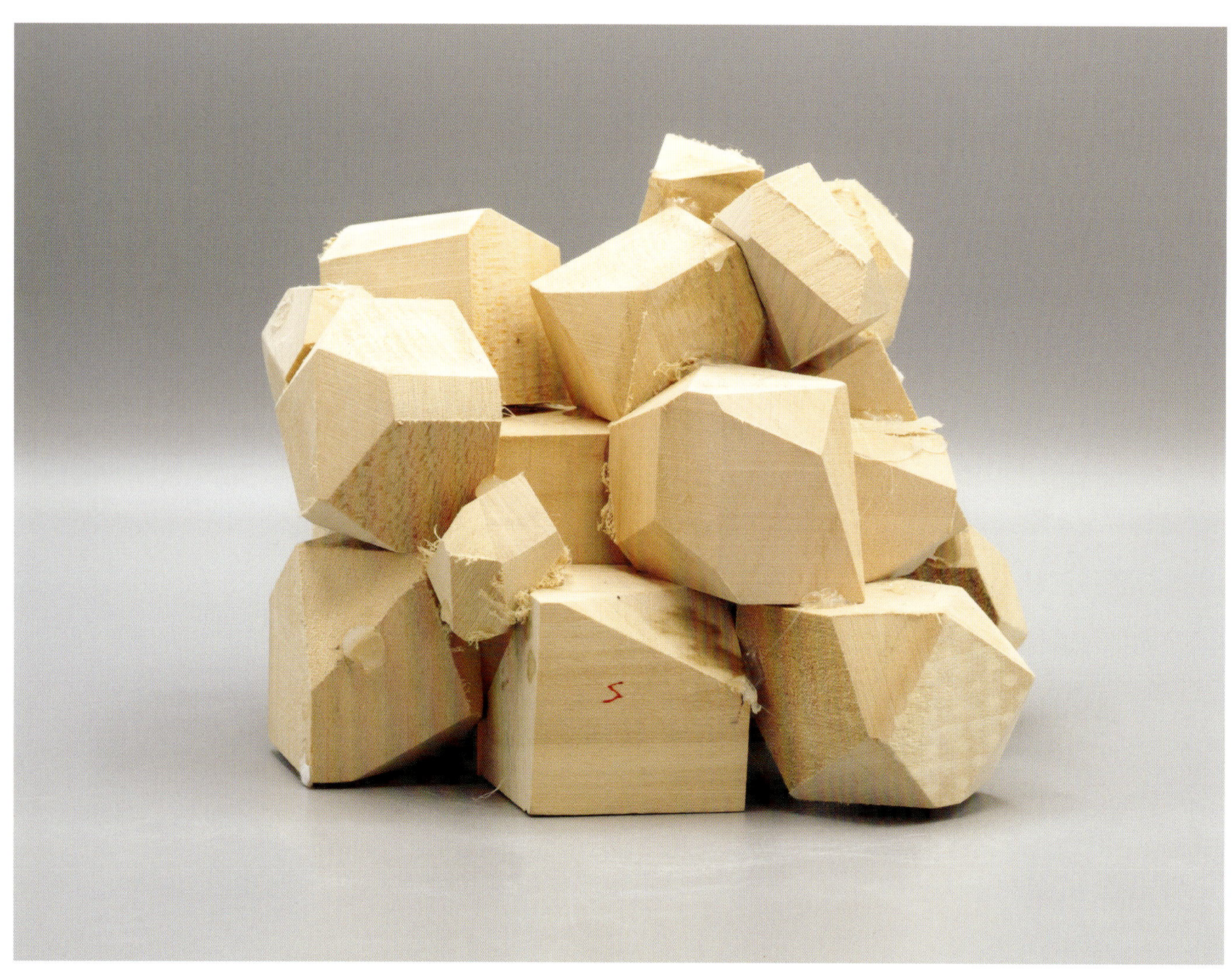

LOU RUVO CENTER FOR BRAIN HEALTH
FRANK GEHRY

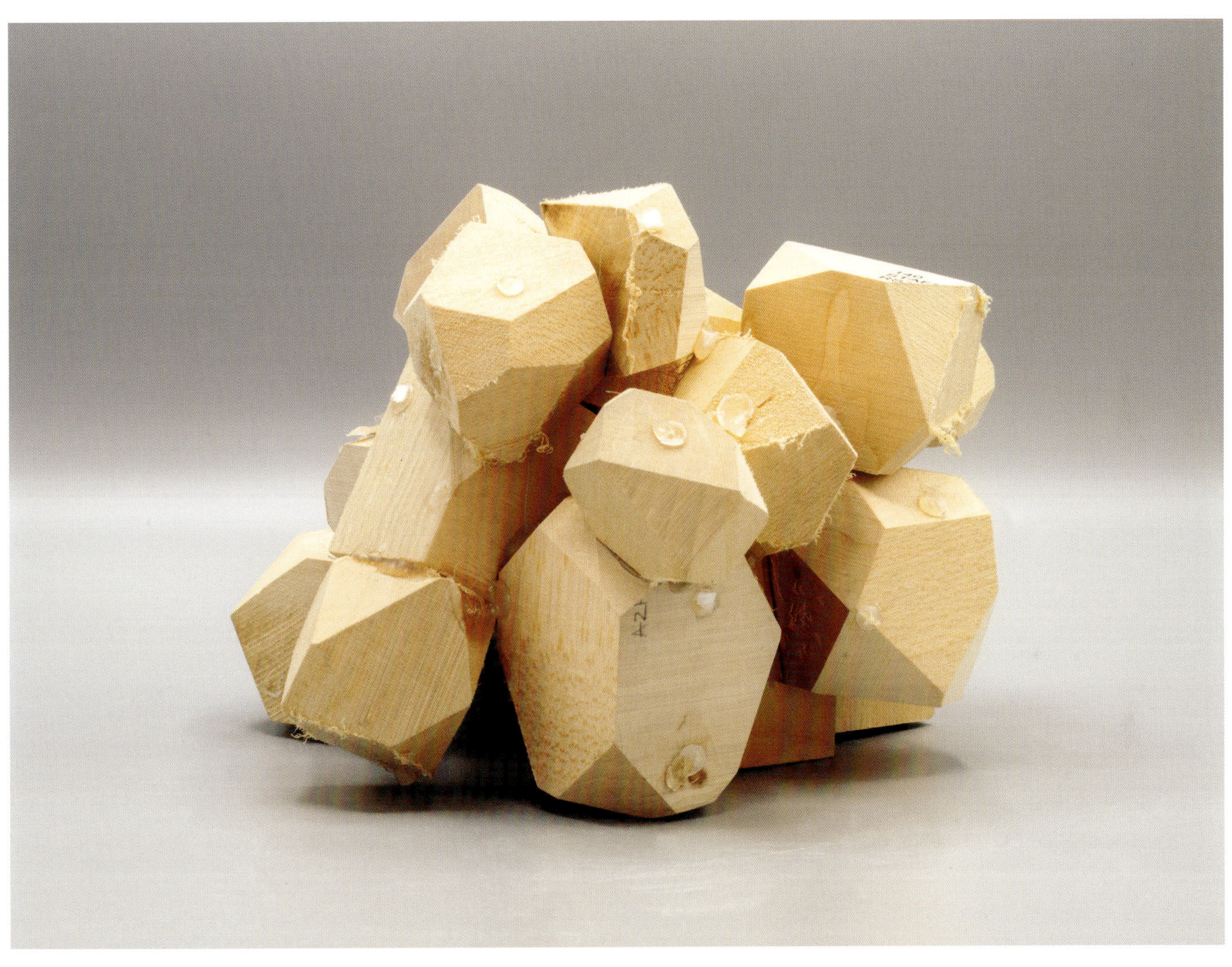

CONCEPT & STRUCTURAL DESIGNS
FRANK GEHRY

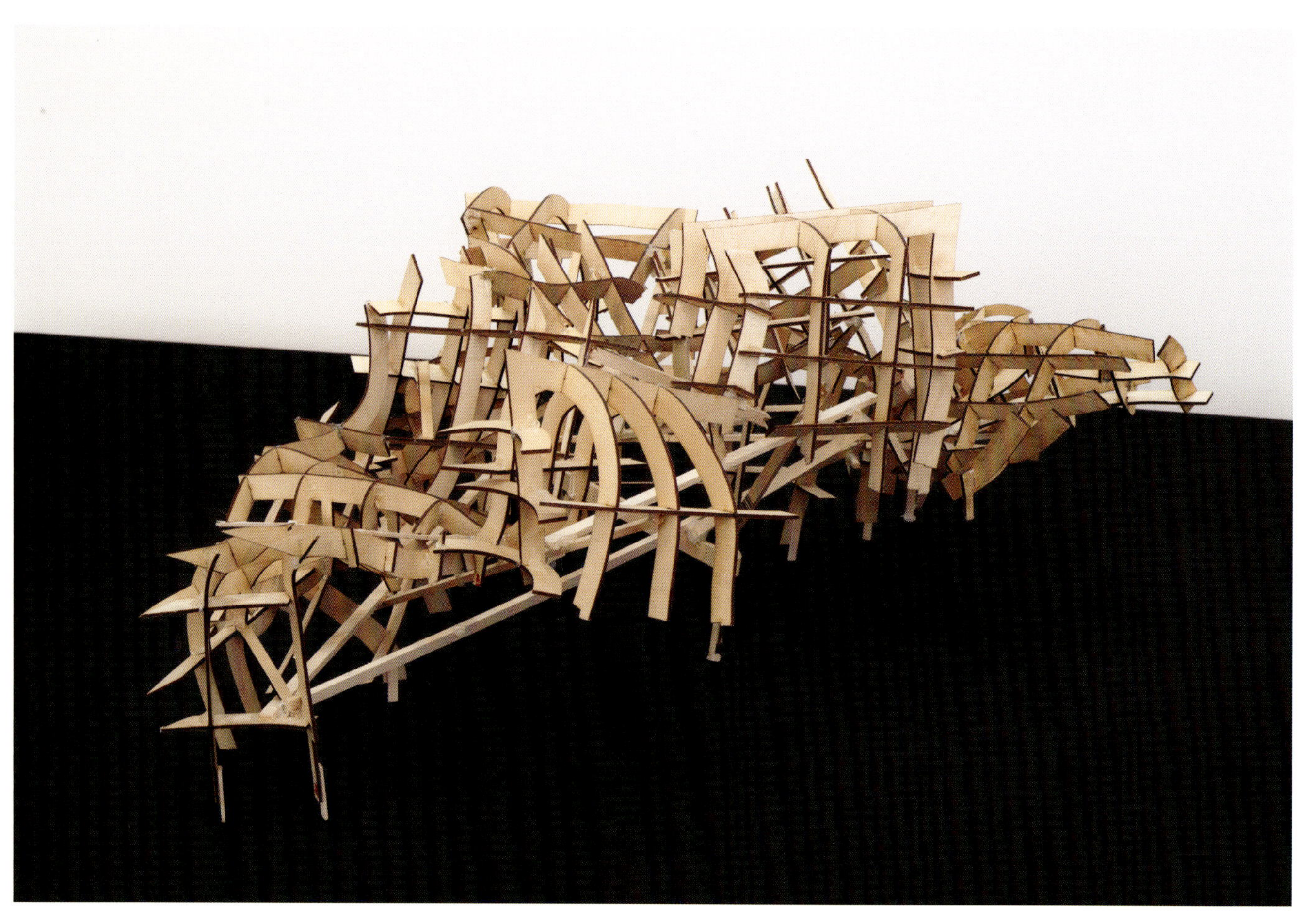

LOU RUVO CENTER FOR BRAIN HEALTH
FRANK GEHRY

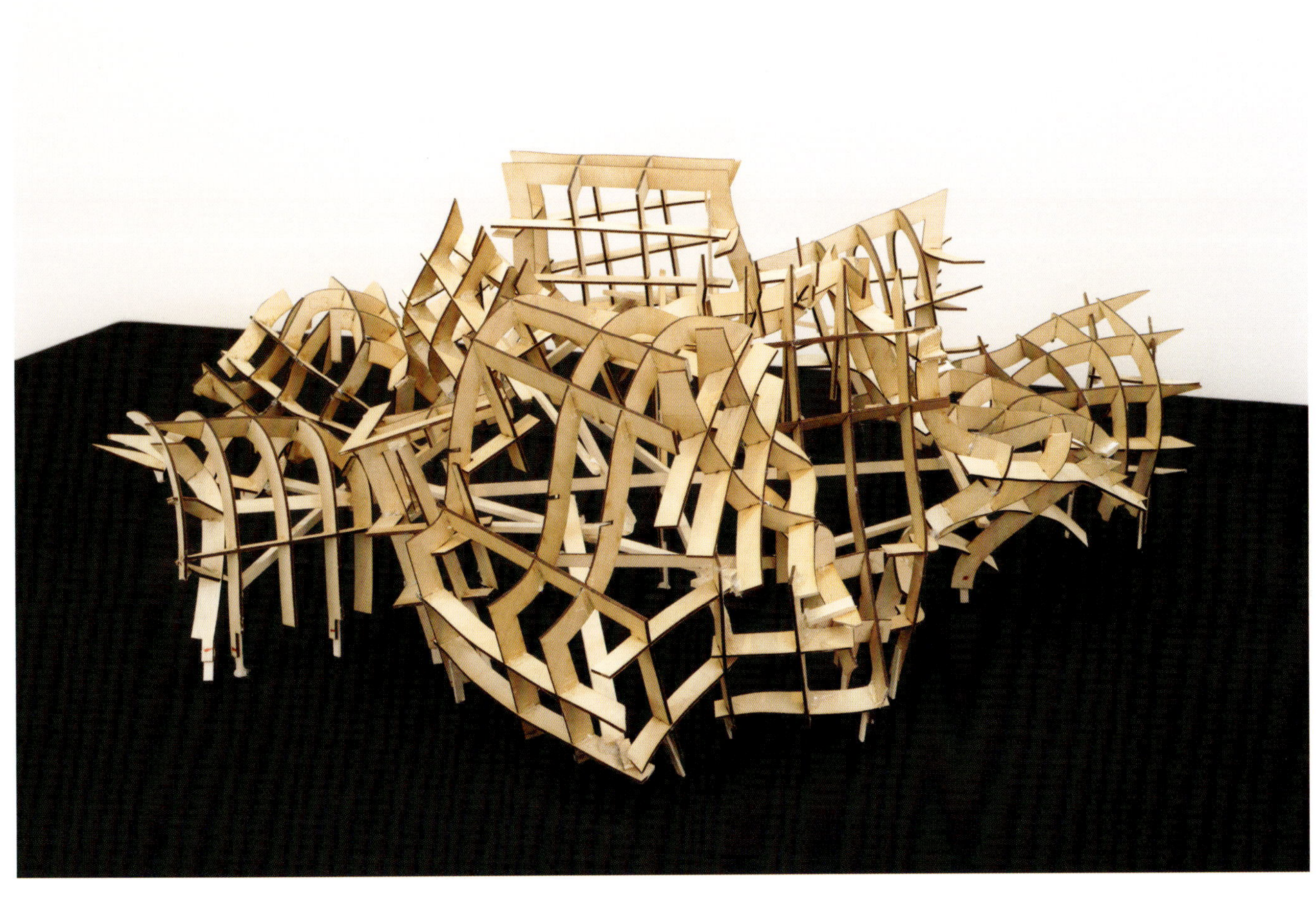

CONCEPT & STRUCTURAL DESIGNS
FRANK GEHRY

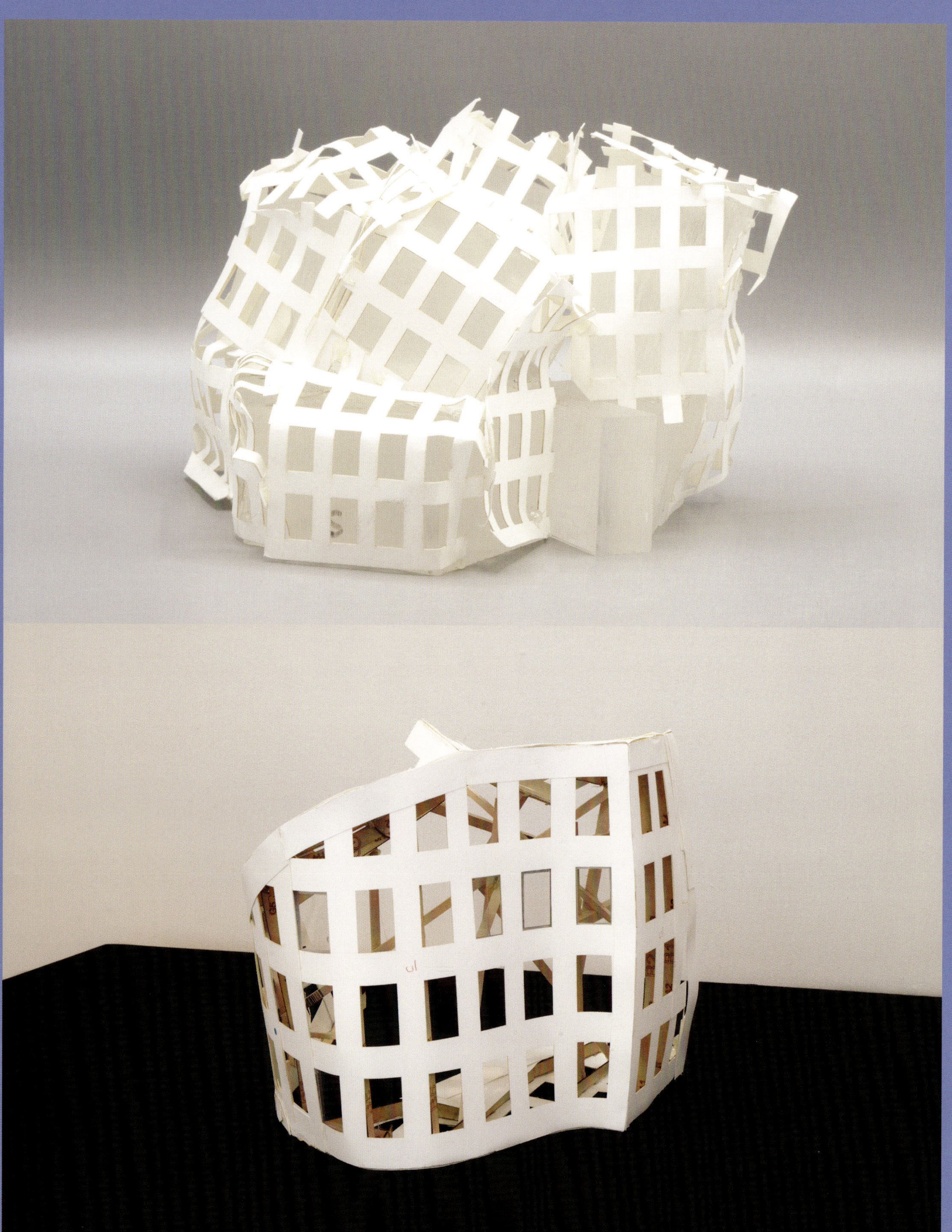

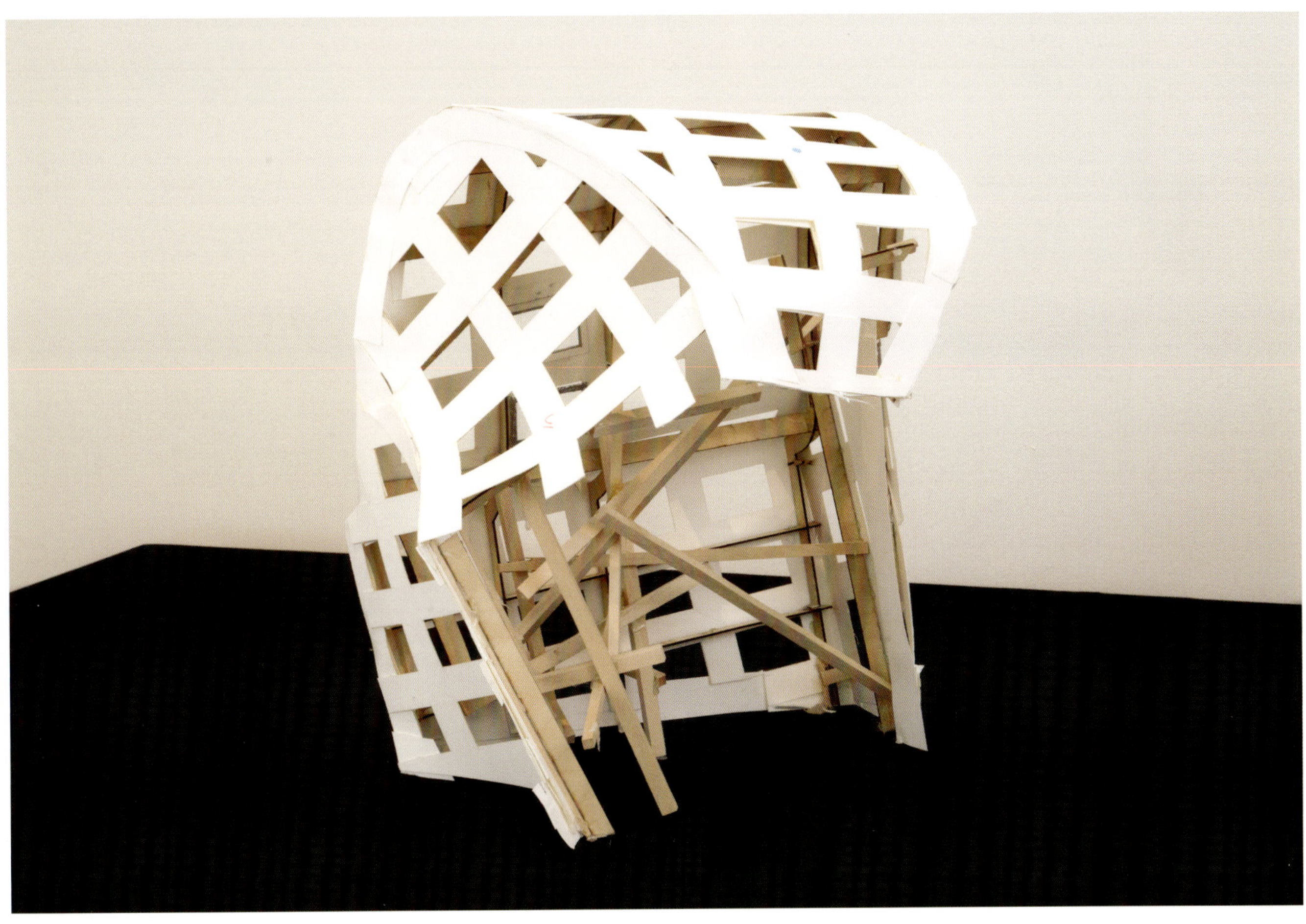

Lou Ruvo Center for Brain Health

2005-2010 (built), Las Vegas, Nevada

The Cleveland Clinic Lou Ruvo Center for Brain Health is located on a prominent "gateway" in downtown Las Vegas. The center provides facilities that bridge all aspects of patient care, research, and education for cognitive disorders. The research facilities, clinical facilities, and offices are located within a four-story block that has been articulated as a series of offset rectangular shapes in white plaster and glass. The more public building uses are detached from the medical facilities across a dramatic covered-trellis courtyard near the corner of the site. The undulating form of the Keep Memory Alive Event Center, which is articulated as a curvilinear metal façade and roof with punched-window/skylight openings, juxtaposes with the white block form of the clinic itself. This center is rented out by the organization to subsidize the clinic and fund ongoing research.

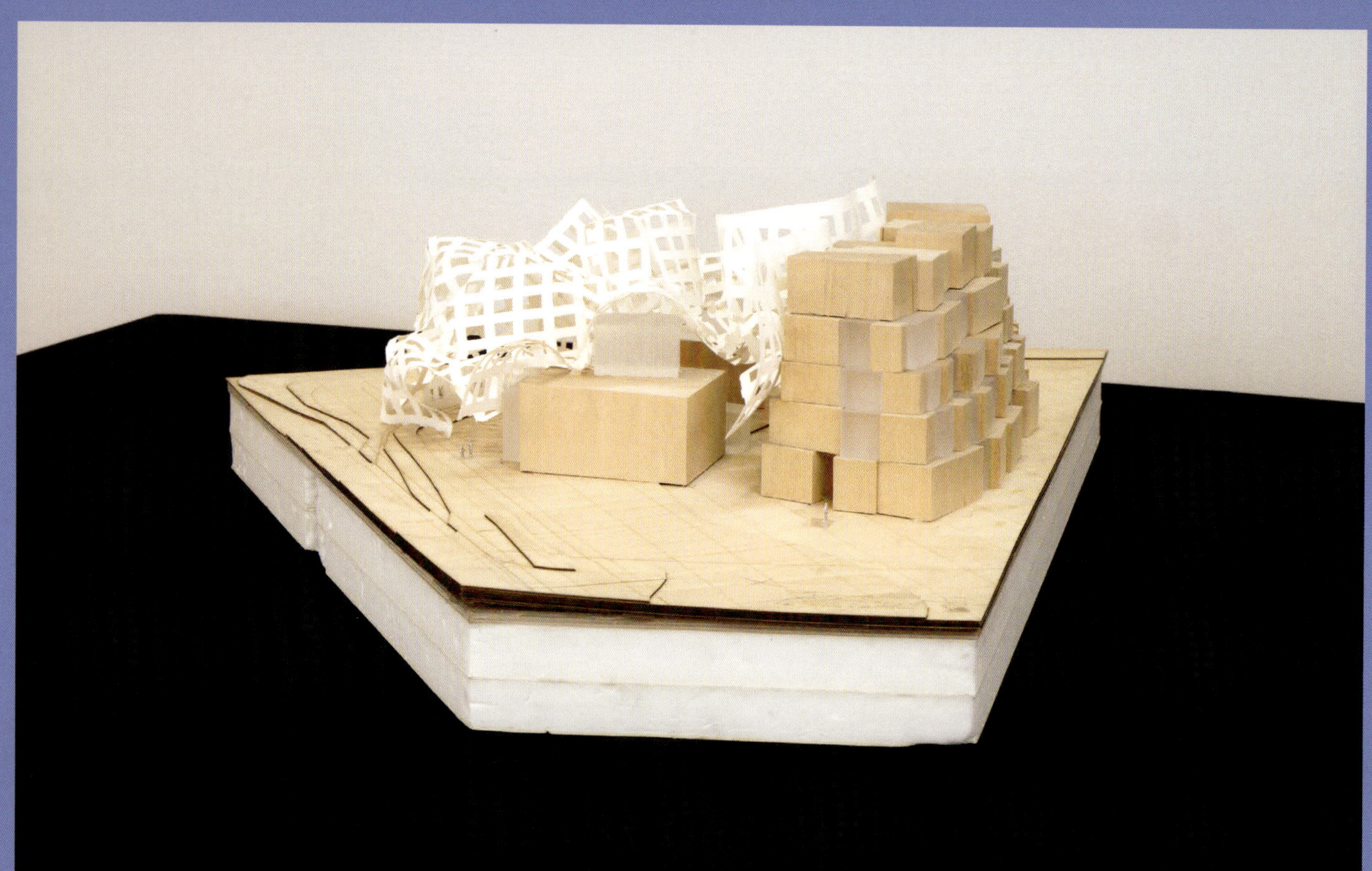

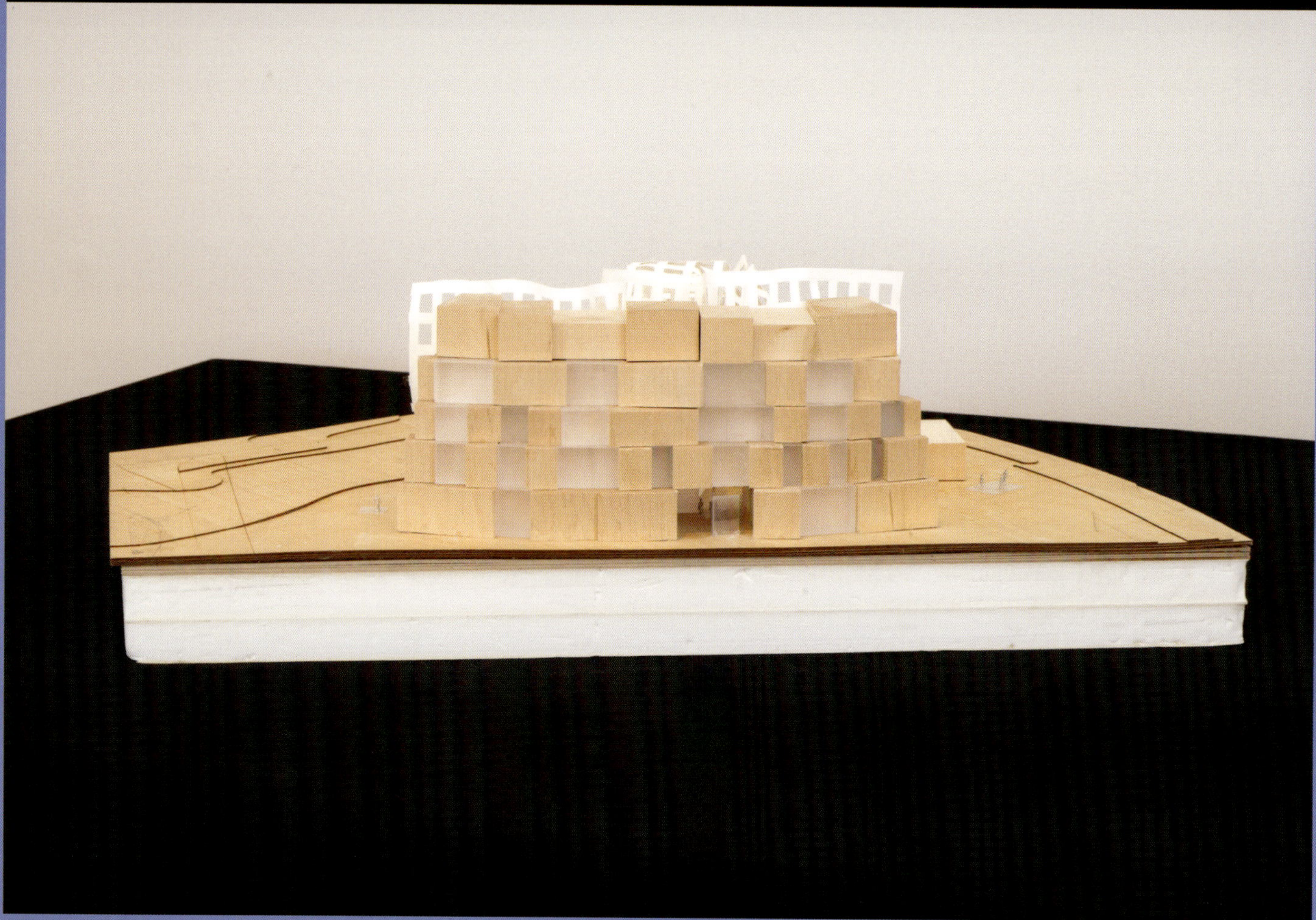

Lou Ruvo Center for Brain Health

2005-2010 (built), Las Vegas, Nevada

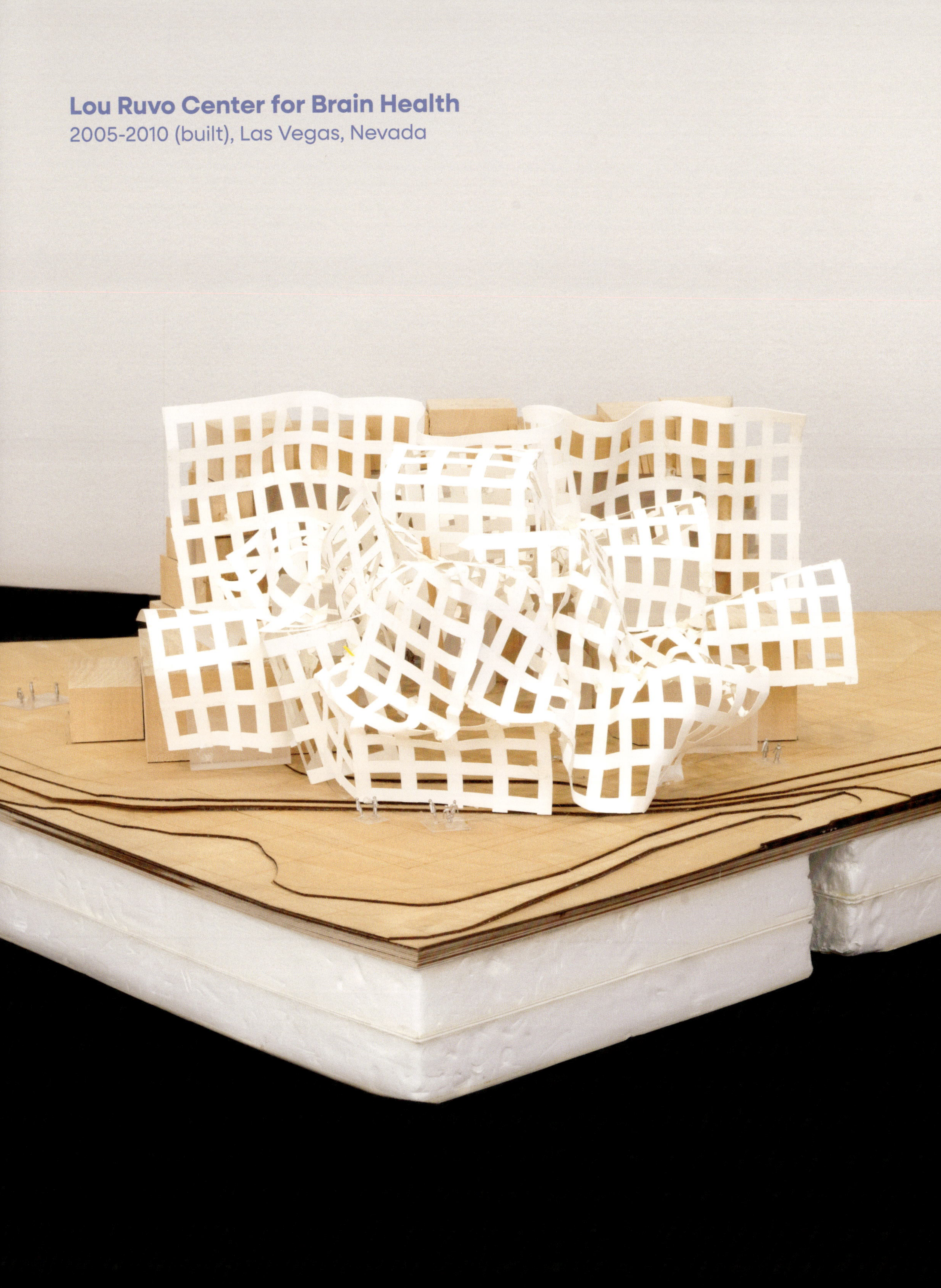

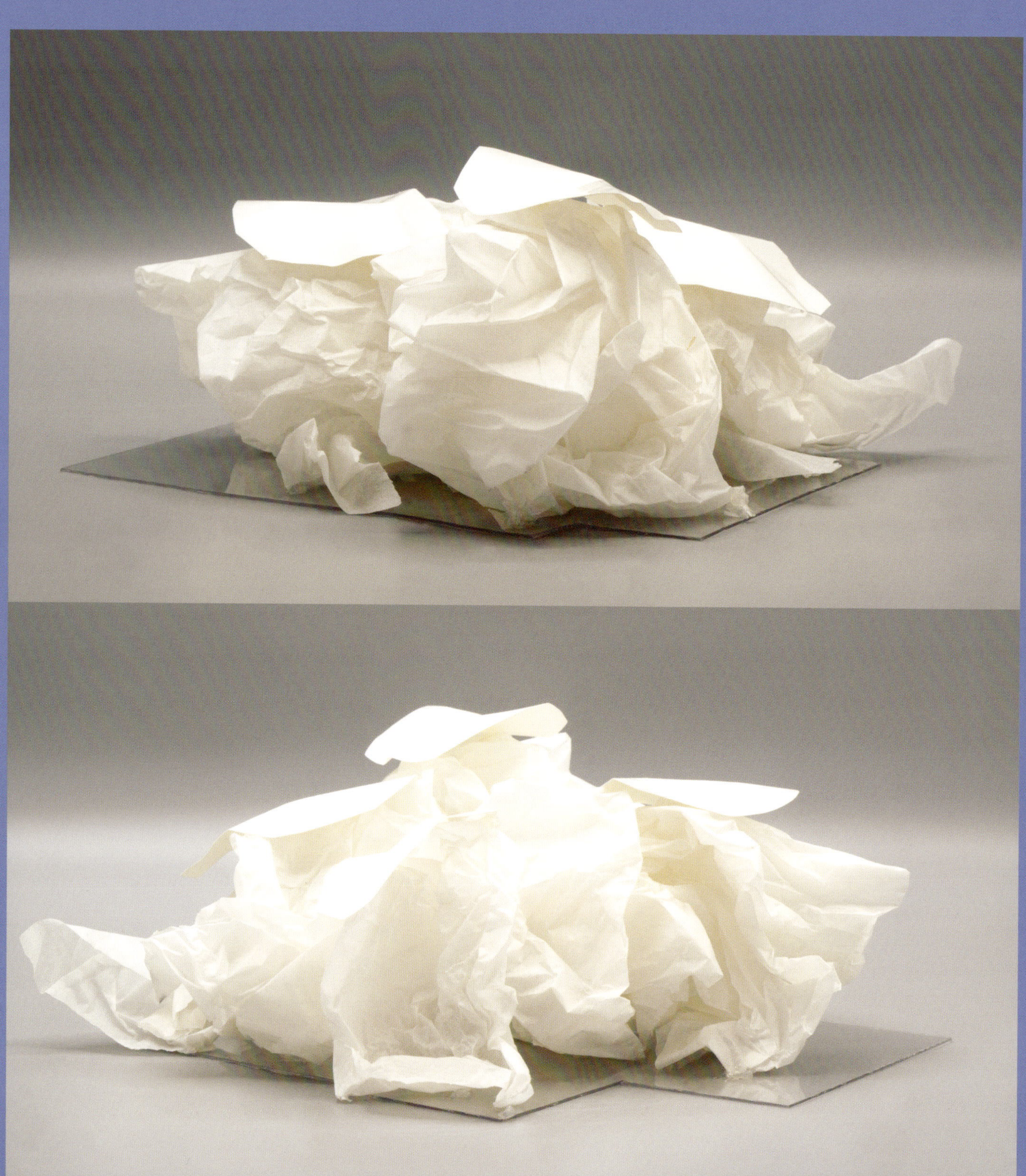

Aspen Meeting House
2013-2018 (built), Aspen, Colorado

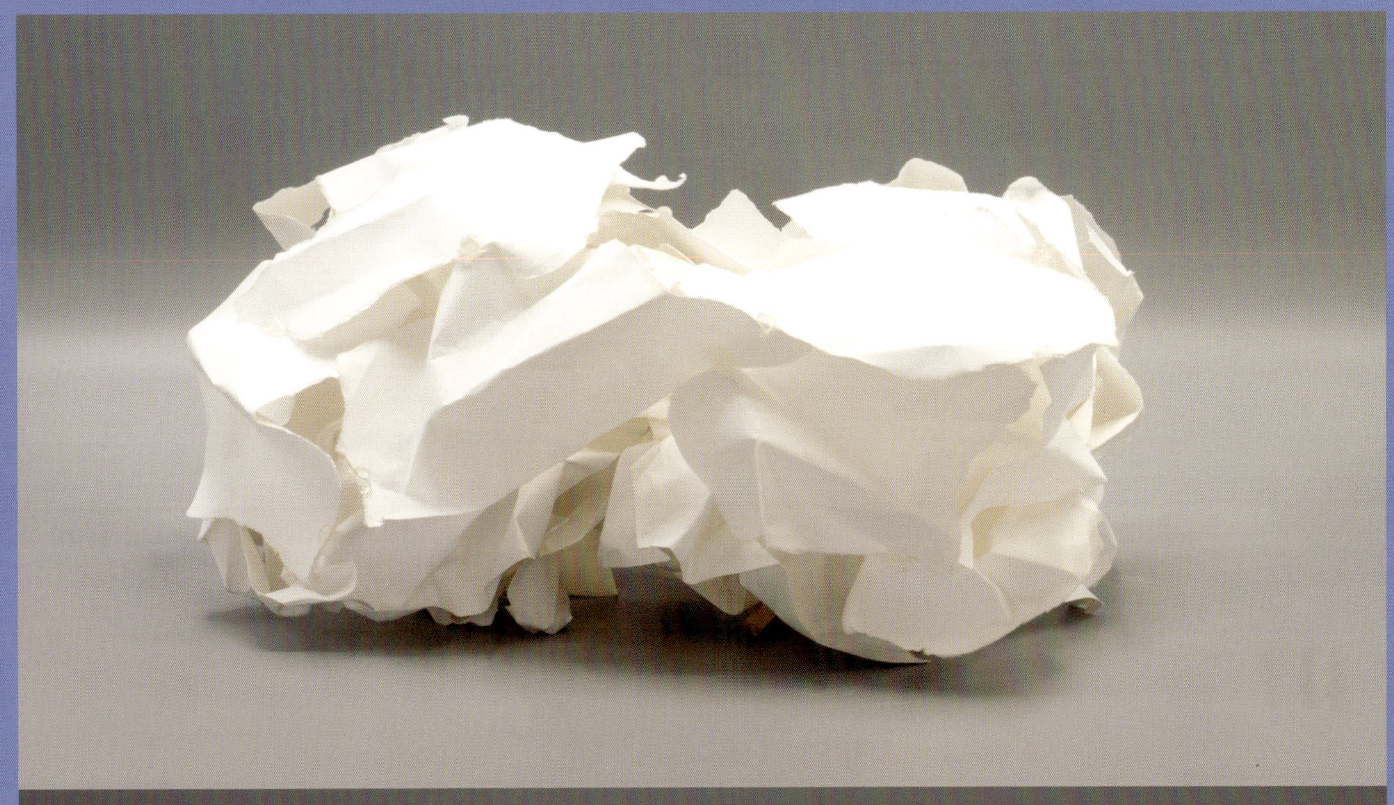

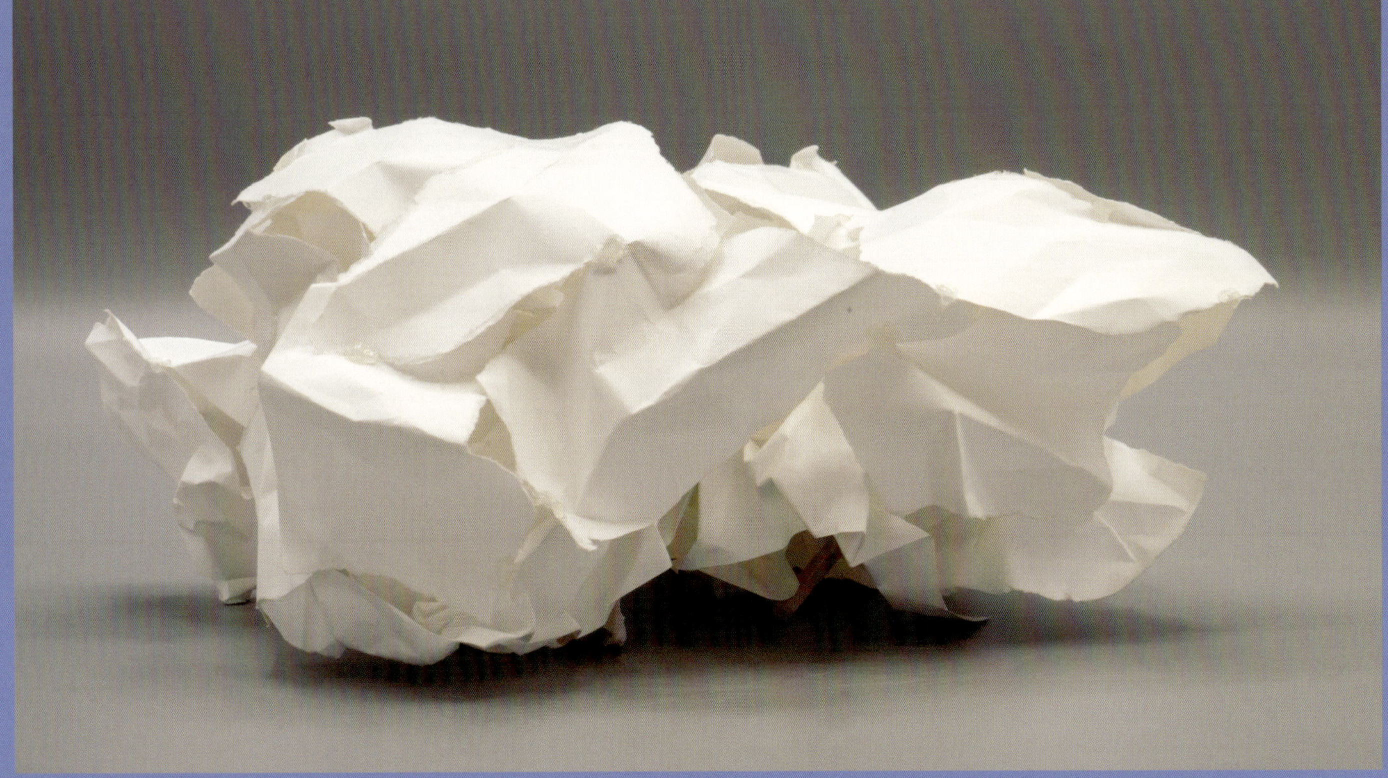

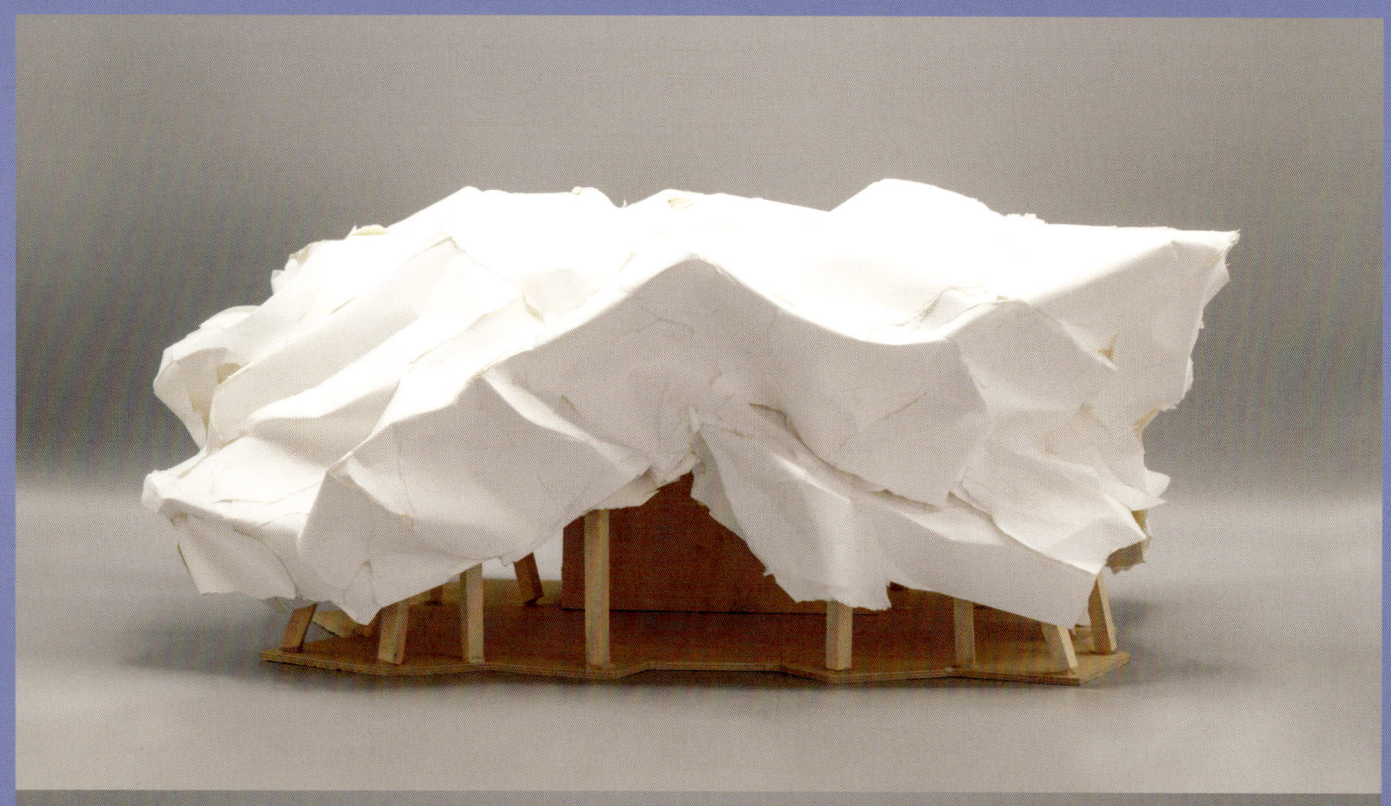

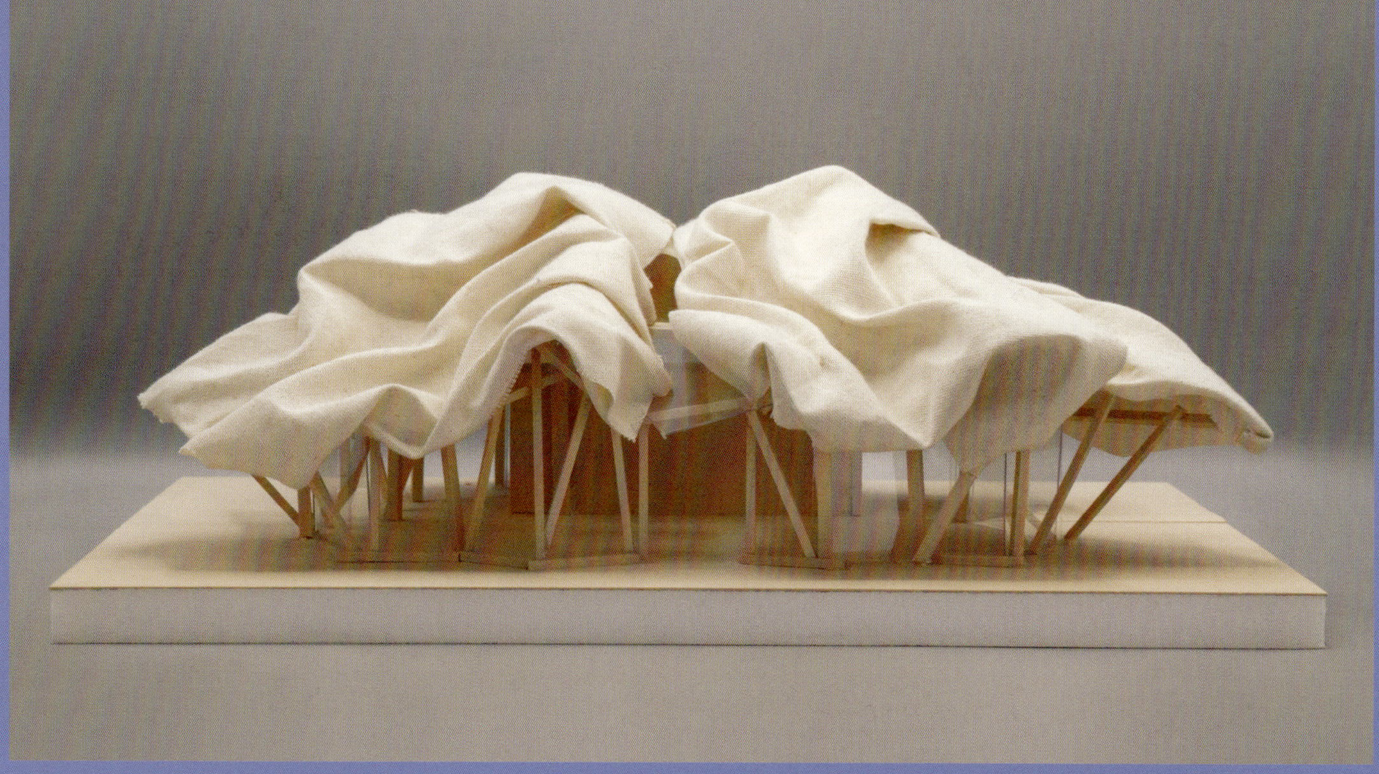

Aspen Meeting House

2013-2018 (built), Aspen, Colorado

The Aspen Meeting House, located in an isolated valley in the mountains of Colorado, was designed to be a place for various gatherings, from casual family events to global business summits. The shape of the roof is inspired by the surrounding mountains—the stainless steel material changes during the day and throughout the year, creating a building that has a different character from day to day. The roof is fabricated as a single piece and was manufactured by shipbuilders in the Netherlands. Approximately 900 uniquely curved stainless-steel panels are welded together to form a weather-proof roof that sits on top of 10 wood columns.

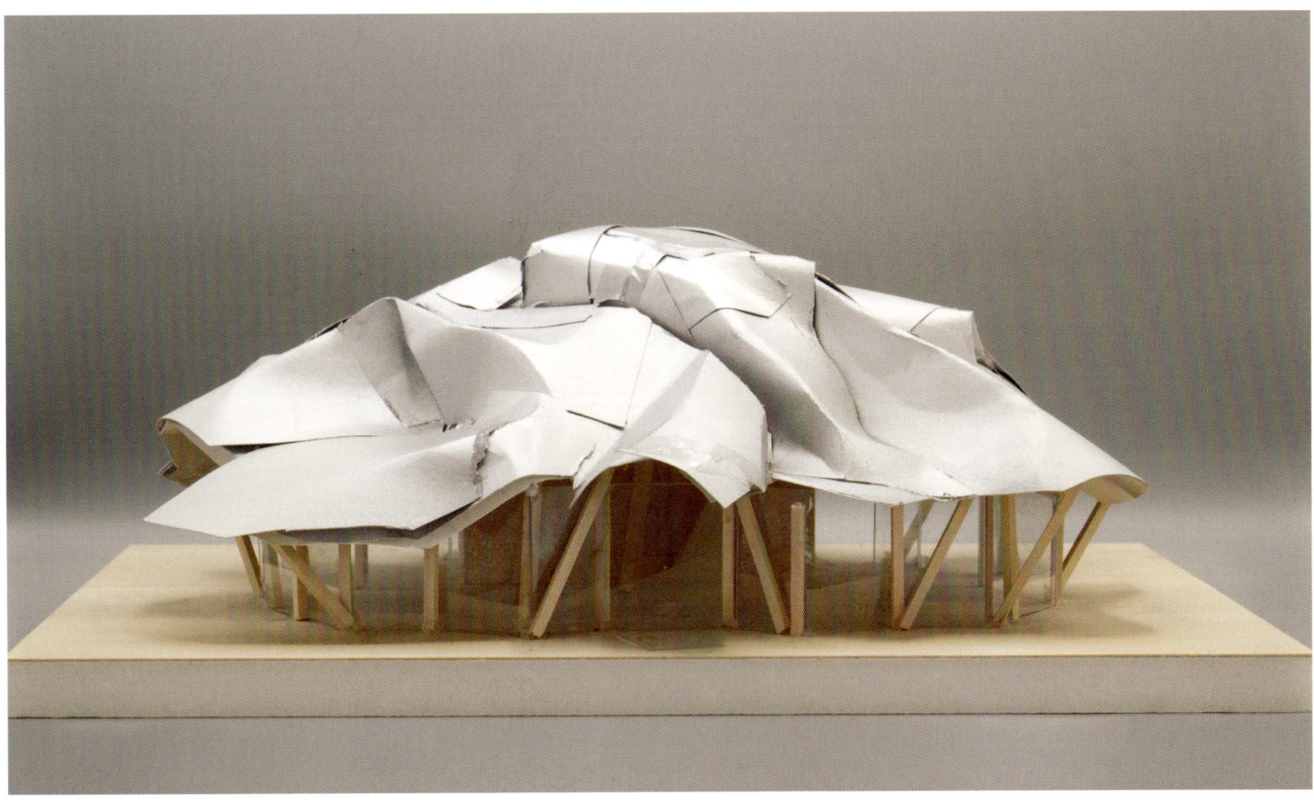

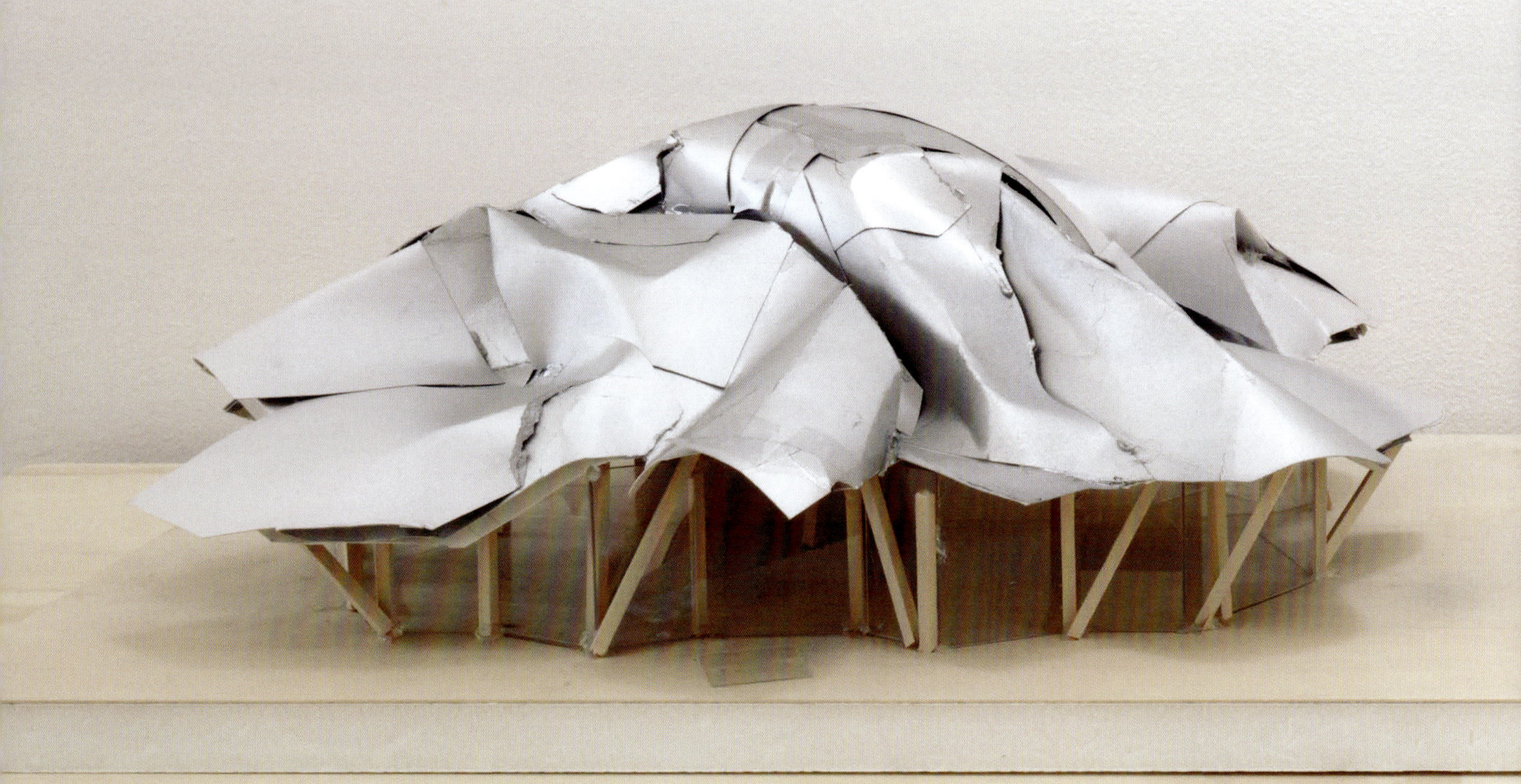

Aspen Meeting House
2013-2018 (built), Aspen, Colorado

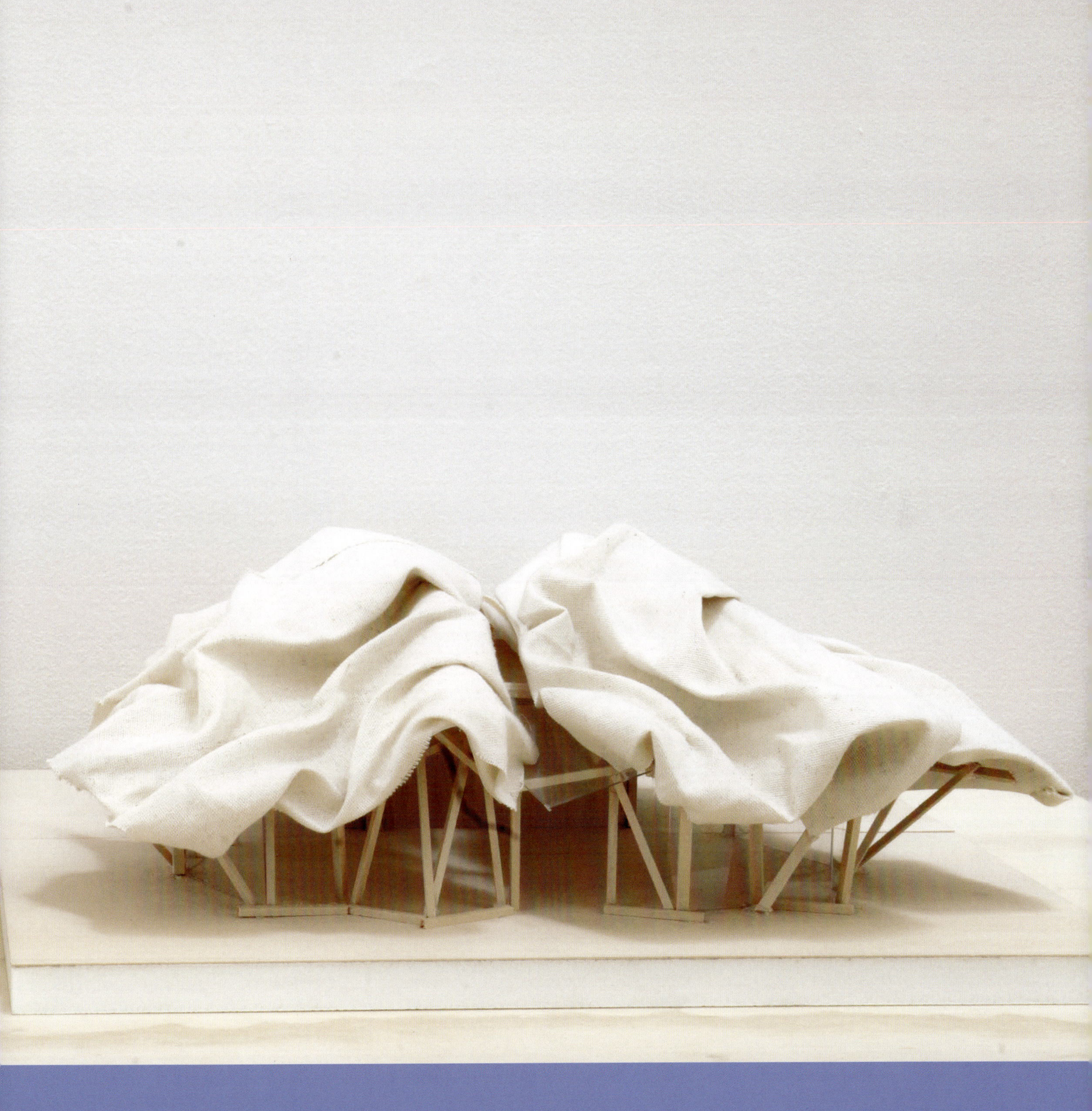

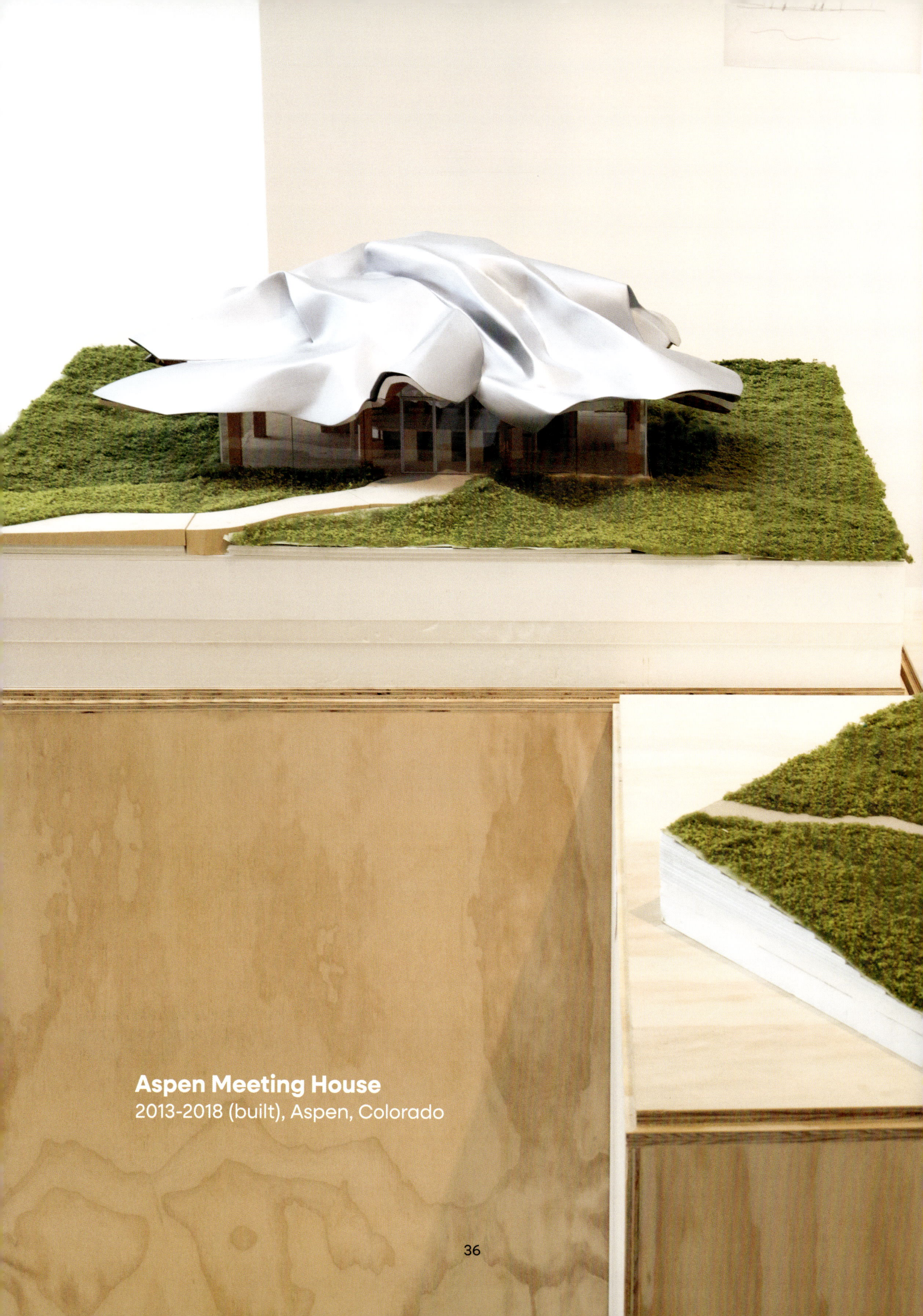

Aspen Meeting House
2013-2018 (built), Aspen, Colorado

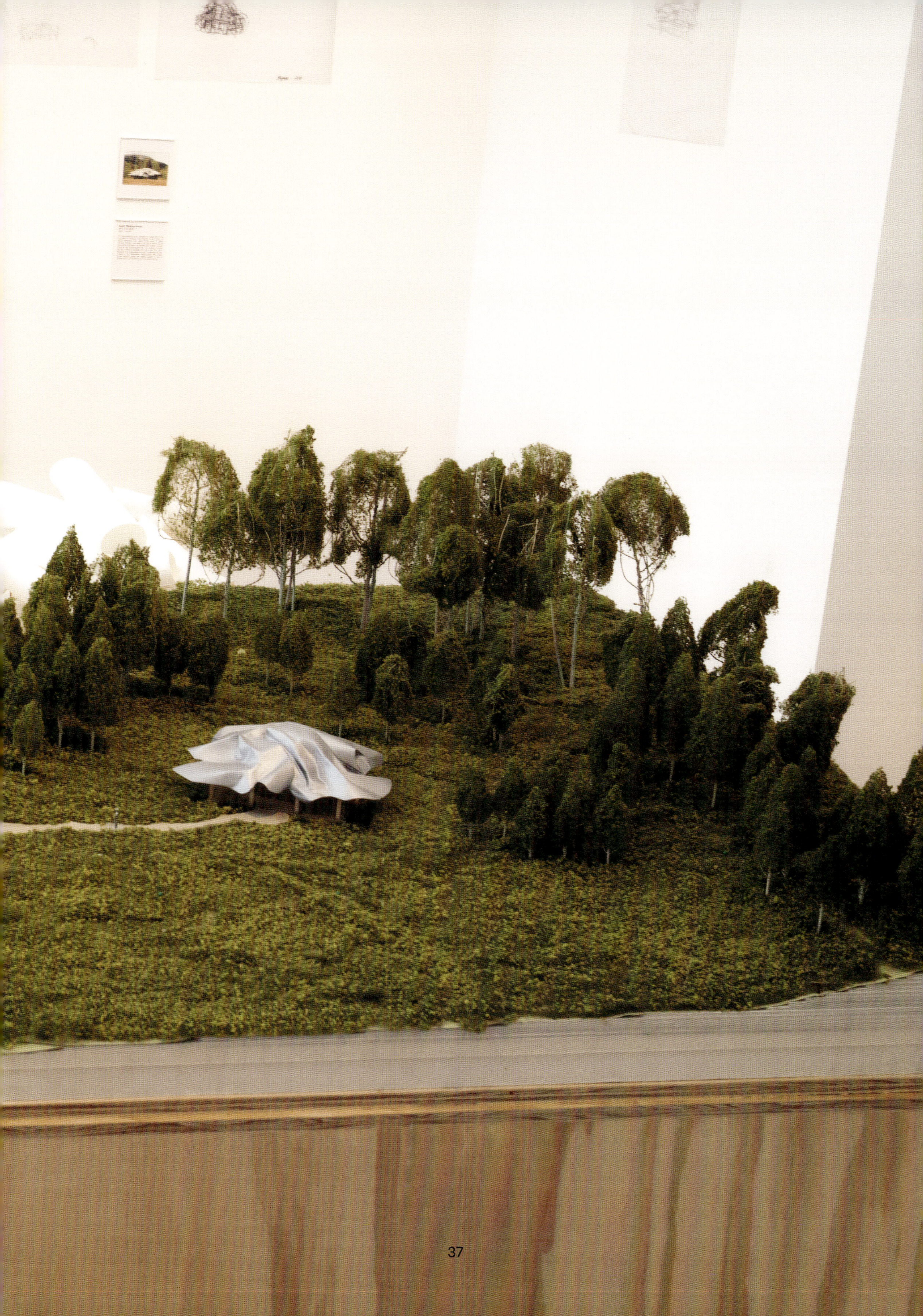

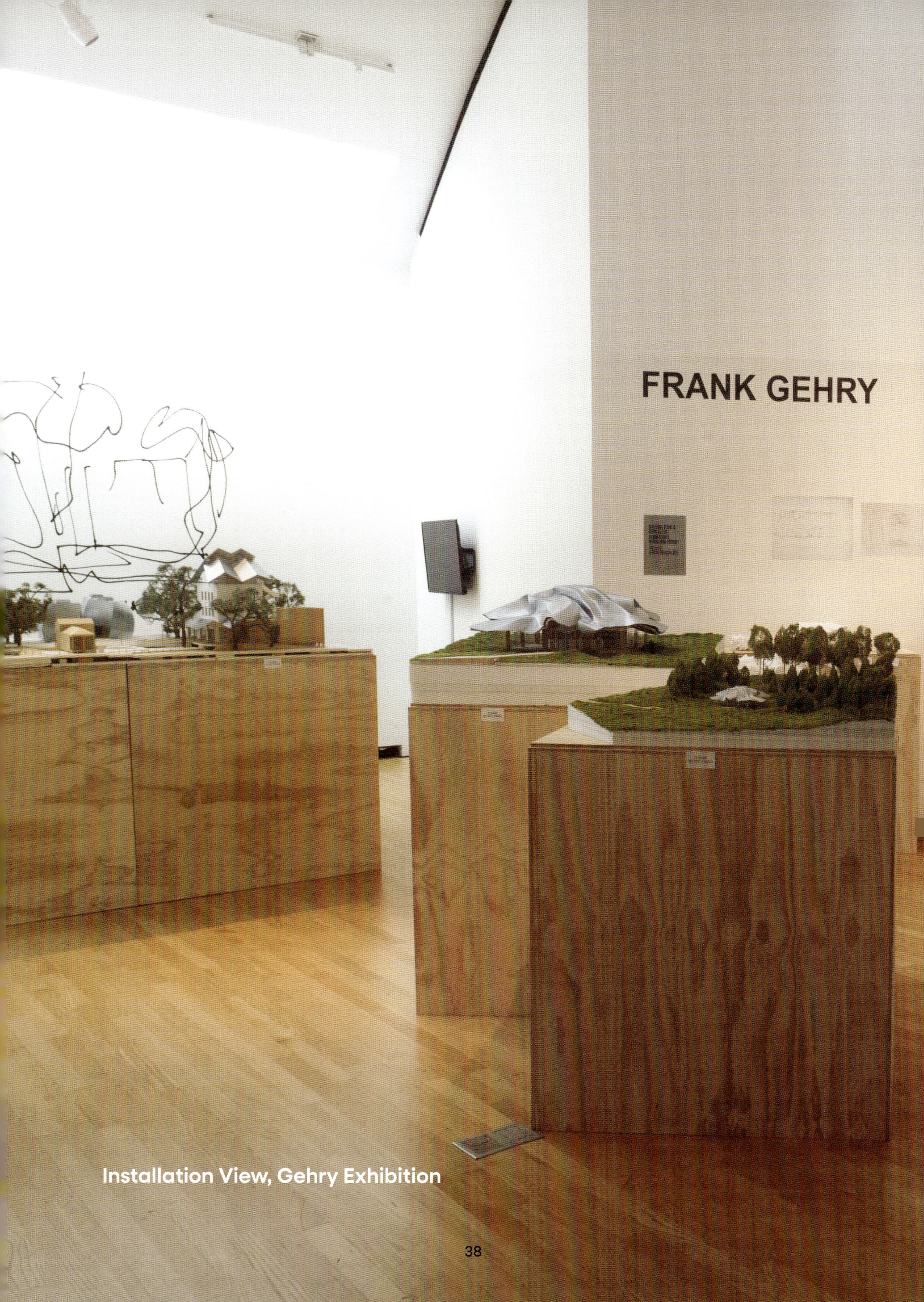

Installation View, Gehry Exhibition

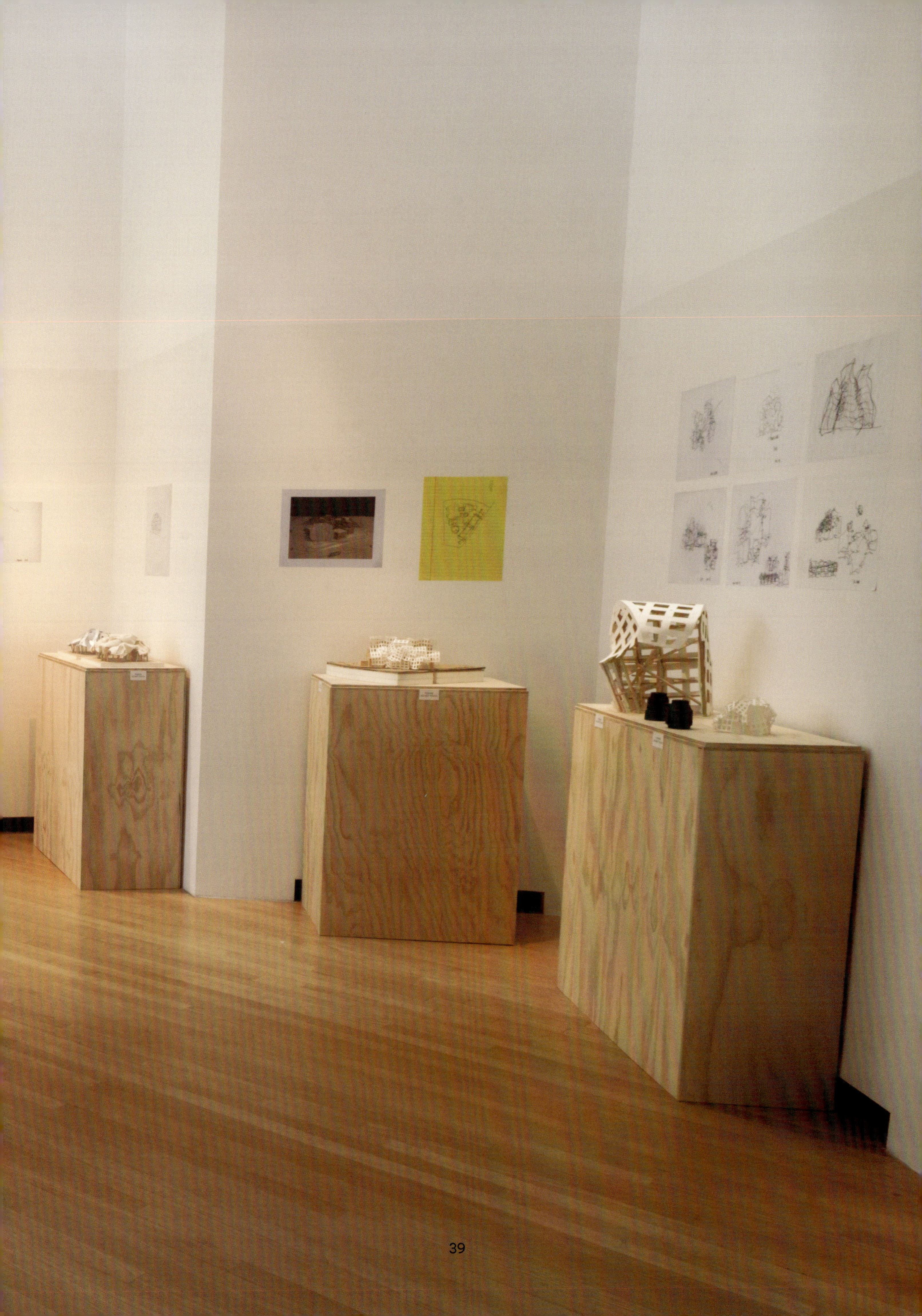

Ohr-O'Keefe Museum of Art

1999-Present (built), Biloxi, Mississippi

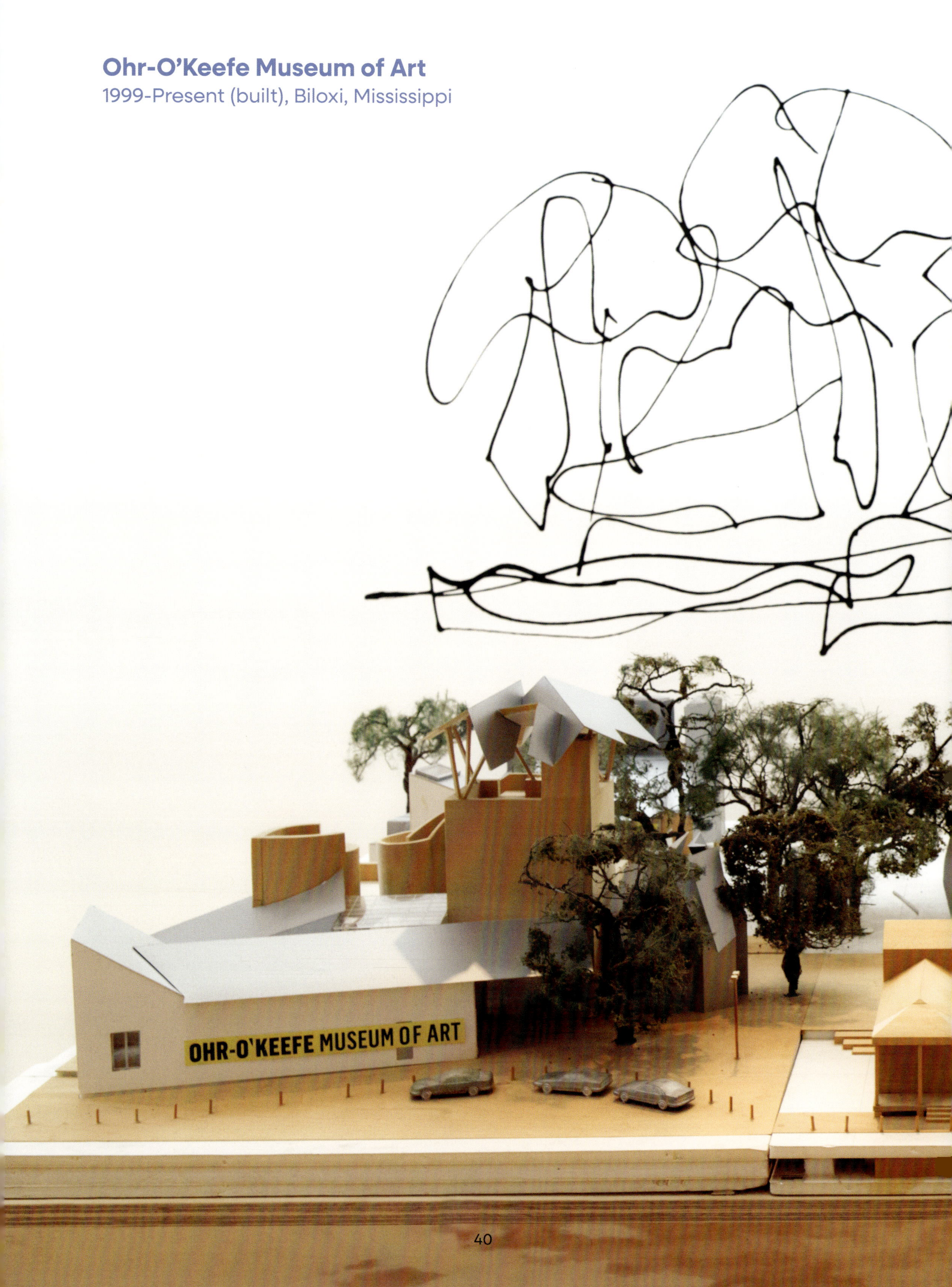

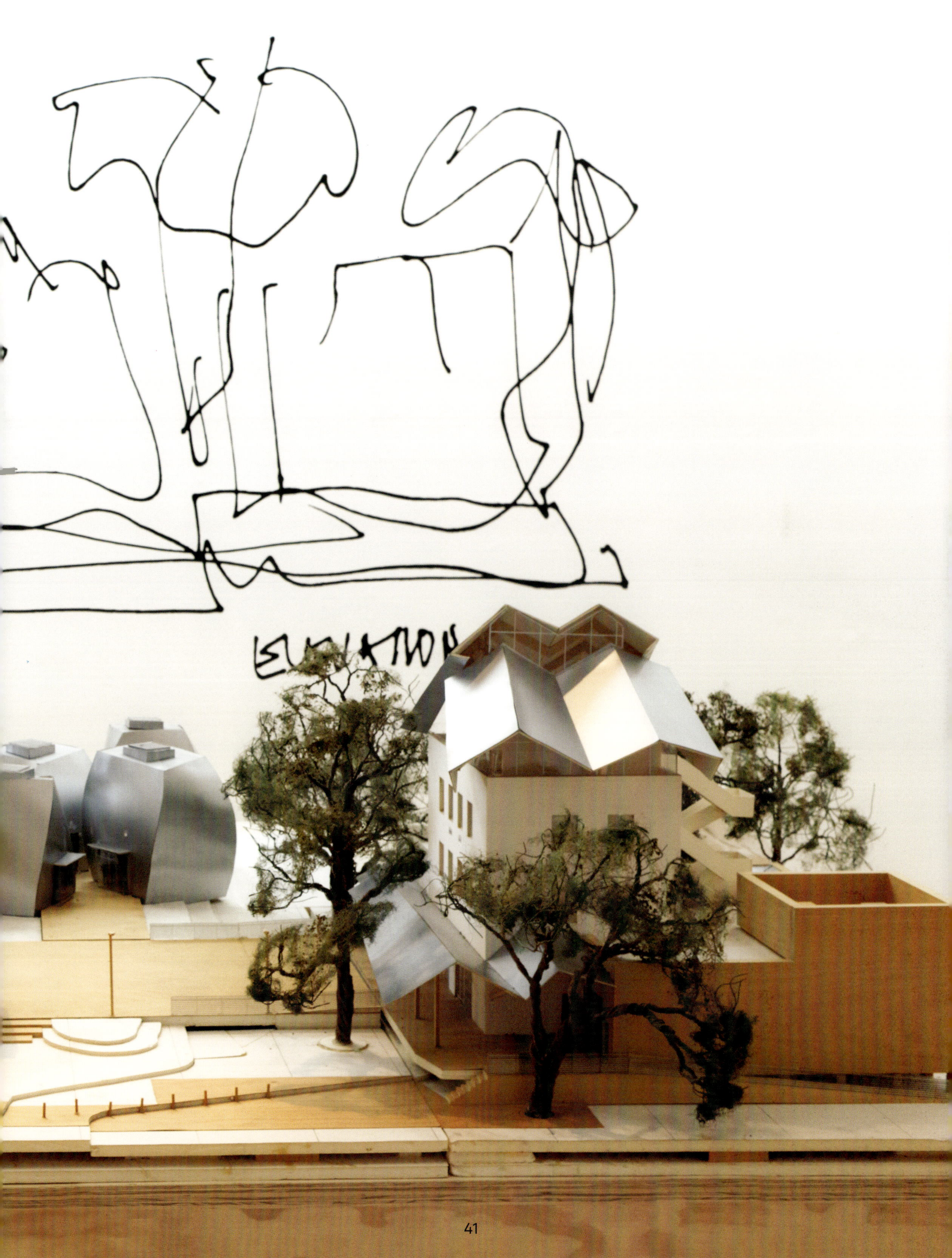

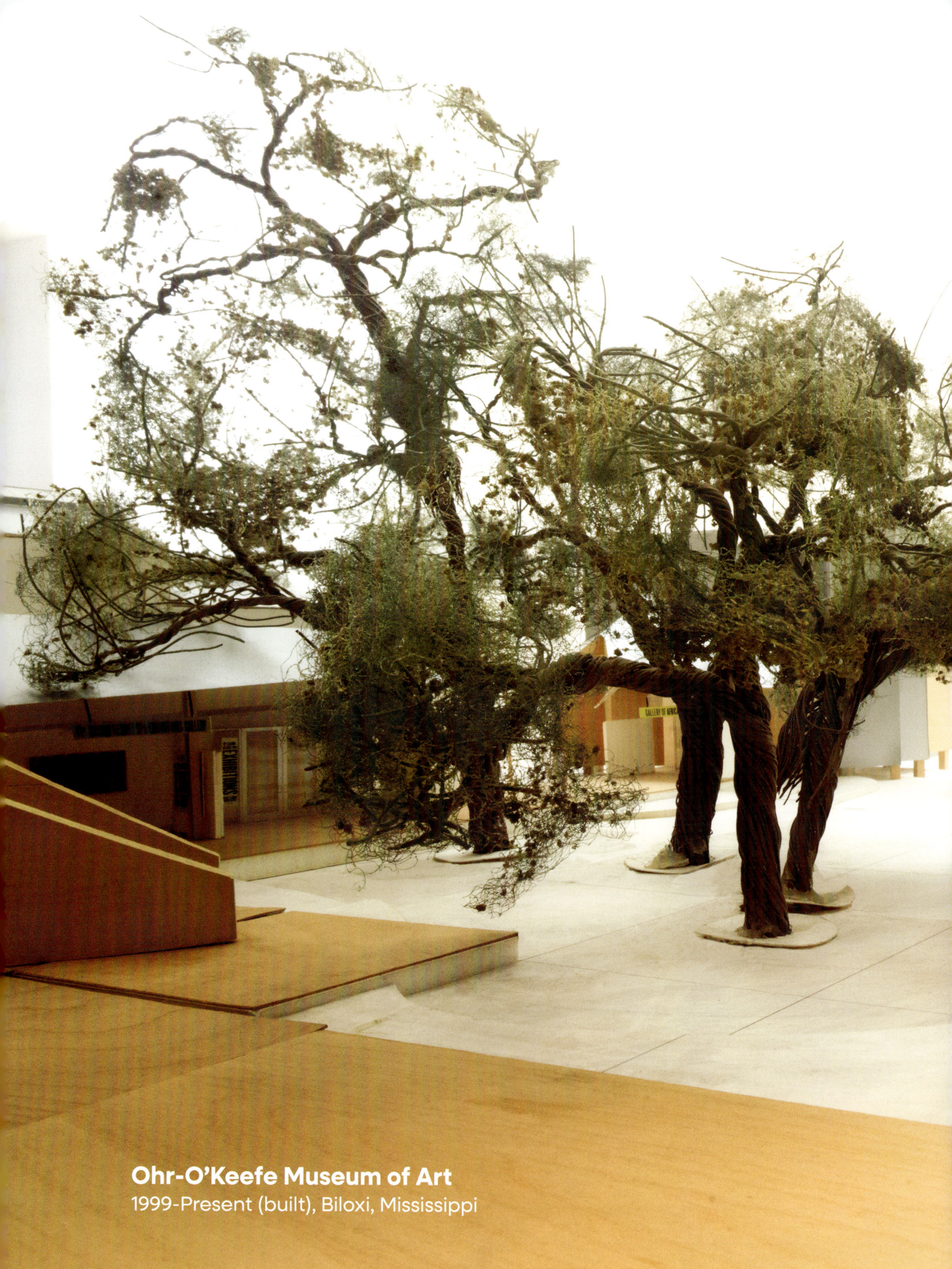

Ohr-O'Keefe Museum of Art
1999-Present (built), Biloxi, Mississippi

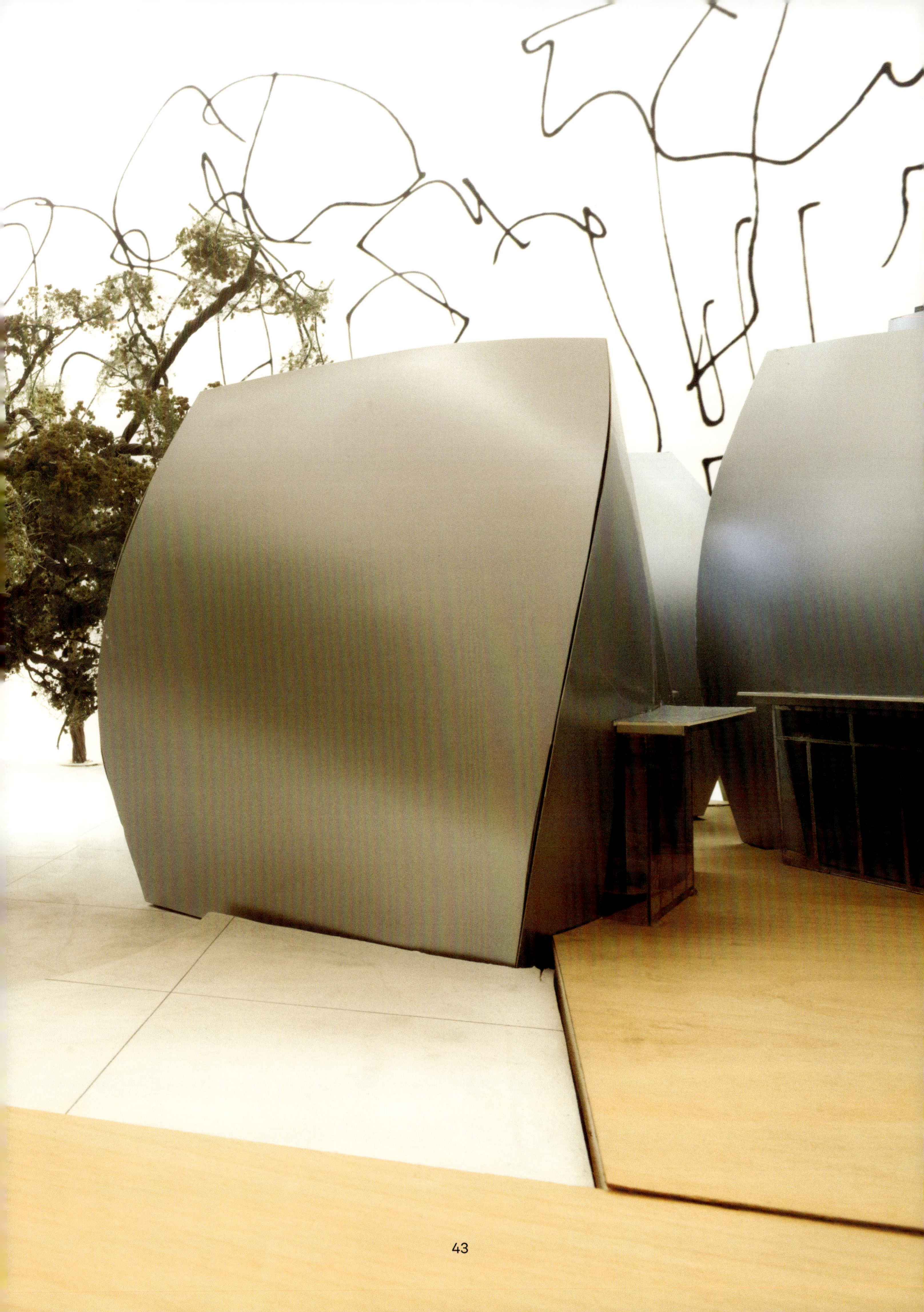

Ohr-O'Keefe Museum of Art

1999-Present (built), Biloxi, Mississippi

Located in Biloxi, Mississippi, in Tricentennial Park, the Ohr-O'Keefe Museum of Art is a small campus of six separate pavilions set within a grove of ancient Live Oak trees and interconnected by a brick plaza promenade. Each of the buildings has a covered exterior porch at the entry, evoking the vernacular domestic forms of the area. The George E. Ohr Museum itself consists of four gently sculptural volumes clad in stainless steel panels and connected by a central glass-enclosed gallery, providing a total of 2,700 square feet of exhibition space devoted to the display of pottery created by Ohr in the late nineteenth and early twentieth centuries. The interiors of the four enclosed galleries are subtly sculpted volumes, that allow the true power of Ohr's pottery to be fully expressed.

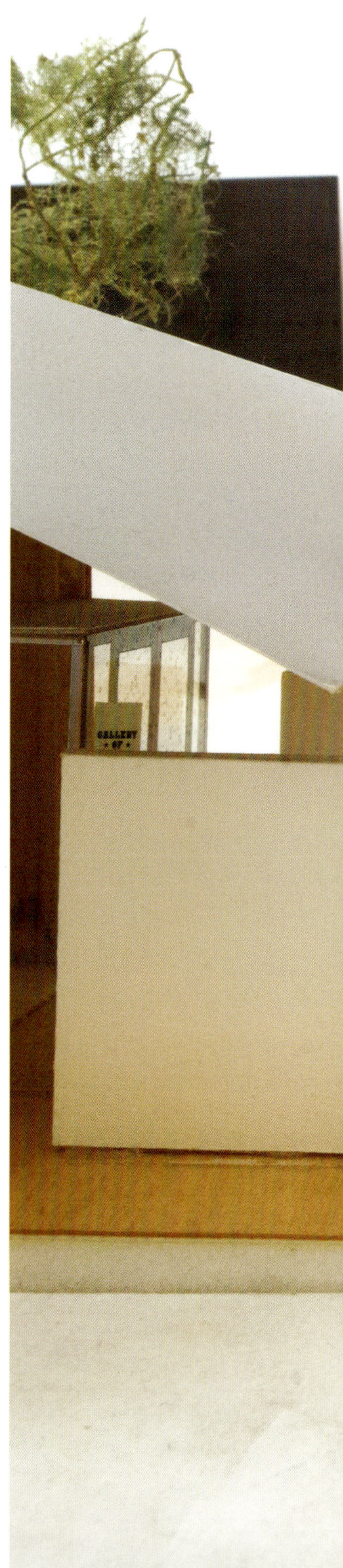

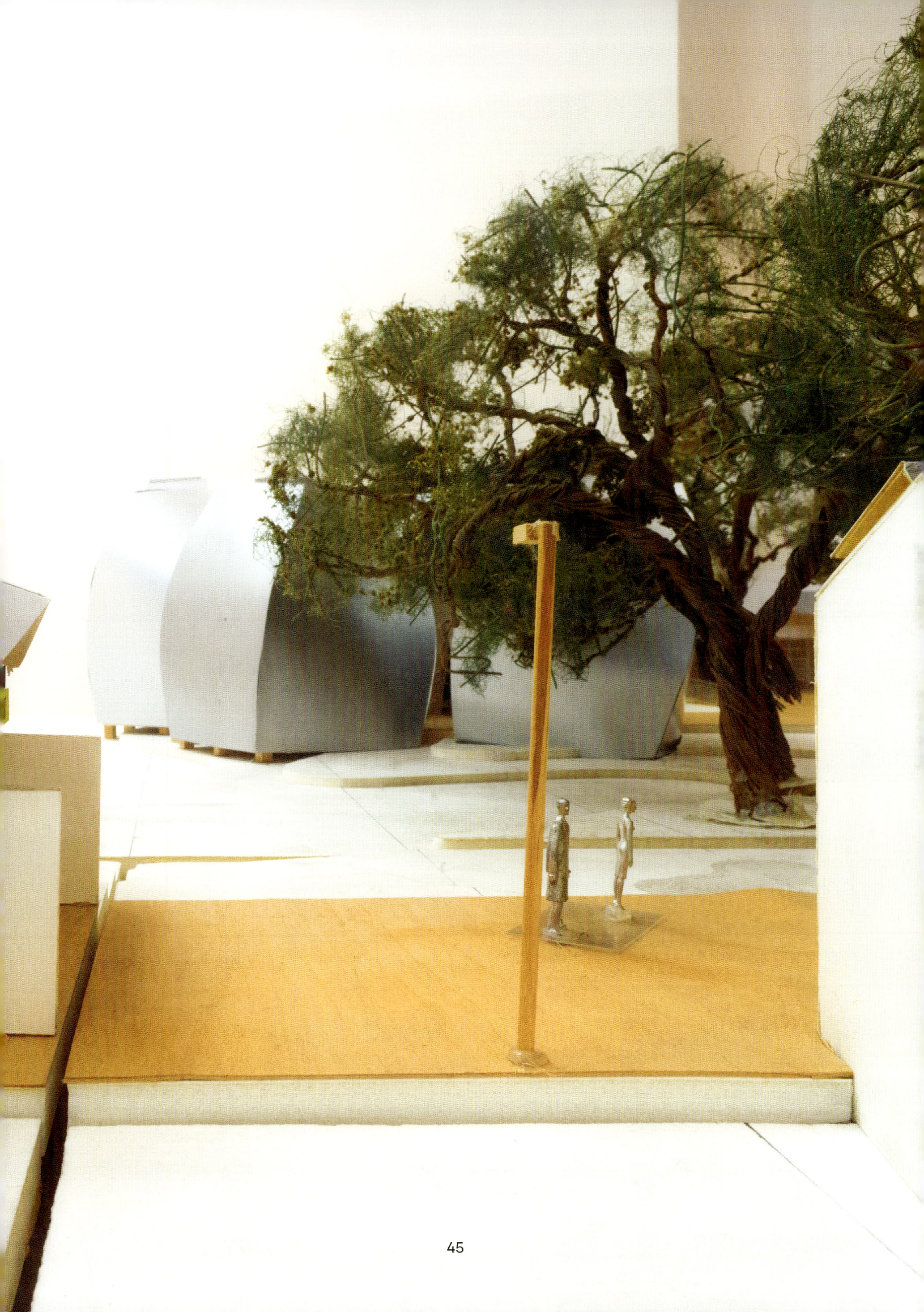

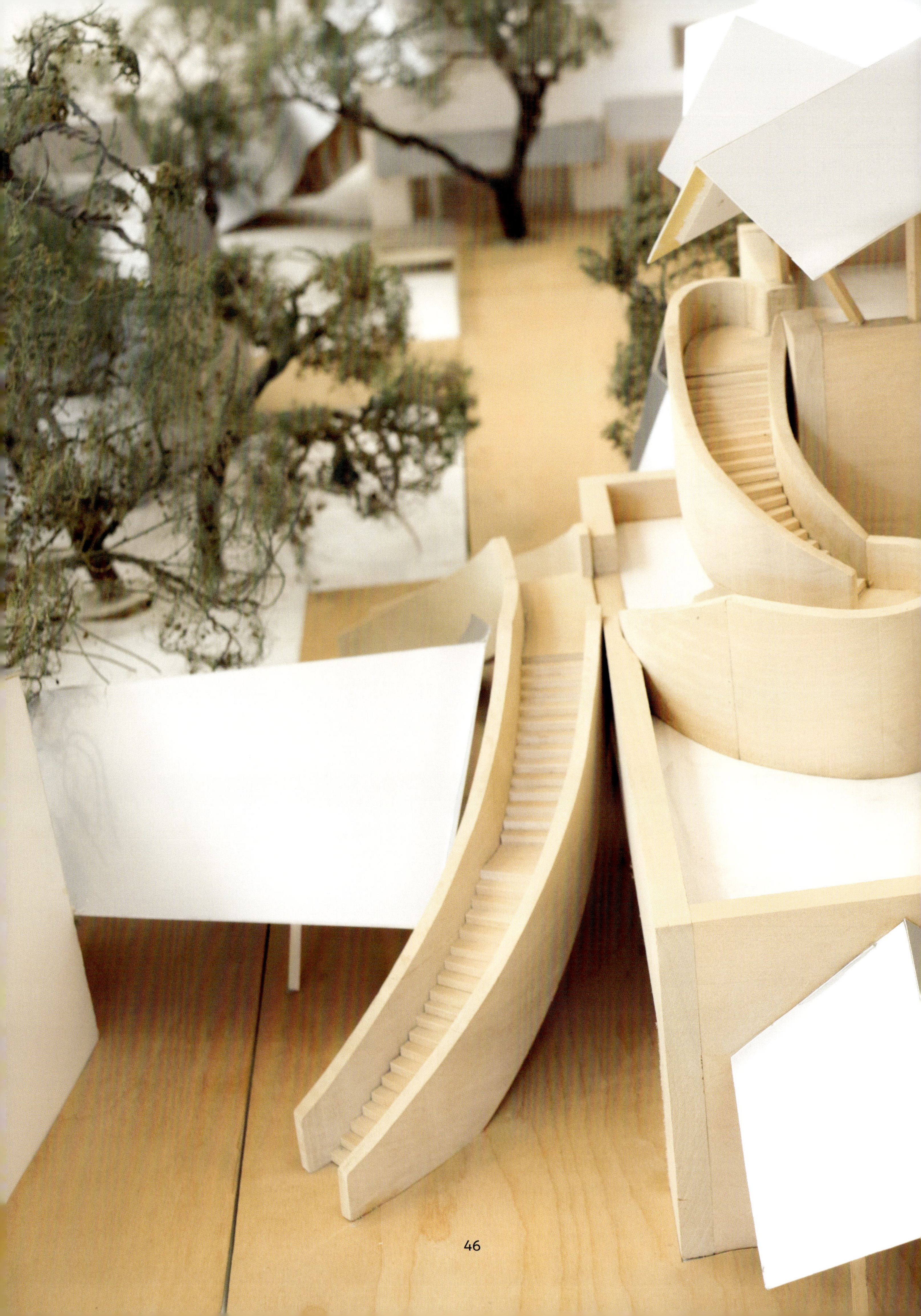

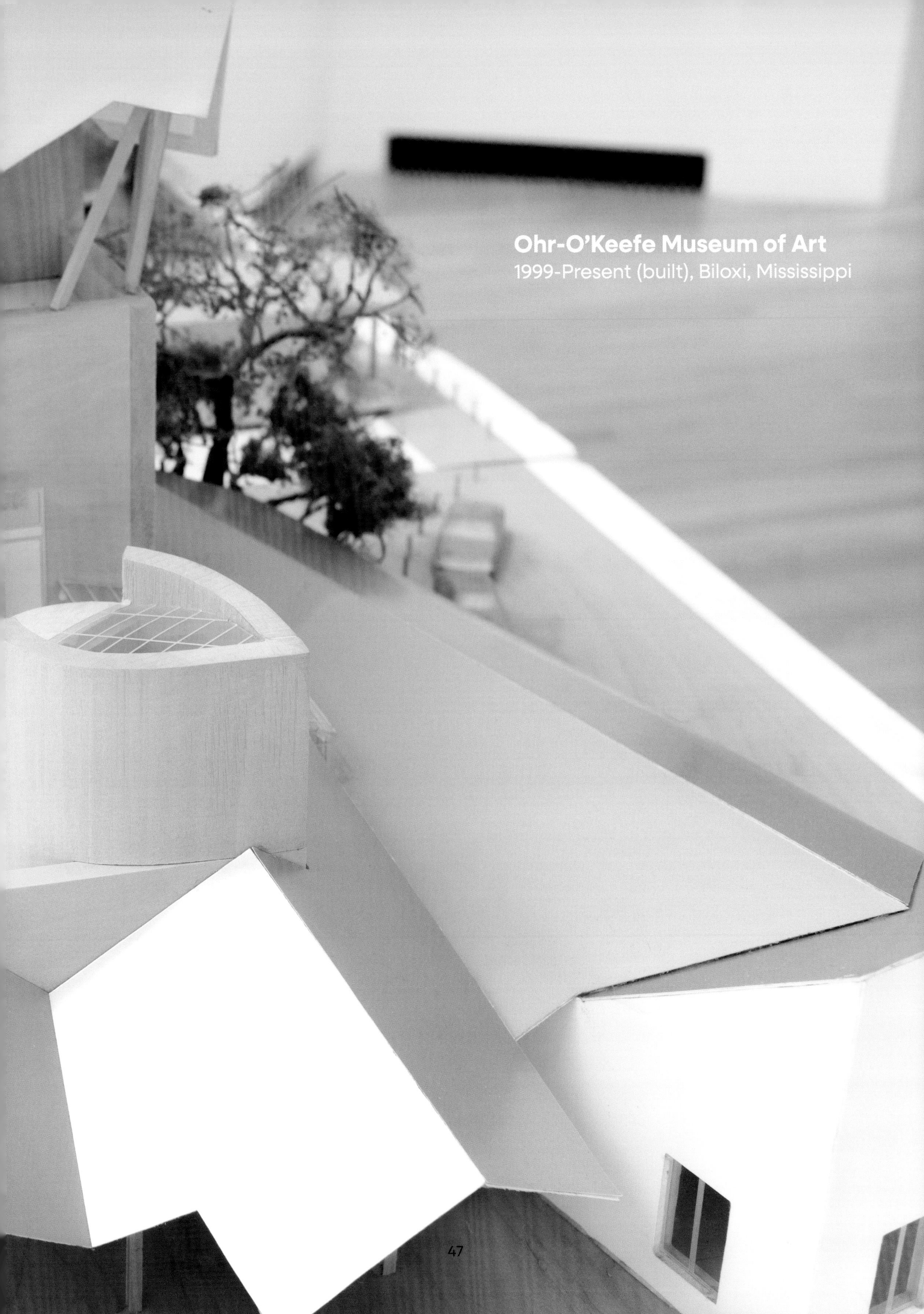

Ohr-O'Keefe Museum of Art
1999-Present (built), Biloxi, Mississippi

Tract House
1982 (unbuilt)

The design for a tract house was commissioned for an exhibition by the Leo Castelli Gallery in Los Angeles. Devised as a solution for American suburban housing, the study disassembles the typical single-family house into separate components, as if it were a series of pavilions based on a nine-square grid. The hope was that entire neighborhoods could be composed of a series of these houses; each house would be distinct because the segments could be placed in different positions and different relationships.

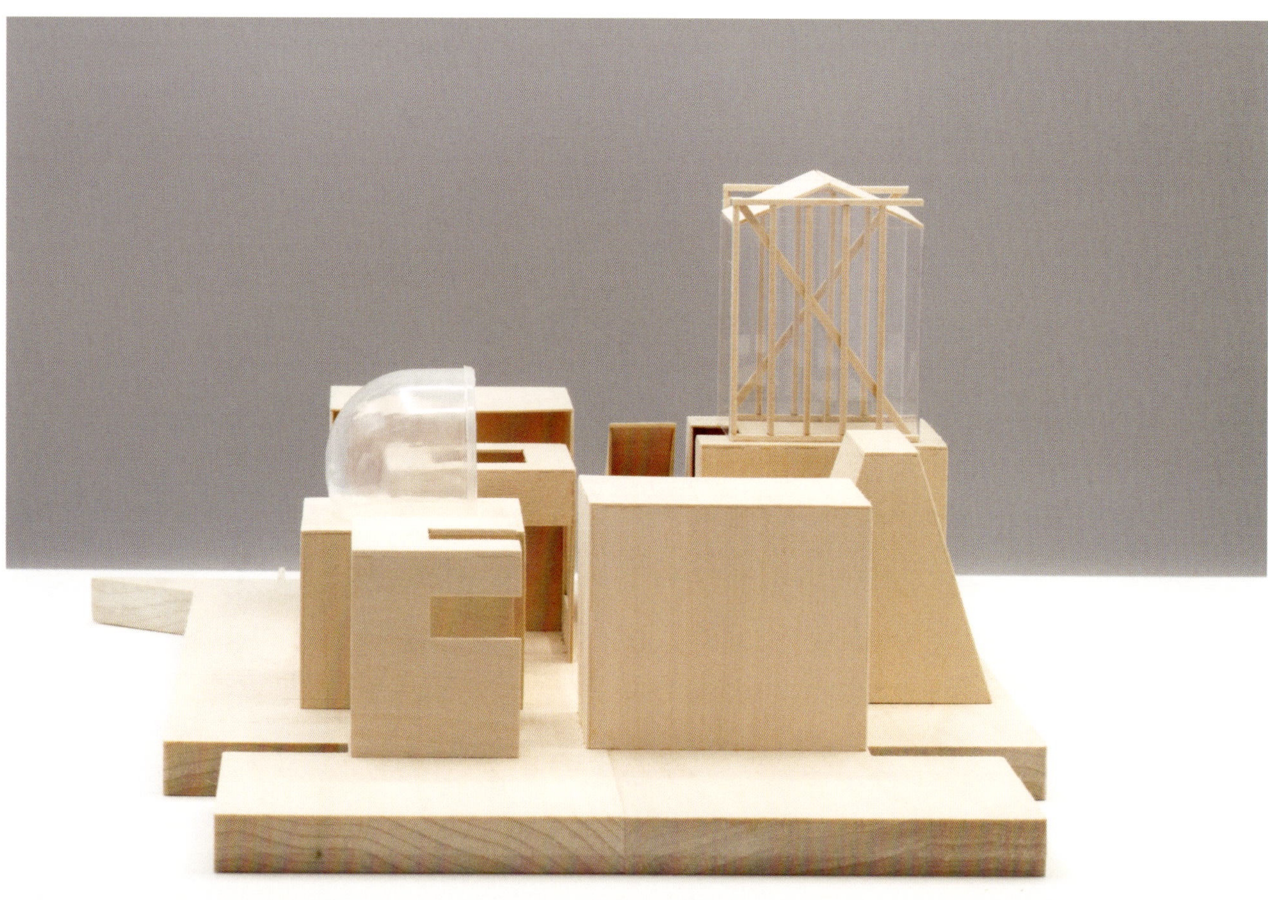

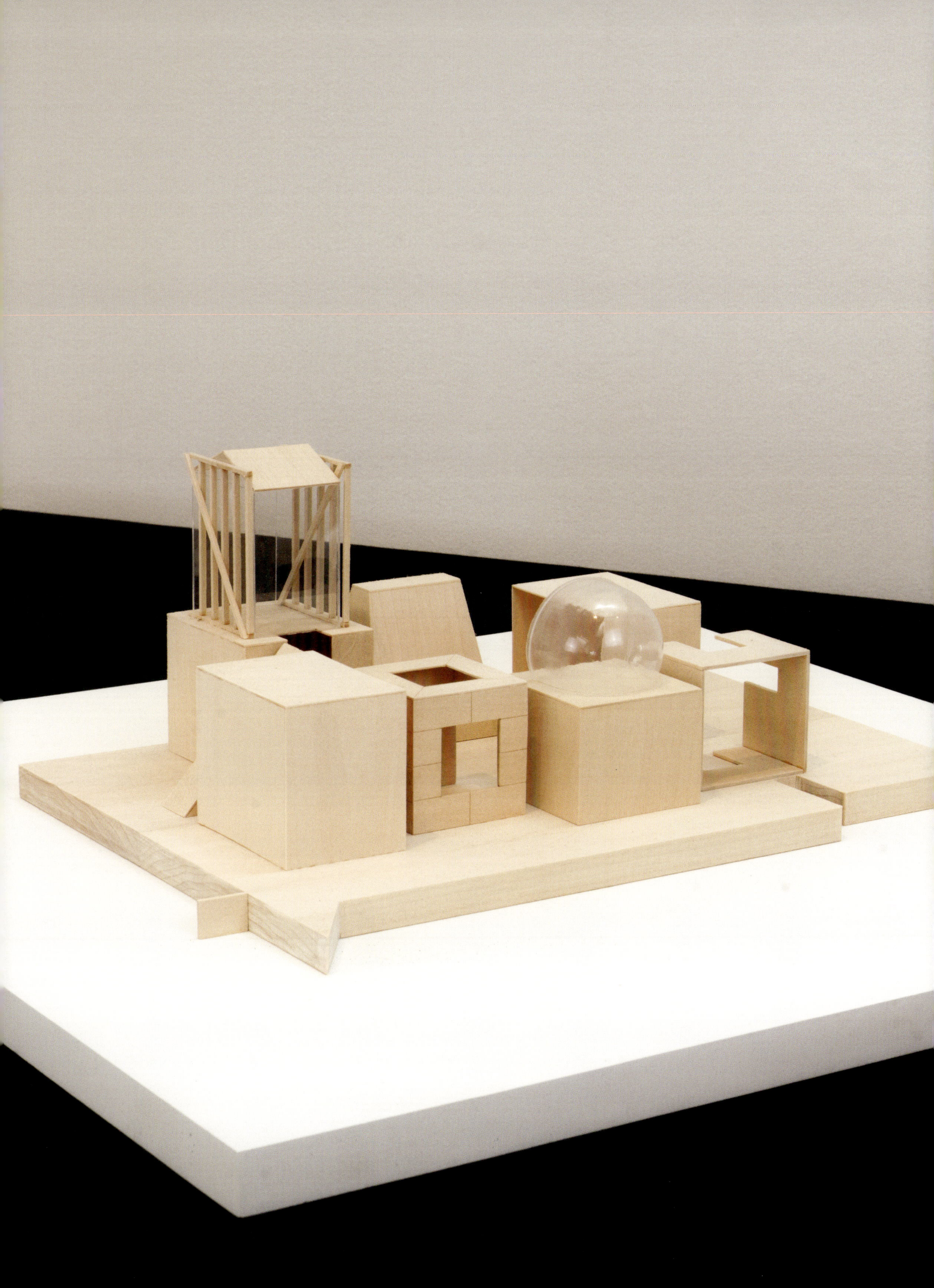

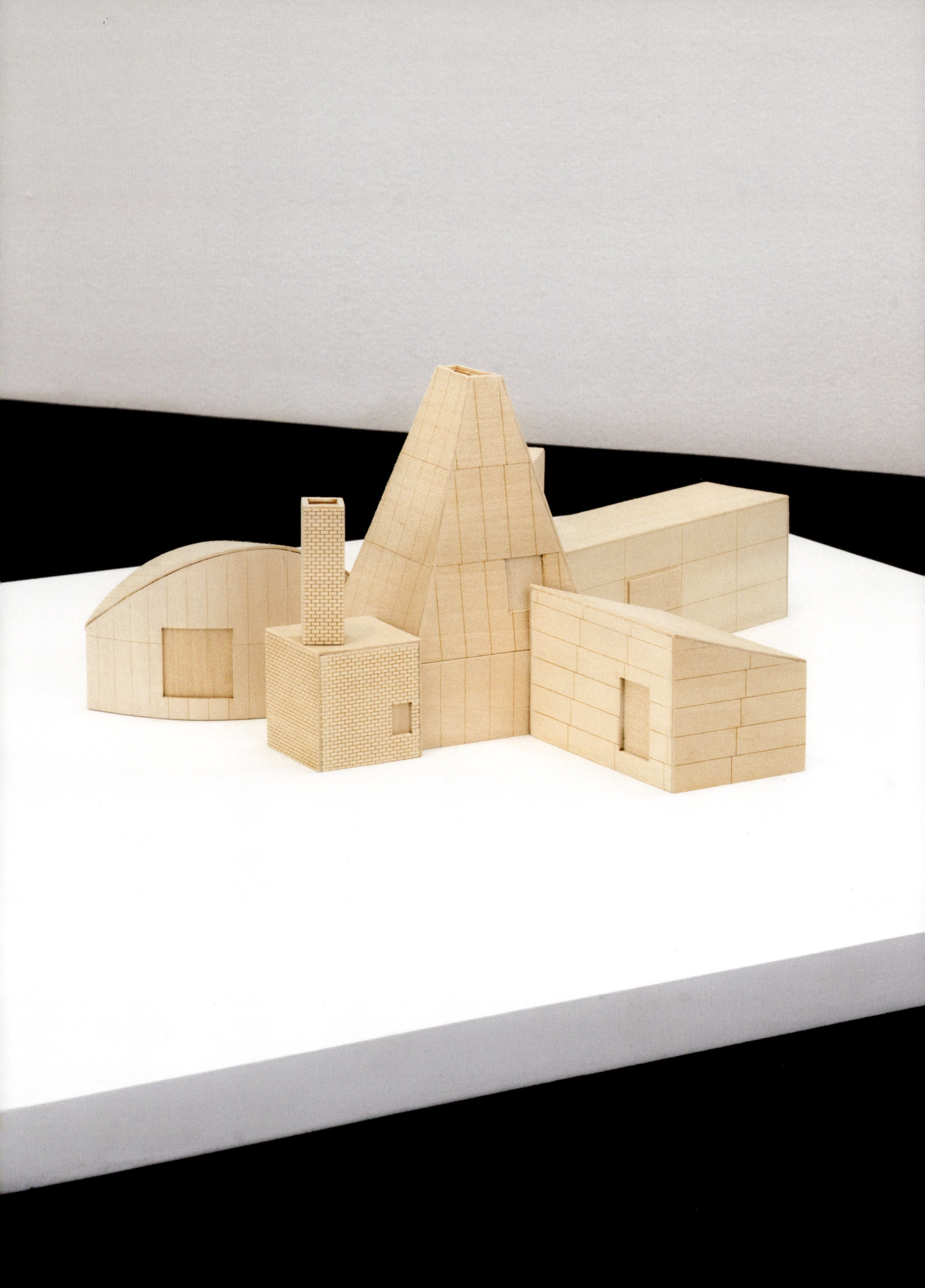

Winton Guest House

1982 (built), Wayzata, Minnesota

This project was located on a heavily wooded lakefront property approximately thirty miles from Minneapolis. The client wanted a modest building that maintained the sense of the natural landscape and complimented the existing main house designed in the early 1950s by Philip Johnson. Like the other early house projects, the parts of the house are very simple differentiated forms. However, the Guest House marks an evolution in Gehry's process: instead of creating a series of one-room buildings, Gehry treats the living room as the tall central organizing form with the bedrooms and service areas arranged around it. The separate rooms are not connected, but they touch, creating tension with the negative space between them. As a result, the Guest House doesn't look as much like a building as it does a large outdoor sculpture. The objects-in-a-landscape are placed together in a tight complex, like a Morandi still-life painting. The Guest House has since been purchased by a new owner and relocated to upstate New York.

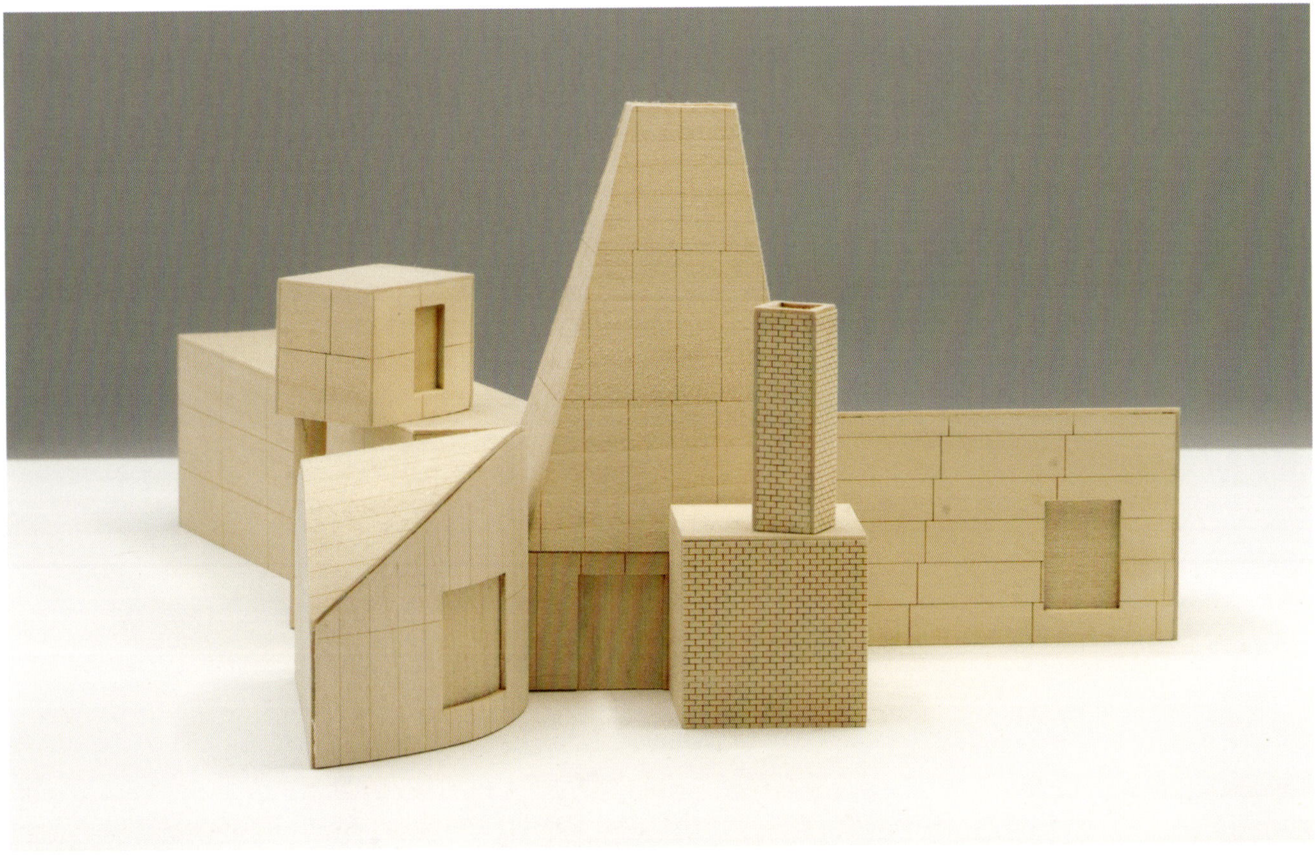

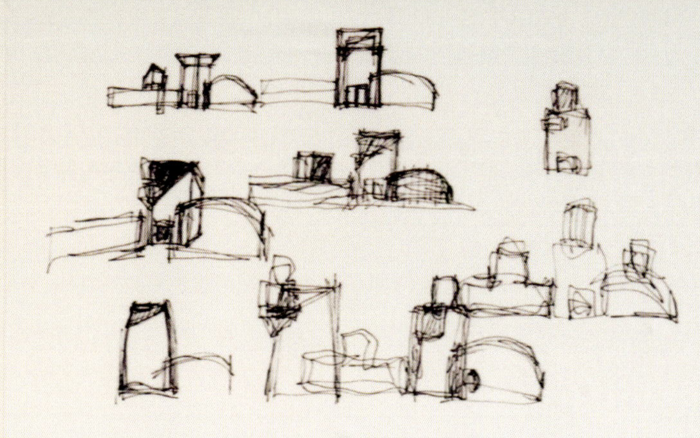

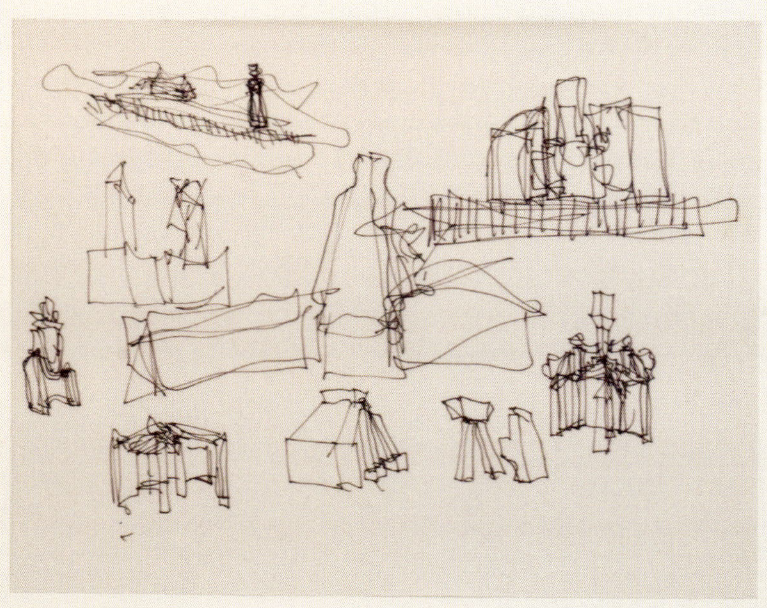

Winton Guest House

1982 (built), Wayzata, Minnesota

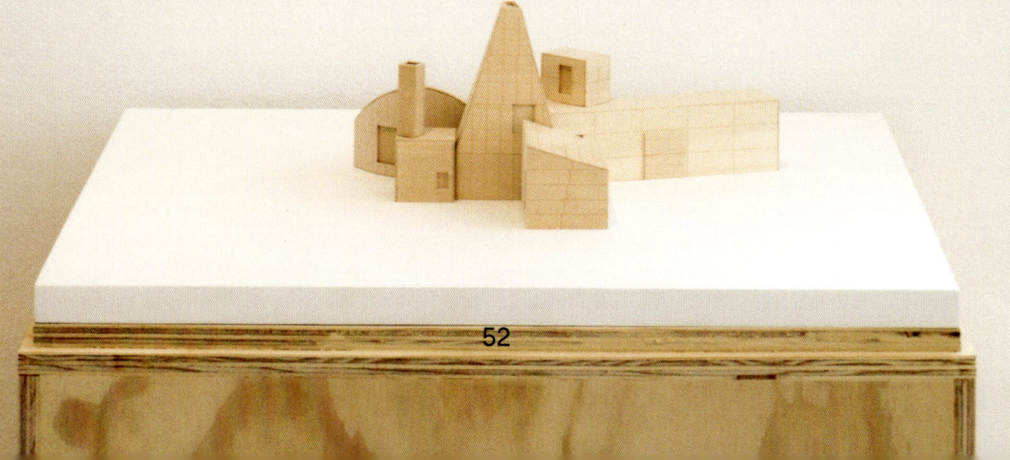

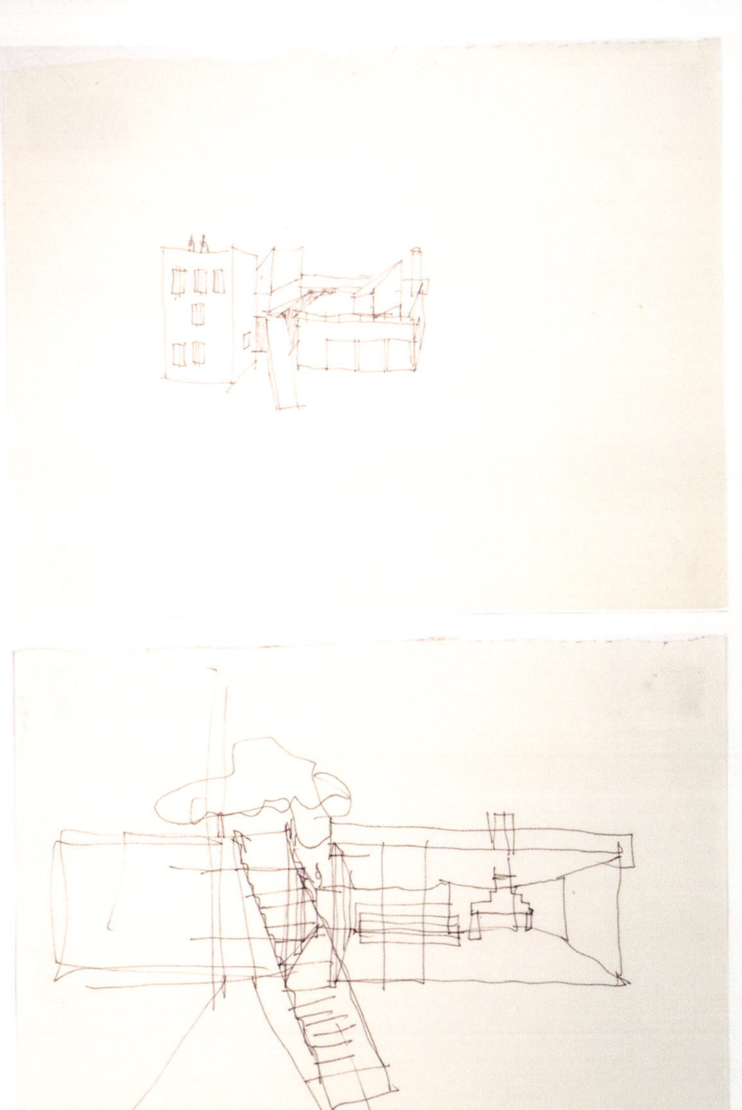

Tract House

1982 (built), Calabasas, California

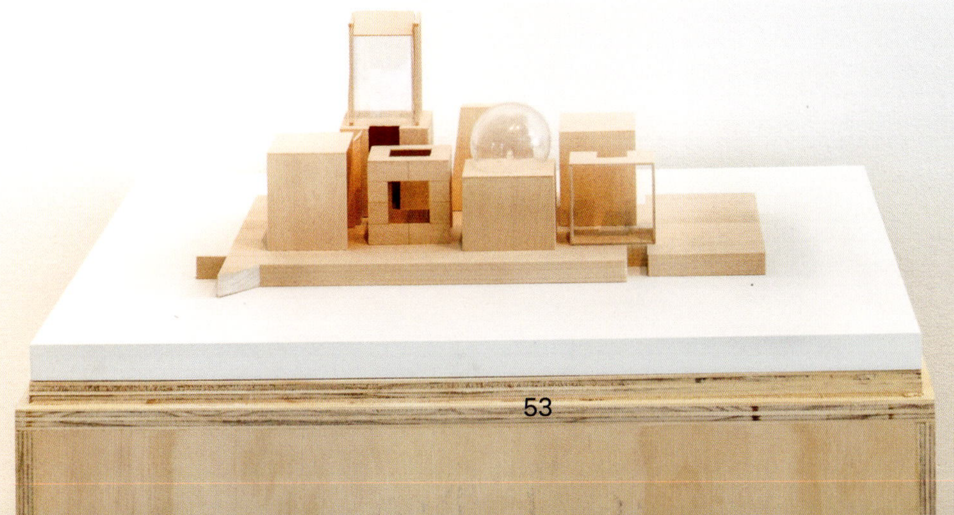

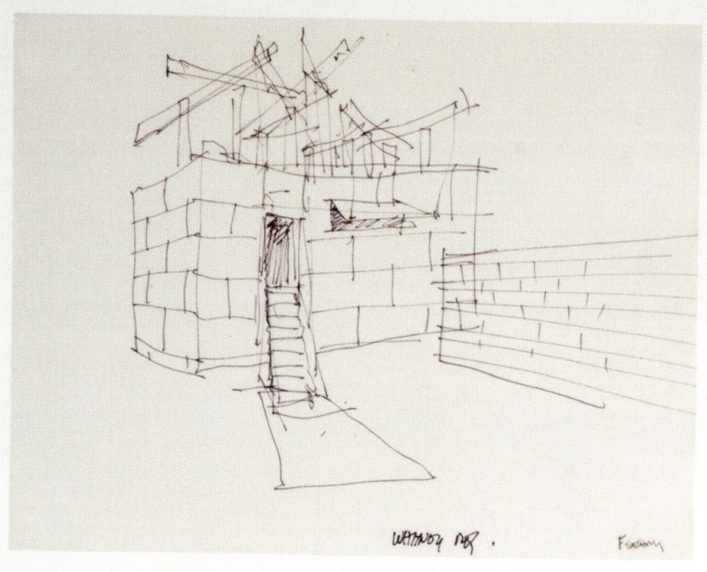

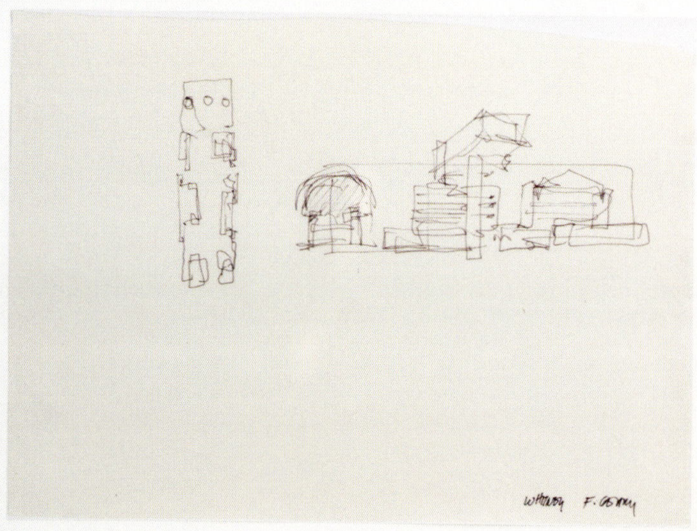

House for a Filmmaker
1981 (built), Los Angeles, California

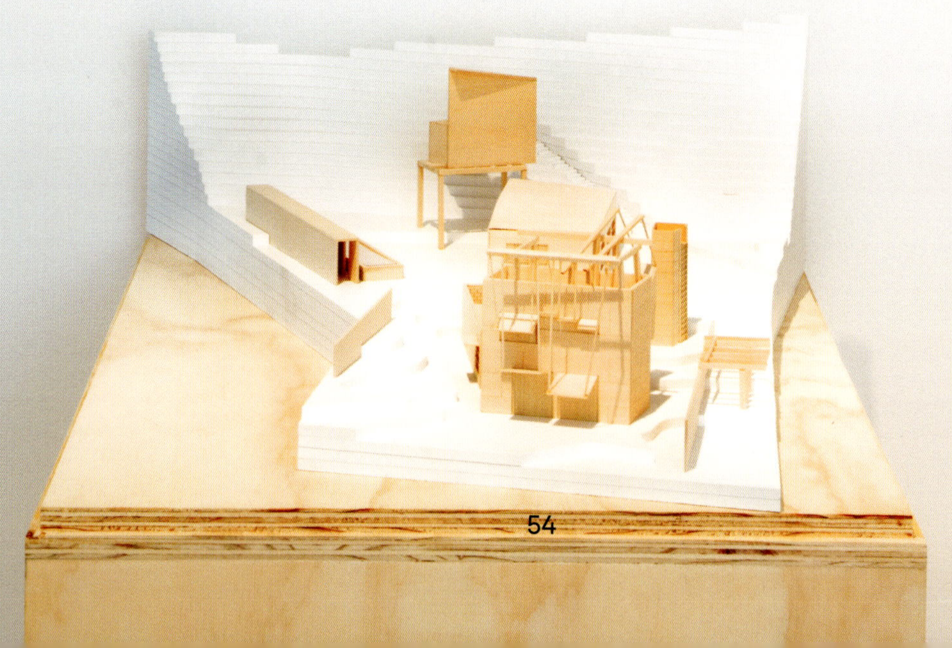

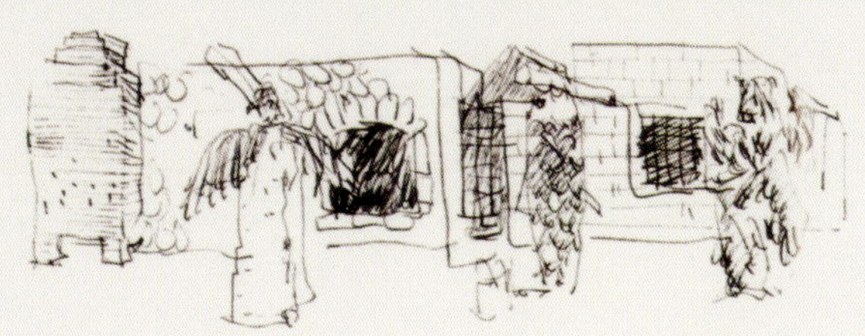

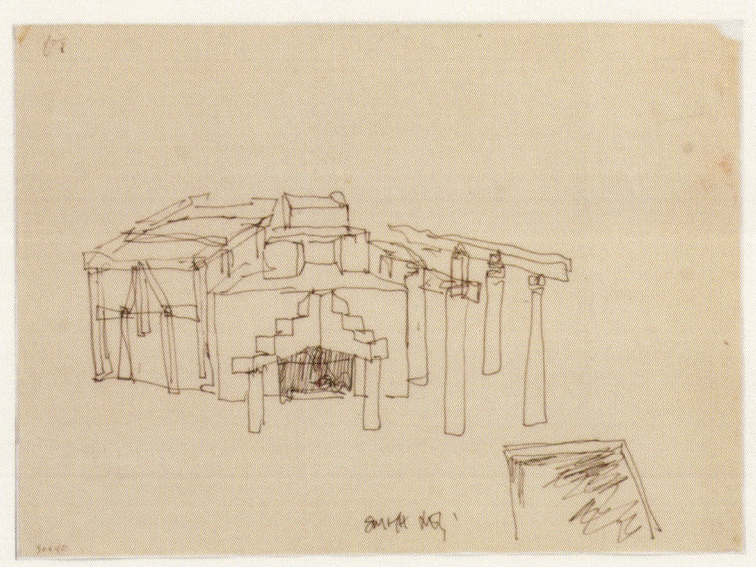

Smith House
1981 (unbuilt)

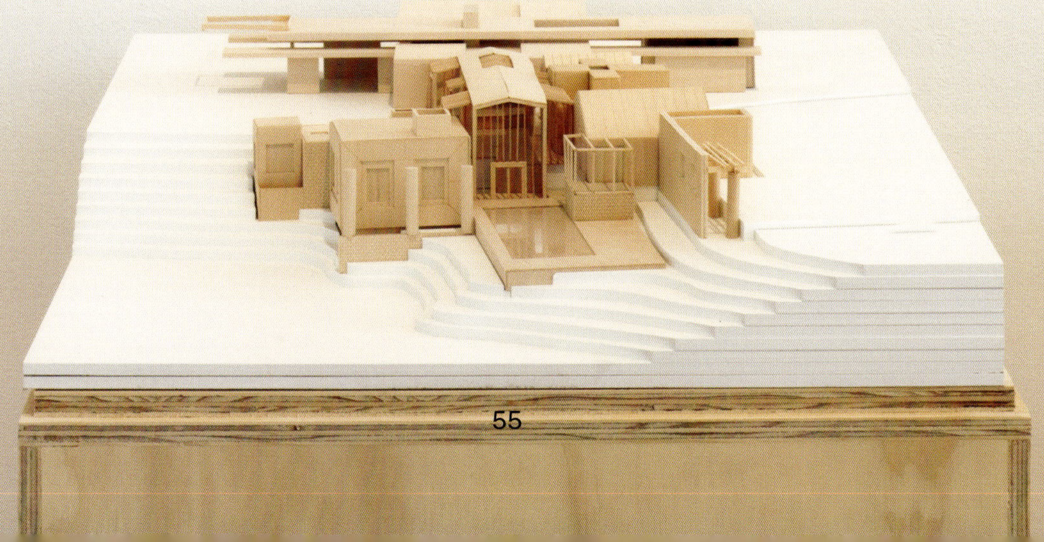

Smith House

1981 (unbuilt)

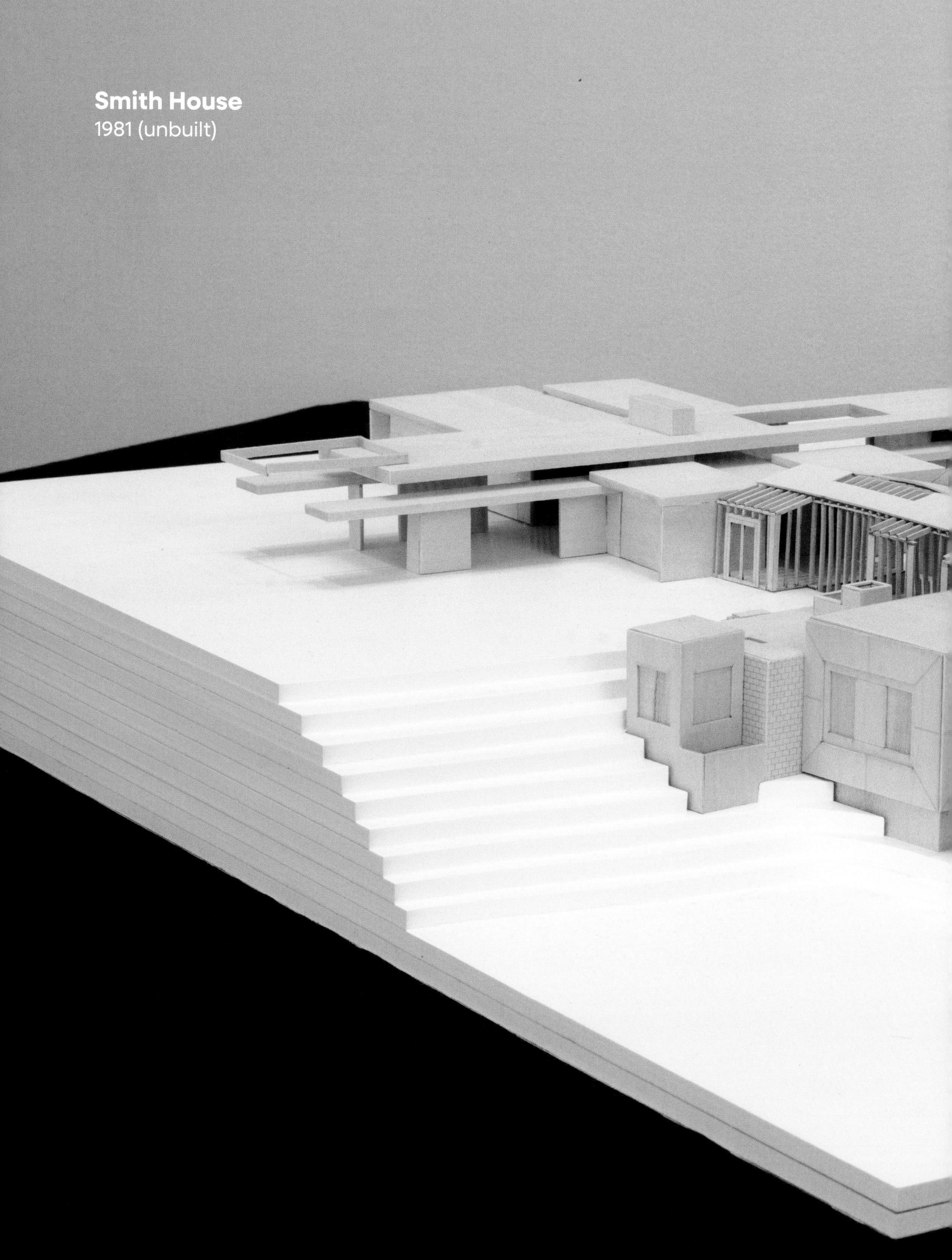

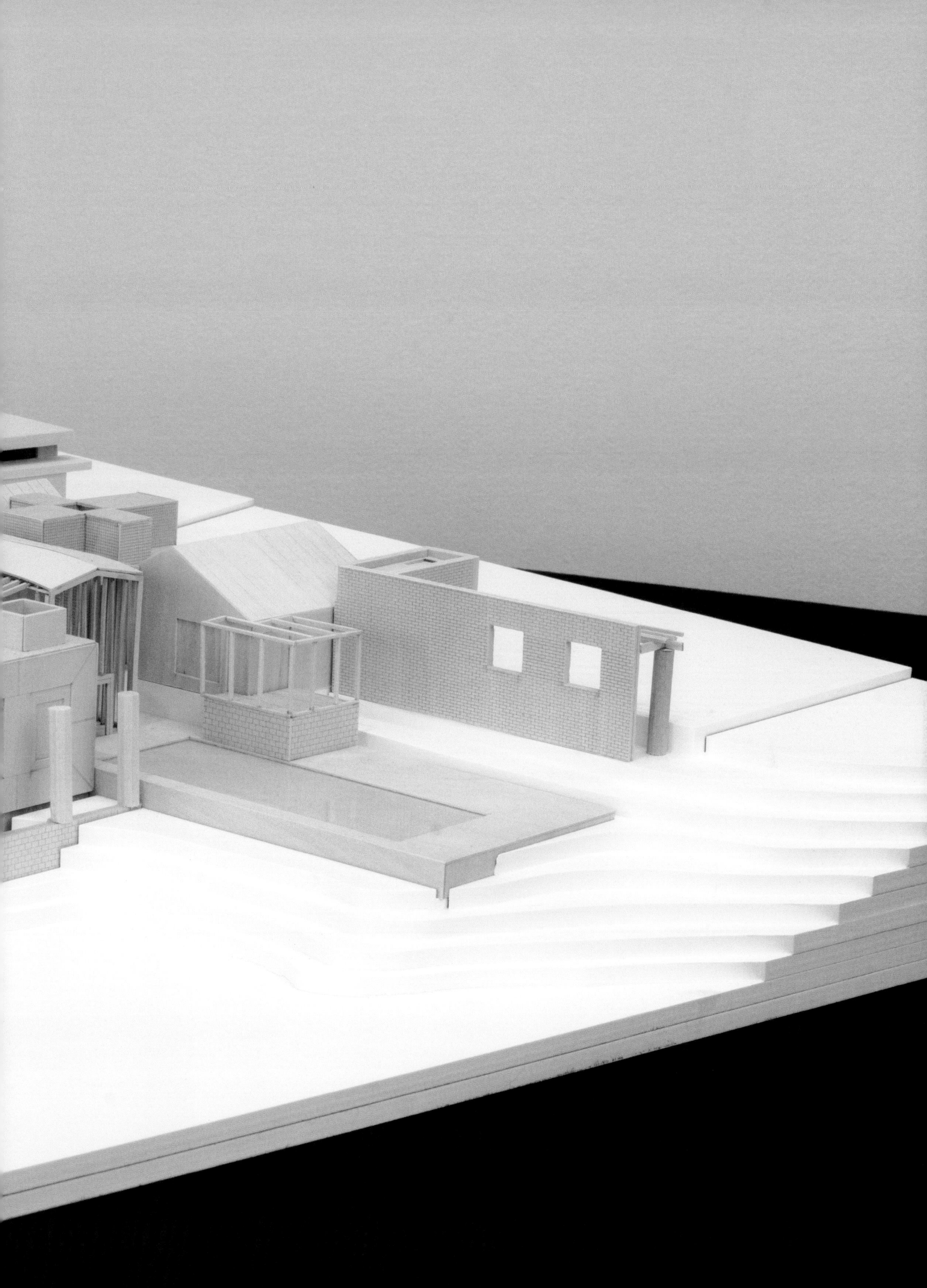

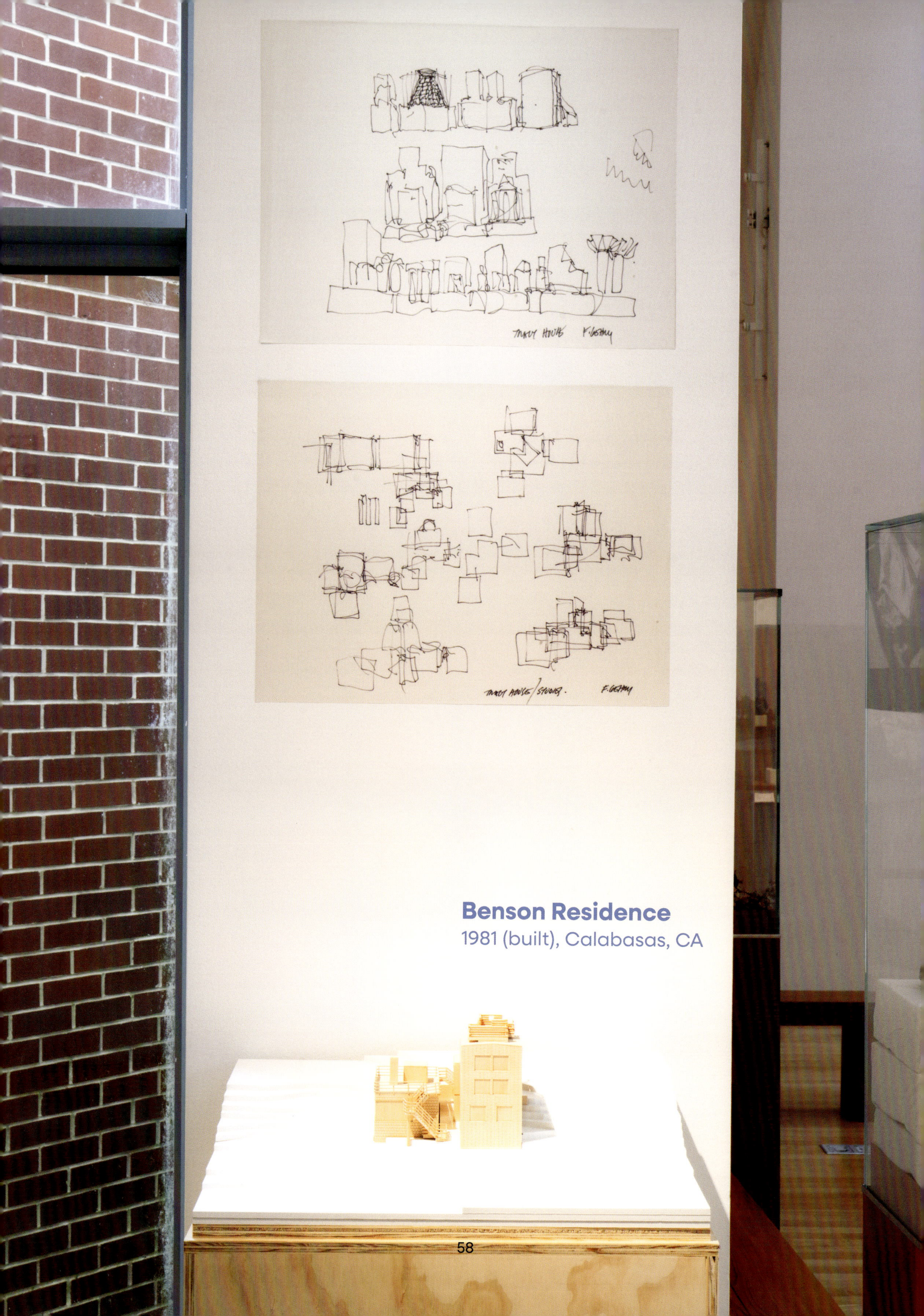

Benson Residence

1981 (built), Calabasas, CA

Benson Residence

1981 (built), Calabasas, CA

The house was designed for a Loyola Law School professor and his young family. The project was challenging because the site was situated on a steep hillside and the budget was extremely tight. The solution was to create two separate buildings joined by second-story bridges—the taller building is the sleeping area (the kids on the bottom floor and the parents upstairs), while the other is the living area. By breaking down a house into two simple boxes, it was cheaper than a single building. This configuration also allowed Gehry to treat them like two objects in a still-life painting, exploring the relationship of the two objects as well as the space between them. To keep the cost down, rough carpentry was left exposed and each of the buildings were clad in a different color of asphalt shingles, which ended up giving the simple boxes a visual richness. The Bensons loved the playful house and lived there for thirty years. The house is now a historic landmark.

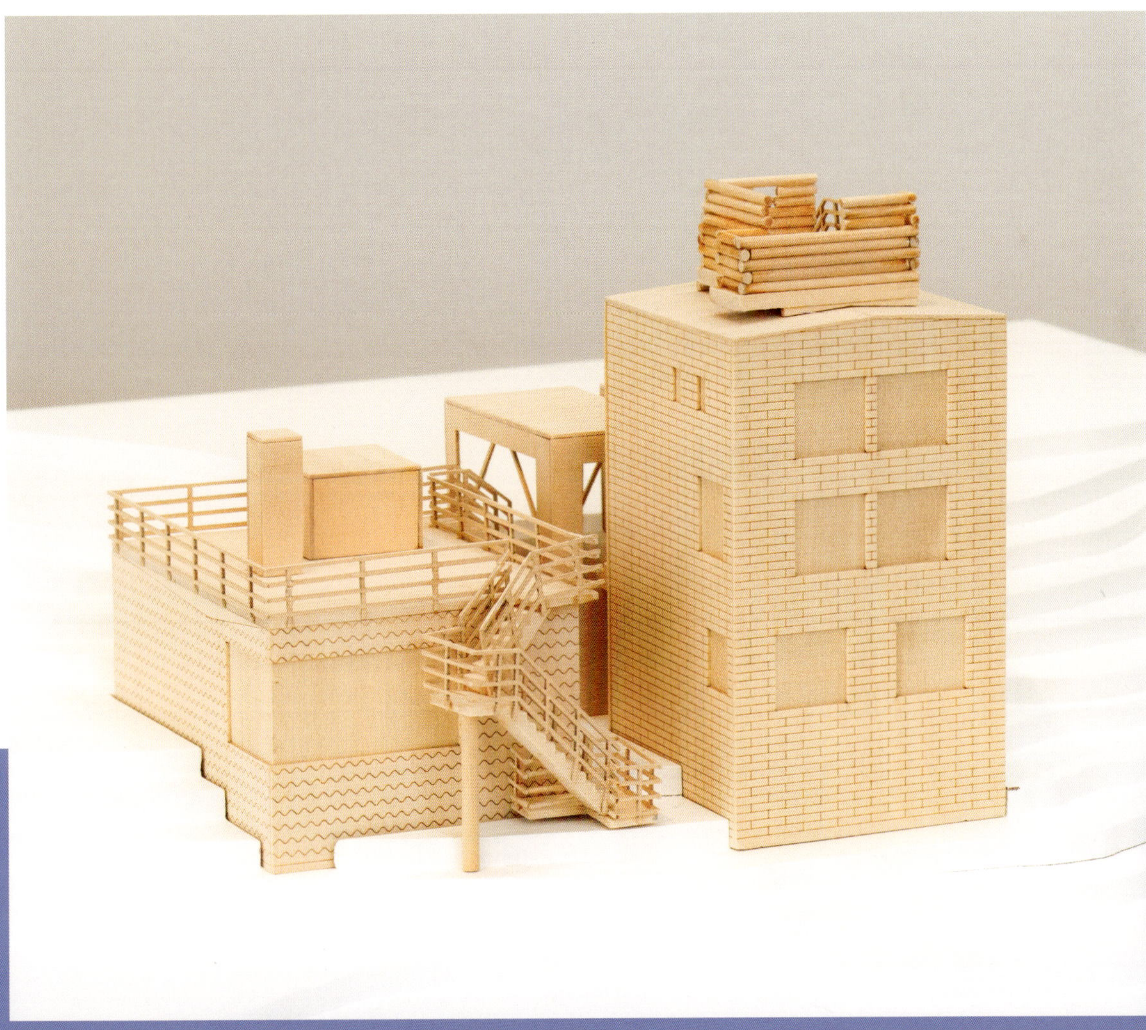

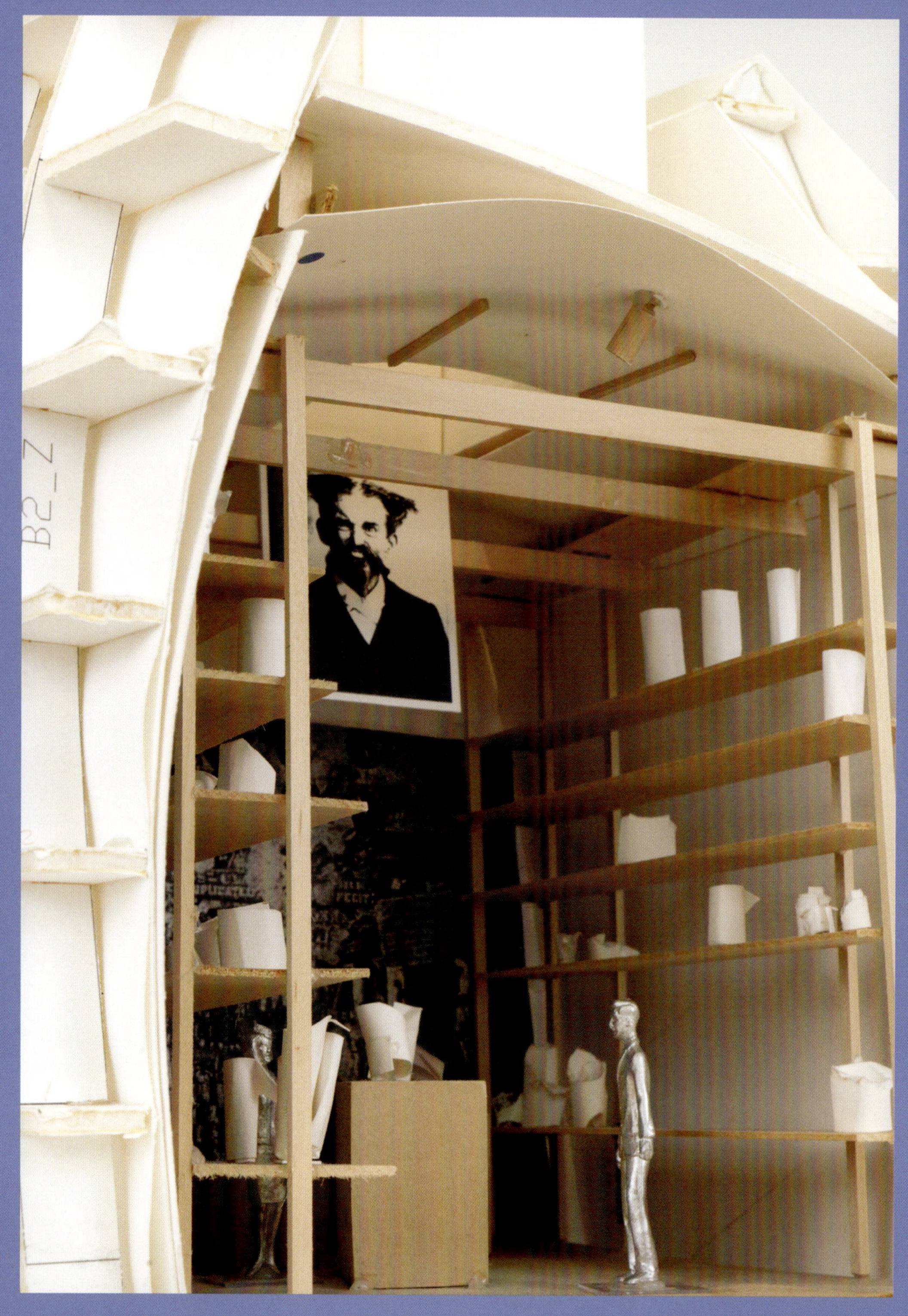
B2_Z

INTERPRETATION OF GEORGE OHR'S STUDIO (MODEL, ½" = 1'-0")
WOOD, GATORBOARD, FOAMCORE, PAPER
FRANK GEHRY

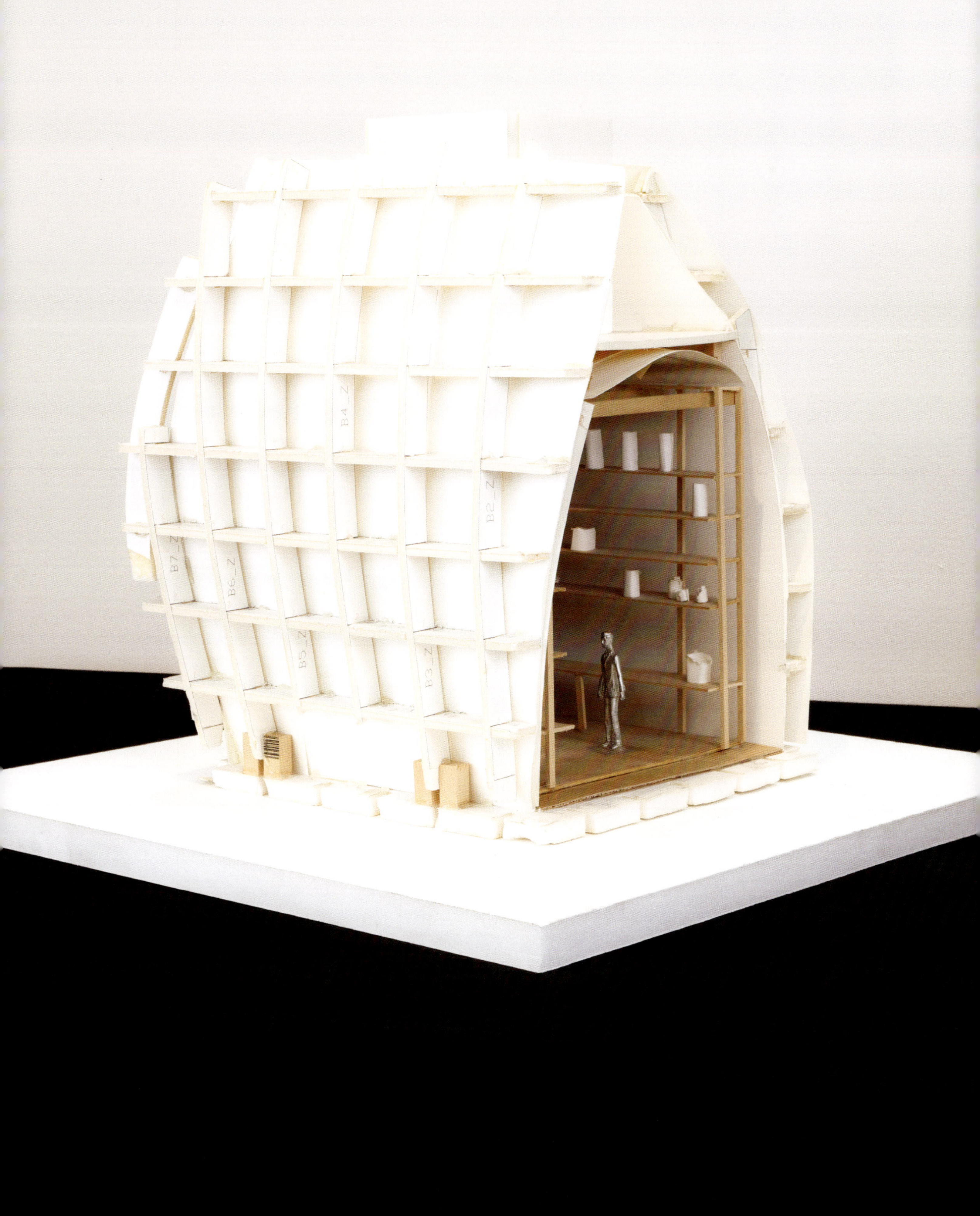

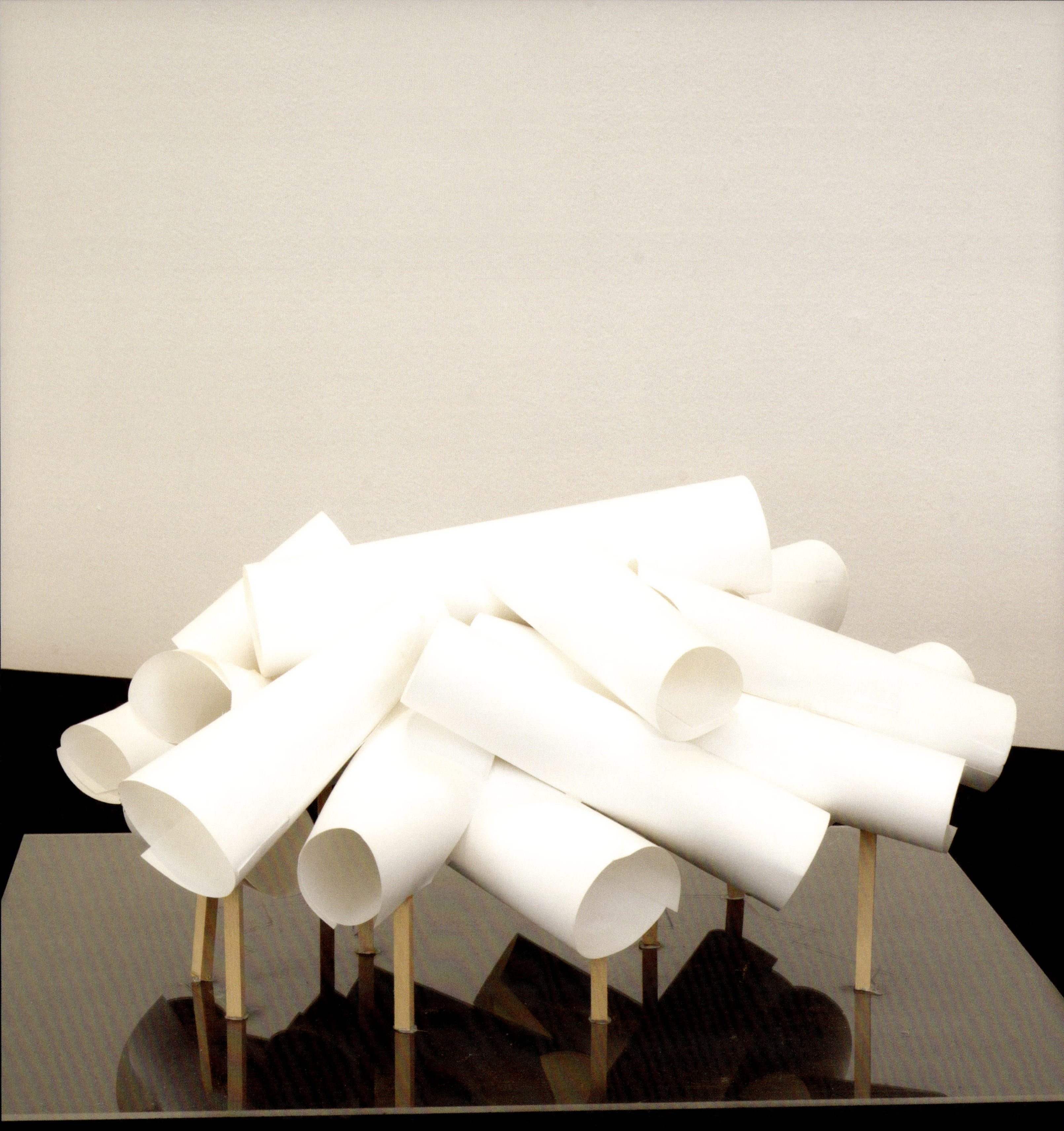

ABOVE:
ASPEN MEETING HOUSE (PROCESS MODEL, 18" × 18" × 8.5")
WOOD, PAPER TUBES, PLEXIGLASS
FRANK GEHRY

RIGHT:
TIFFANY & CO. TABLETOP COLLECTION
GRID OBJECT
FRANK GEHRY

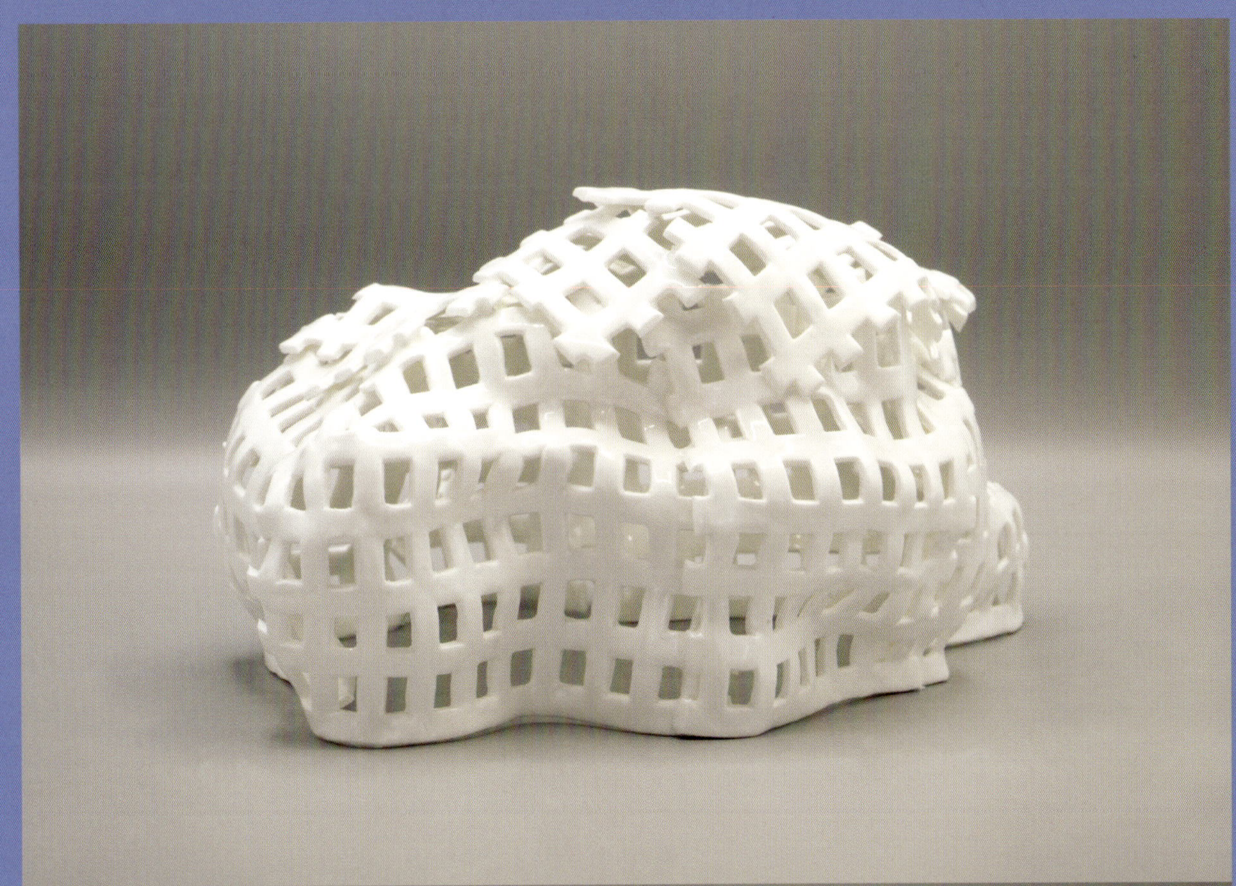

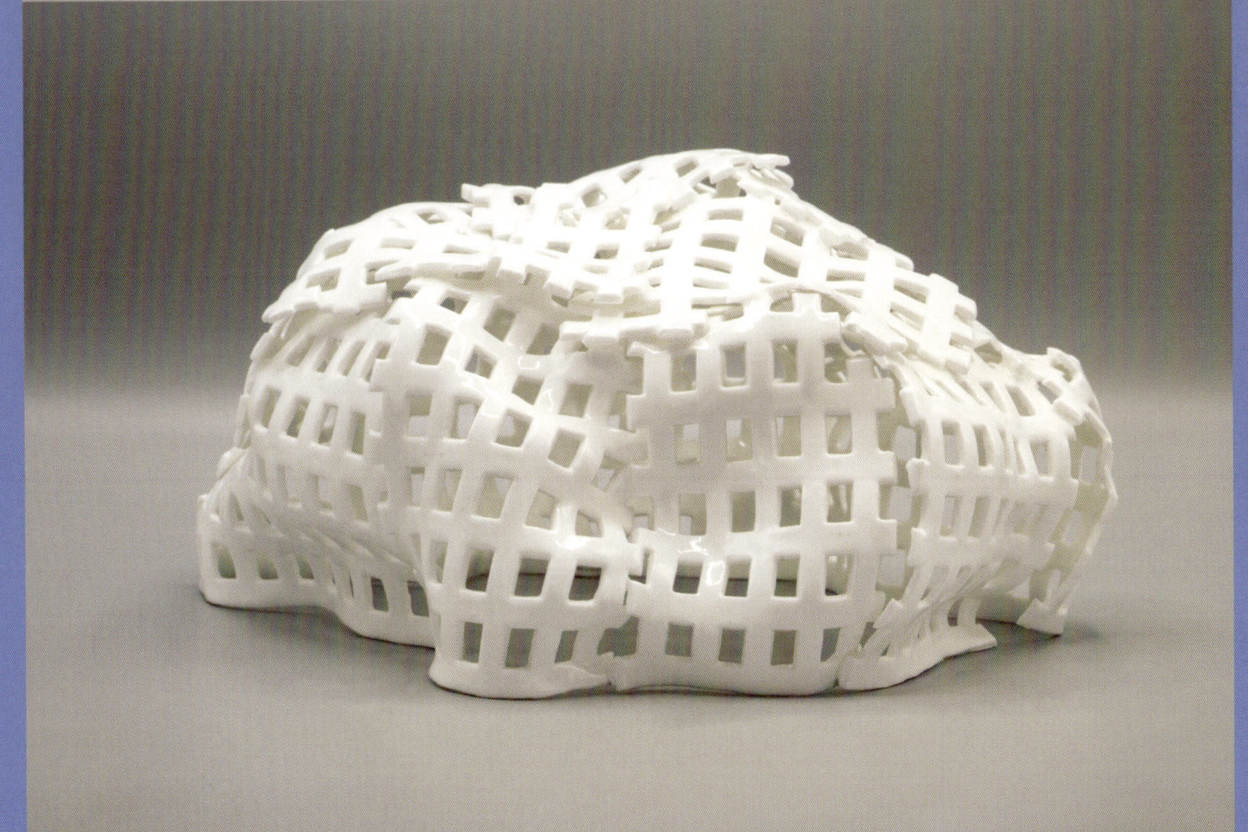

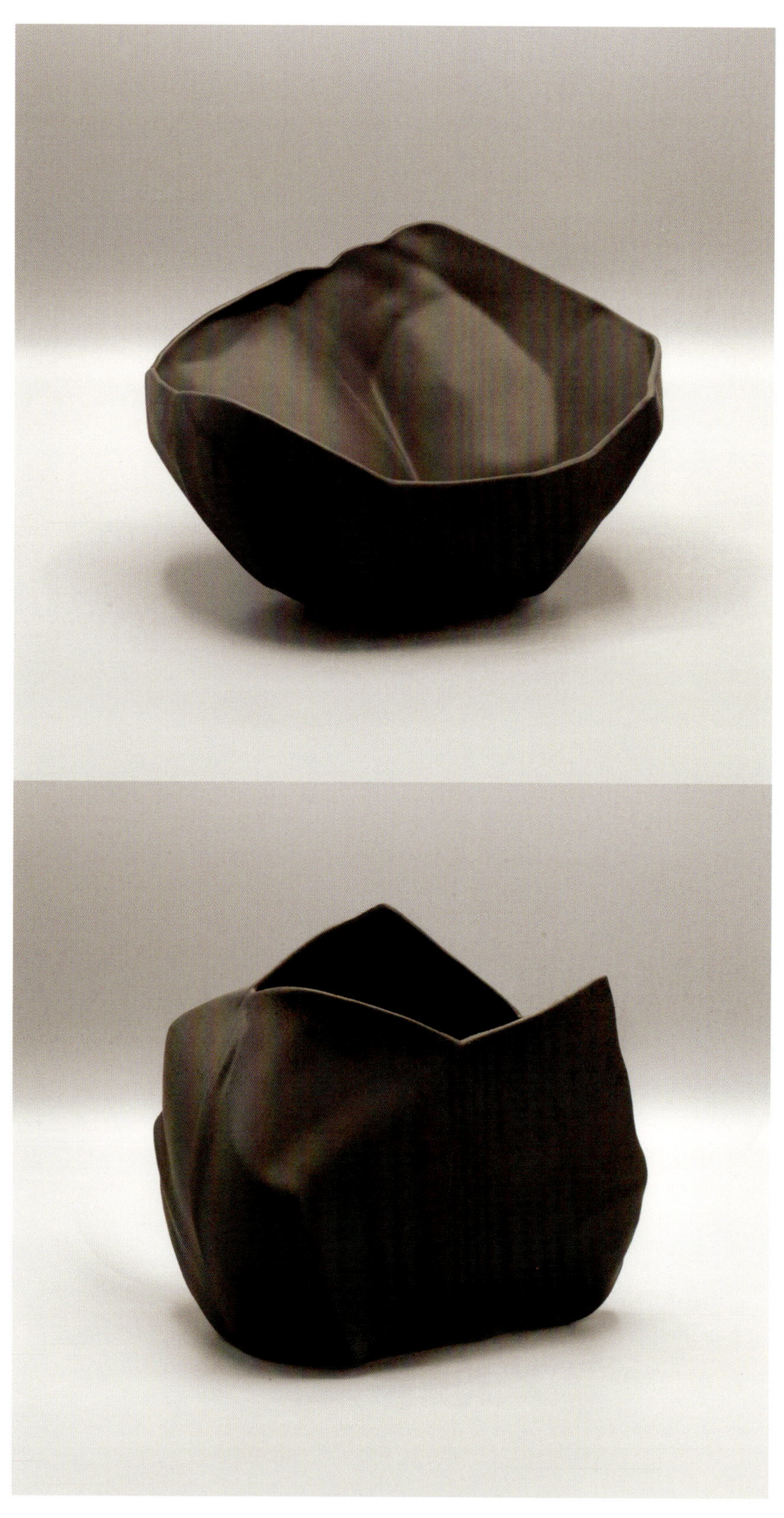

TIFFANY & CO. TABLETOP COLLECTION
ROCK BOWLS
FRANK GEHRY

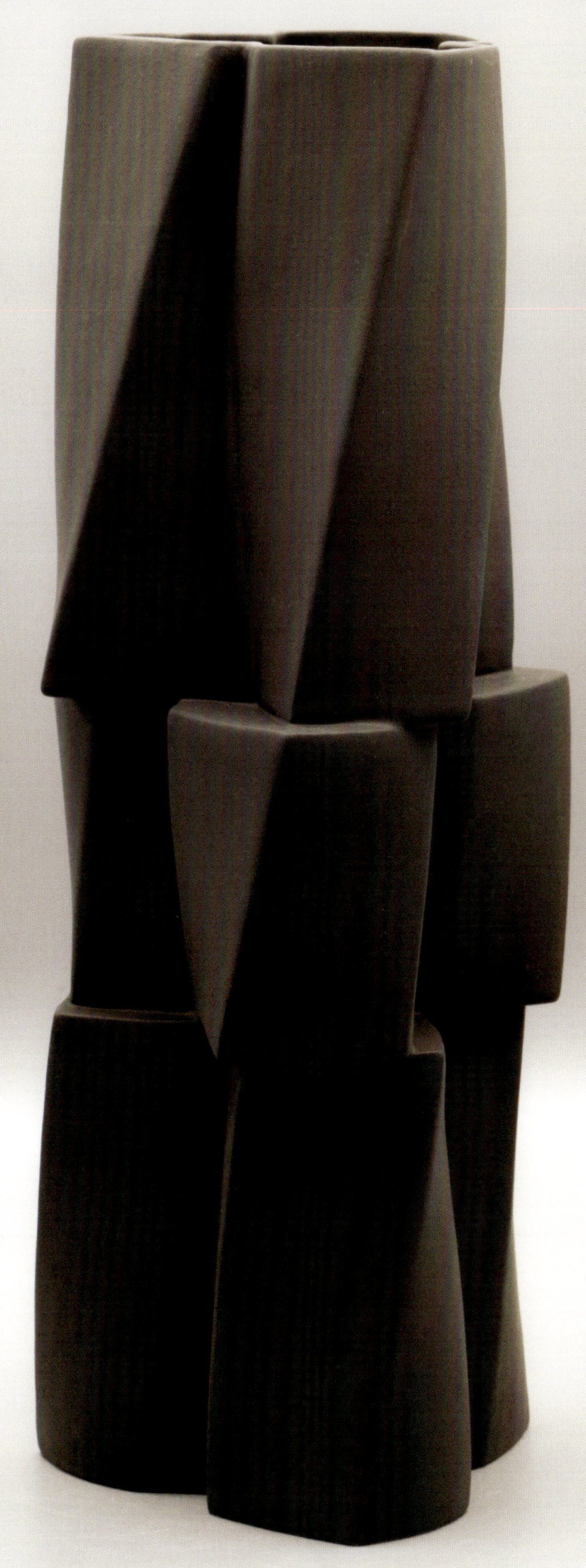

TIFFANY & CO. TABLETOP COLLECTION
ROCK VASE
FRANK GEHRY

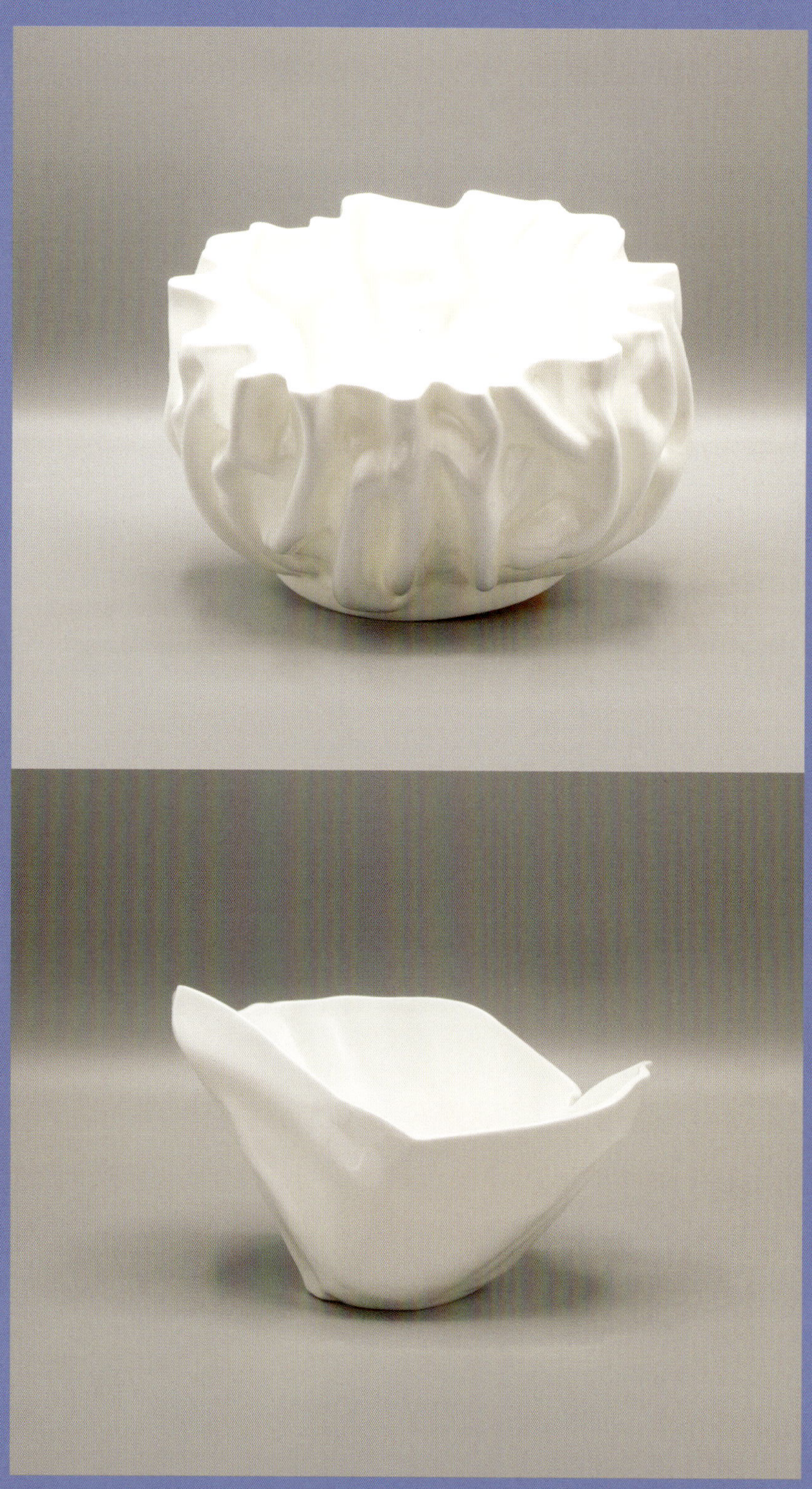

TIFFANY & CO. TABLETOP COLLECTION
ROCK BOWLS
FRANK GEHRY

TIFFANY & CO. TABLETOP COLLECTION
ROCK VASE
FRANK GEHRY

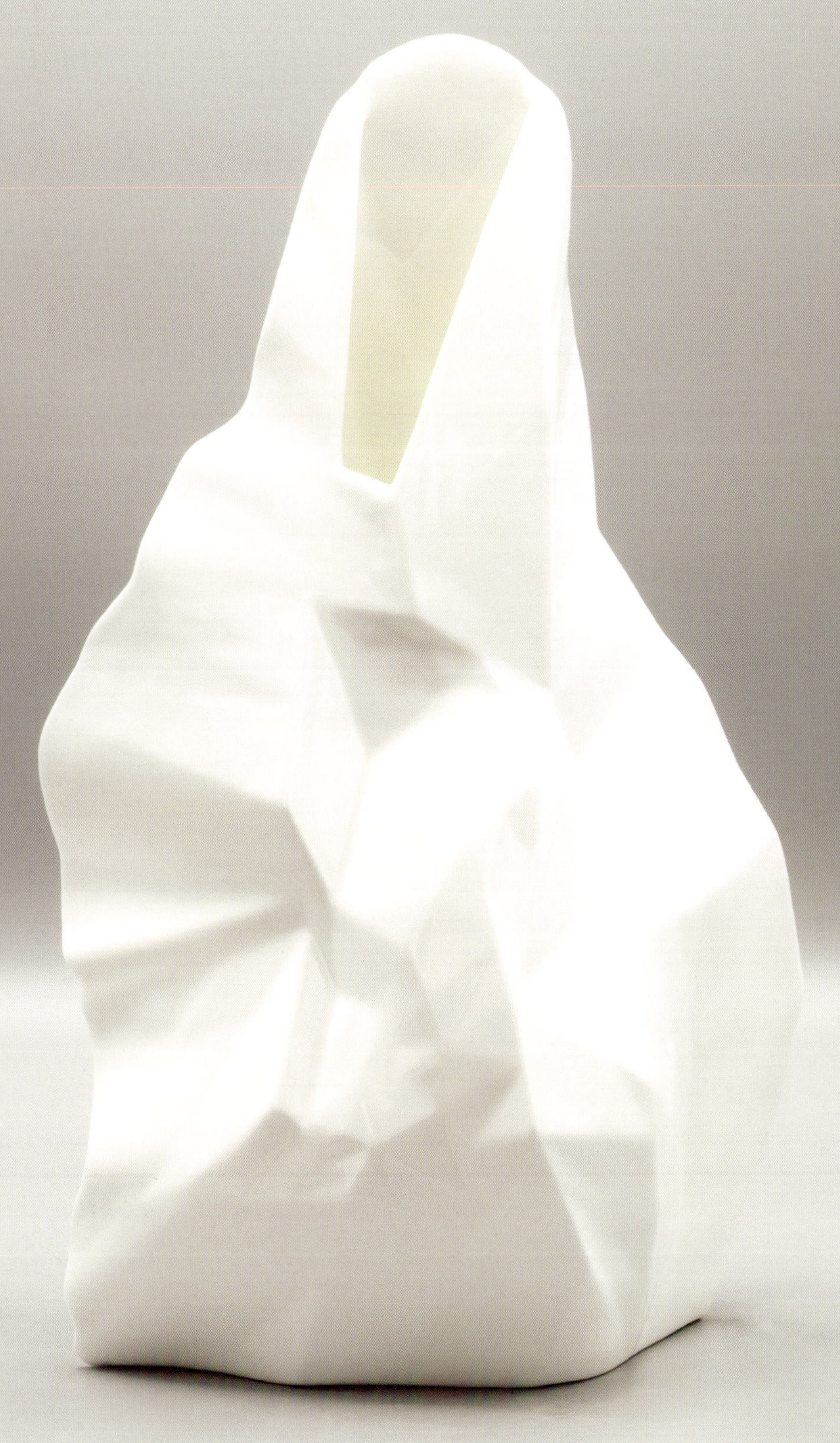

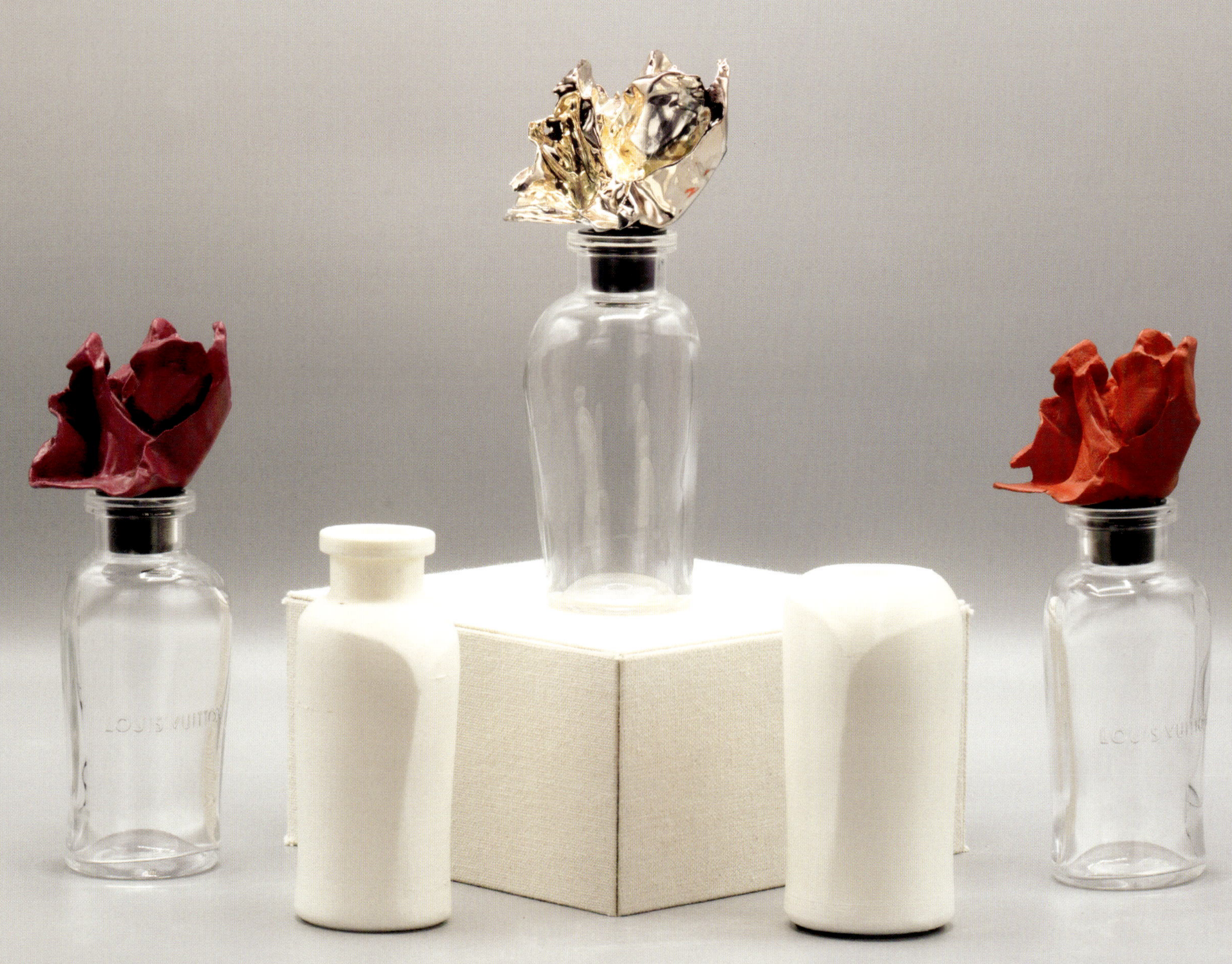

LOUIS VUITTON: LES PERFUMES
BOTTLE STUDIES
FRANK GEHRY

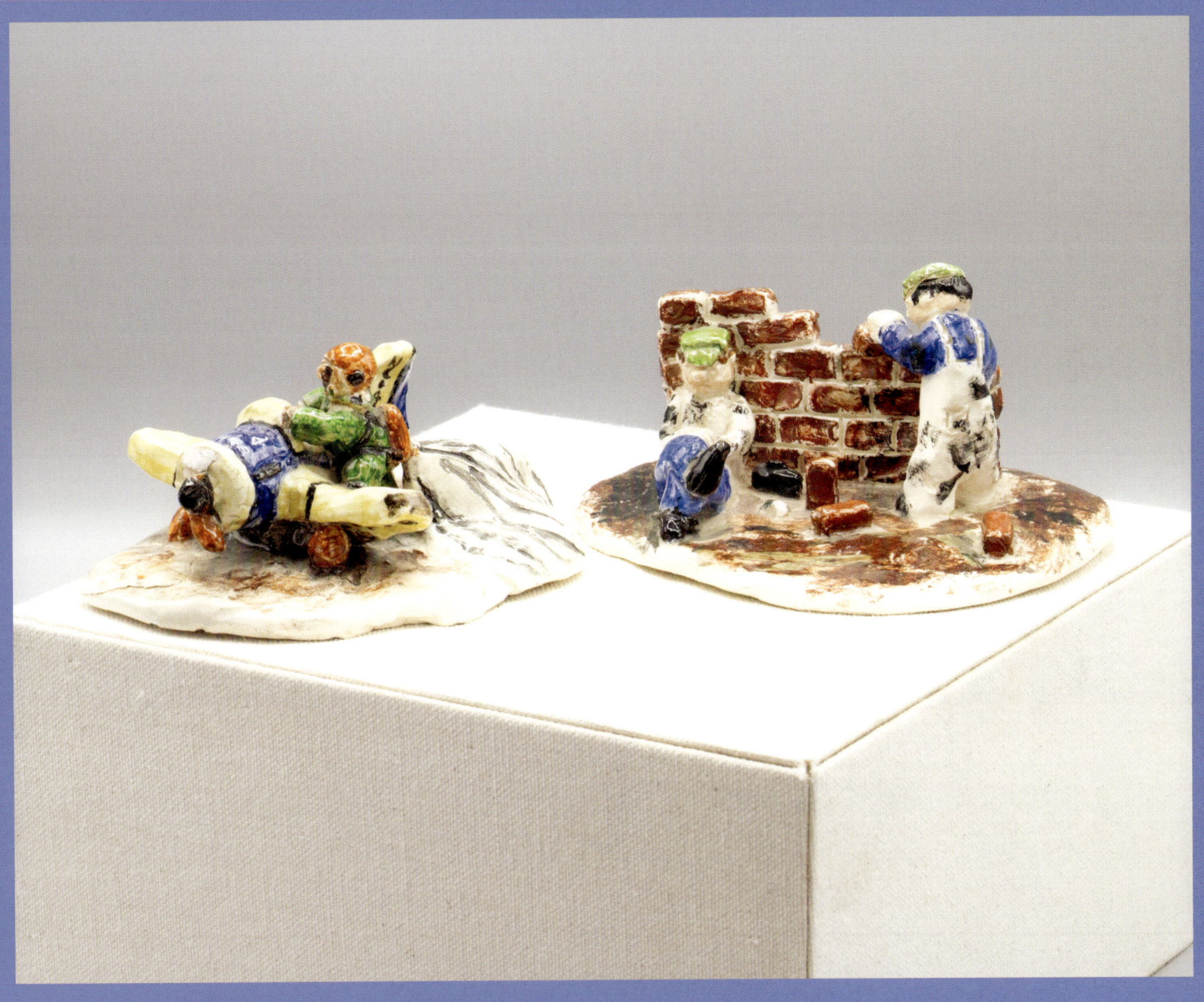

EARLY, NEVER-BEFORE SHOWN CERAMICS
FRANK GEHRY

FRANK GEHRY & ROBERT TANNEN

Text by Robert Ivy

TOGETHER

Like an unexpected flash of summer sheet lightning, Jeanne Nathan and Robert Tannen telephoned at *Architectural Record* in Manhattan, and I invited them for a chat at my brownstone on Hicks Street in Brooklyn Heights. Interesting people whom I had not seen in years, always bubbling with ideas, they had a notion to float. After trundling up to the third floor and sharing the requisite Brooklyn and New Orleans stories, they broached the topic: Biloxi, Mississippi was going to build a museum for George Ohr, the consummate American potter, and wouldn't Frank Gehry be the perfect choice as architect?

He would be perfect. Yet Gehry's star had risen, in part thanks to the Guggenheim Museum in Bilbao, Spain. The digitally fueled, gritty yet sculptural project changed the course of three-dimensional design and launched new museums as pilgrimage sites. In fact, Gehry kept a small, crumpled tissue-like vase by Ohr near his desk in Santa Monica, an impossibly fragile object among his hundreds of cardboard, paper, and metal models, nearby. A physical link from the hands of the potter to another like-minded spirit in Louisiana, Robert Tannen.

The small object memorialized a friendship. According to Gehry, the two had met in the late 1970s in New Orleans, when Gehry had been approached to reenvision Lafayette Square, a downtown urban park near the upcoming World's Fair site. Each saw kinship in the other and remained friends.

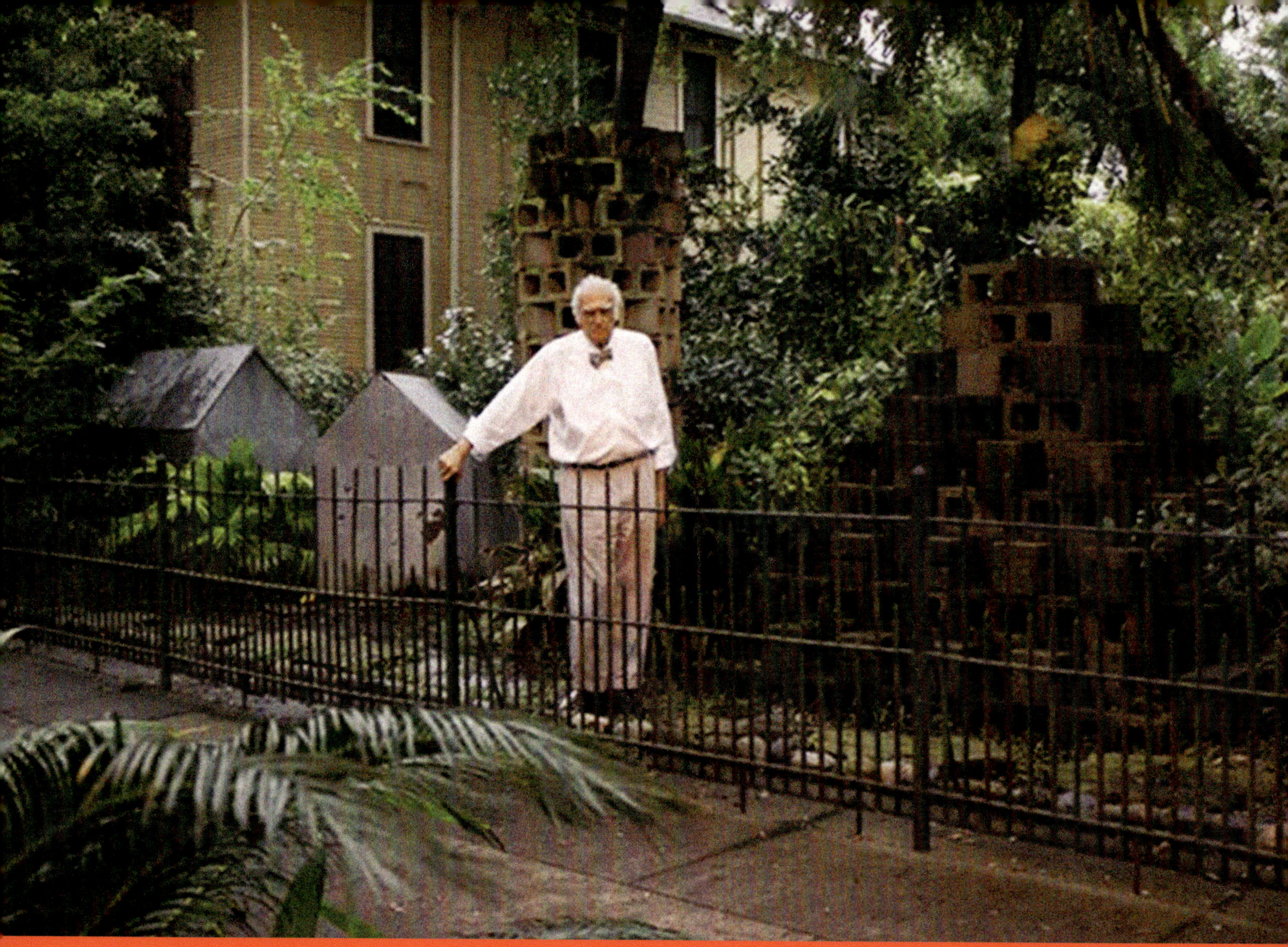

And what did they recognize? Two artists, both iconoclasts. Iconoclasts in the sense that they refused to accept institutional norms. They constantly observe the world and challenge expectations of artists in the translation of their ideas into material objects that represent larger truths as they understand them. One, an architect, ultimately creating sculptural forms that cradle experience; the other, an artist and urban planner, creating cities that enhance experience.

The tactile arts continually serve as repositories of their thinking and dreaming. Each has been drawn to what others might consider the ordinary, reinterpreted. Tannen has taken telephones, wrapped them in their own cords and painted them red. Who would expect that? Both Gehry and Tannen have reinterpreted fish. Tannen's modus operandi has sometimes been to literally upend the familiar, such as his sculpture of shotgun houses, stacked on his lawn on Esplanade Avenue. No one can foresee their next acts.

(LEFT) ROBERT TANNEN IN HIS SCULPTURE GARDEN BEFORE HURRICANE KATRINA (2005)

(BOTTOM) FRANK GEHRY AT THE OPENING OF THE OHR-O'KEEFE MUSEUM OF ART

Their hungry minds and their interests wander from the maquette to the drone's-eye view. Both are scale-shifters, from the immediacy of the sculptural to entire cities. Gehry devised a plan for Los Angeles, and Tannen has counseled cities from the neighborhoods and movement systems of his chosen New Orleans home to international urban centers. Together, they worked on a reinterpretation of a familiar house type, the New Orleans shotgun, as a potential replicable housing solution after Hurricane Katrina.

Gehry ultimately accepted the commission for what became the Ohr-O'Keefe Museum, a brilliant choice for the Mad Potter of Biloxi. Despite having been destroyed in Hurricane Katrina by an errant casino barge that crashed into the initial buildings in 2005, today the individual pavilions representing Gehry's homage to Ohr's genius dot the parkland housing the museum. Tannen and Gehry's ongoing dialogue floats around the site, wondering what's next.

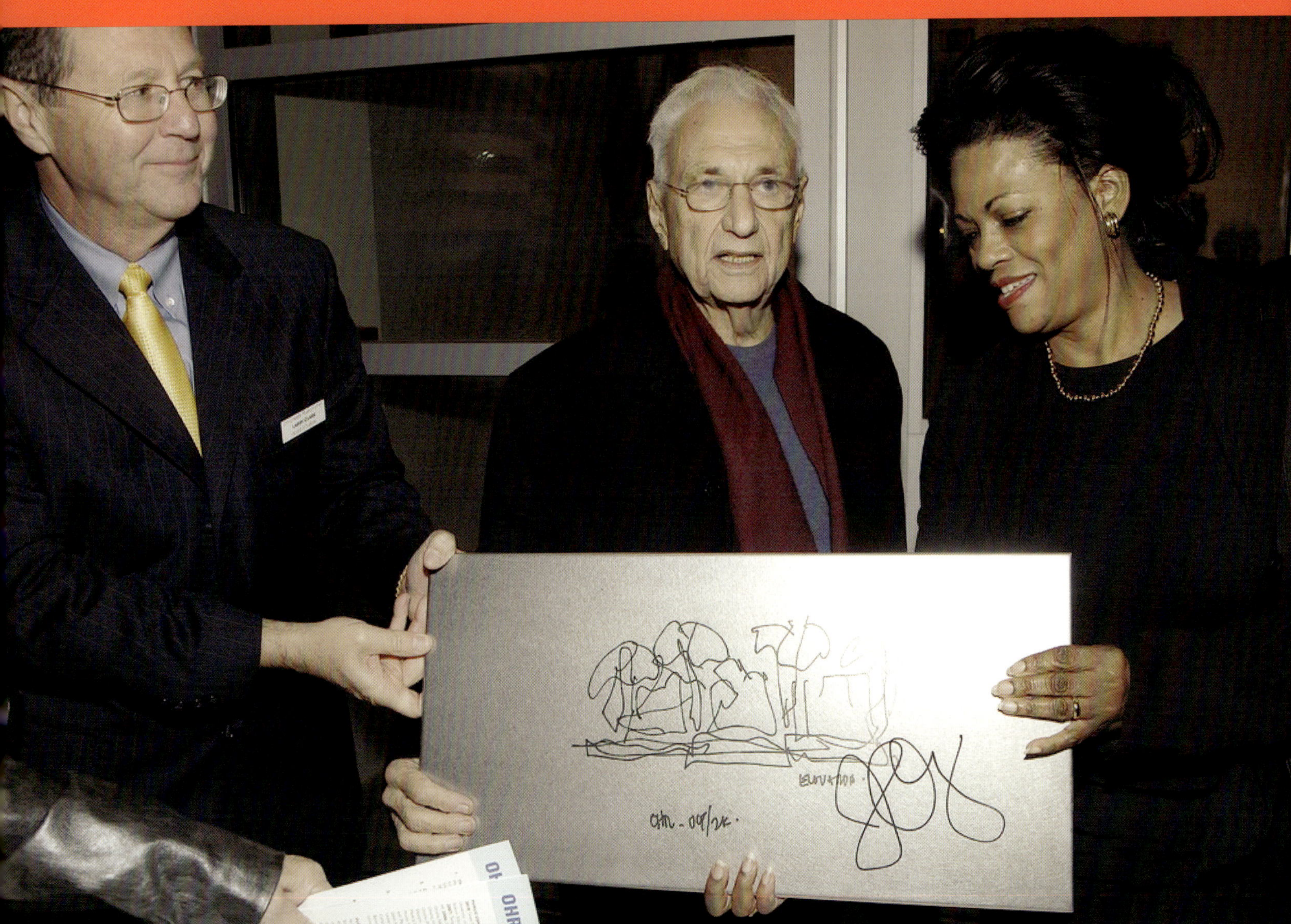

ARCHITECTURAL RECORD | JULY 15, 2009 | TEXT BY SHAWN KENNEDY

It appears that Frank Gehry, FAIA, is finding fertile ground in New Orleans

In addition to designing a duplex for Brad Pitt's "Make It Right" project, Gehry has teamed with urban planner and artist, Robert Tannen, to create a modular shotgun house that they say will be affordable, sustainable, and compatible with the city's historic housing types.

The duo's concept, dubbed Mod Gun, is an expansion of a one-room, emergency-housing prototype that Tannen designed in 2006 as an alternative to the typical FEMA trailer. (The structure was displayed at the Ogden Museum of Southern Art but it was never reproduced.)

The new one- and two-bedroom models—1,000 and 1,200 square feet, respectively—are designed to fit the long, narrow lots common throughout New Orleans. But the Mod Guns will not share the room-into-room-into-room floor plan of the shotgun house. Instead, a screened-in porch will separate the living/dining/kitchen space from the bedroom-and-bathroom suites.

Aspects of the Gehry-Tannen design are still being refined, but a signature feature is fourteen-by-fourteen-foot modular rooms that can be put together to form larger rooms. Many elements like doors, windows, and interior doorways will be consistent in size. "This is part of the economy of the house," says Tannen. "This will also offer the most flexibility for the buyer to configure rooms to suit their needs."

While the final number depends on demand, the developer, New Orleans-based Fortune Development, is expected to build between five and ten houses. The first dwellings will be infill housing on empty lots in Treme, a historic neighborhood bordering the French Quarter that was settled in the early 1800s by free people of color.

New Orleans architect Ray Manning, AIA, of Manning Architects, will be responsible for the final design services.

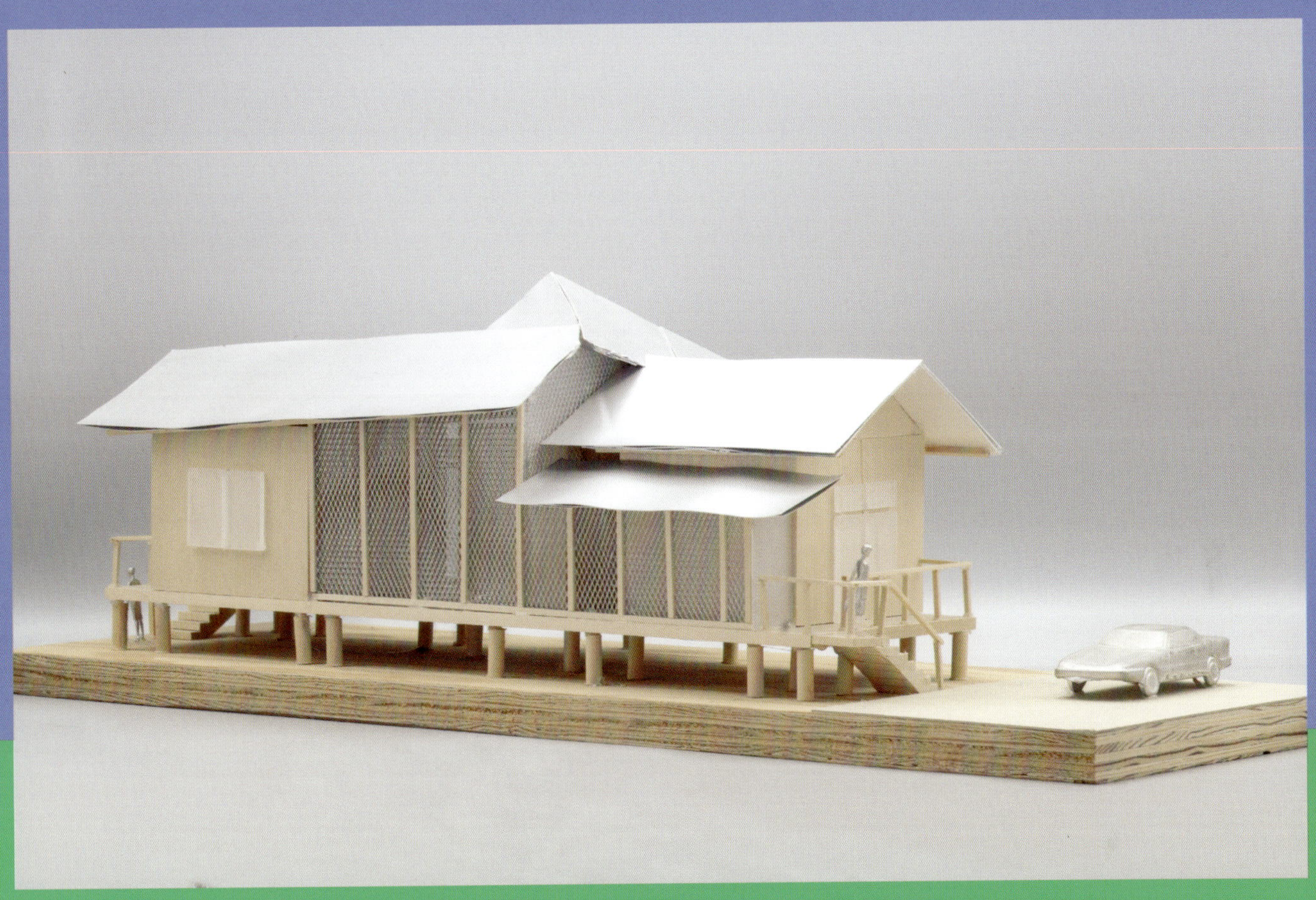

ModGun House

2023 (built)
Pass Christian, Mississippi

Robert Tannen and Frank Gehry's design for a modular shot-gun house, called "ModGun," or "Gehry Gun," was the first experiment using modular technology and the shotgun-style, common to New Orleans and the Gulf Coast. Their goal was to create a modular house that was affordable, sustainable, and compatible with the city's historic housing types. In this coastal variation, the house is separated in the center by a screened-in porch. The duo's concept is an expansion of a one-room, emergency-housing prototype that Tannen designed in 2006 as an alternative to the typical FEMA trailer.

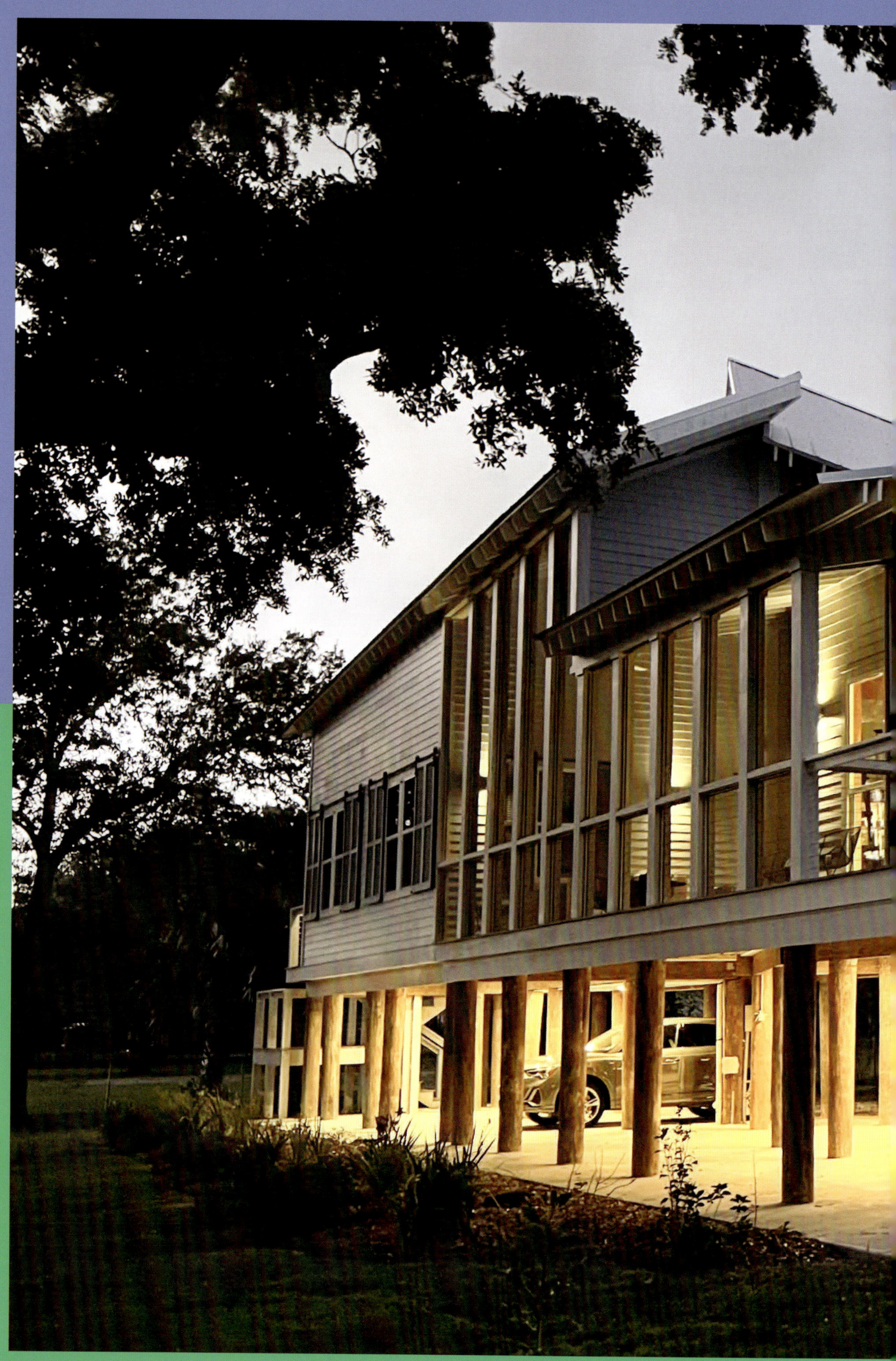

MODGUN HOUSE, 2023 (BUILT), PASS CHRISTIAN, MISSISSIPPI

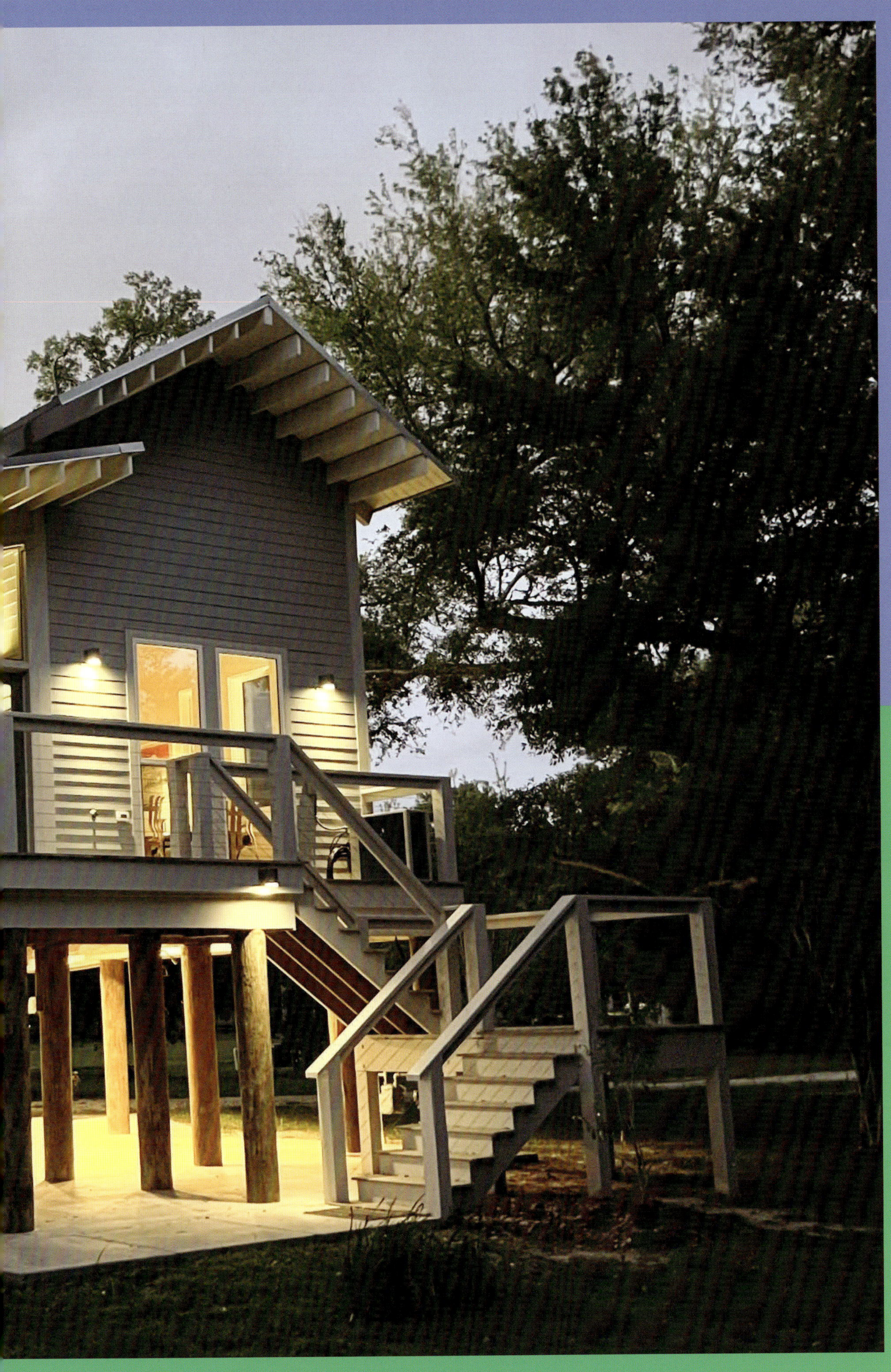

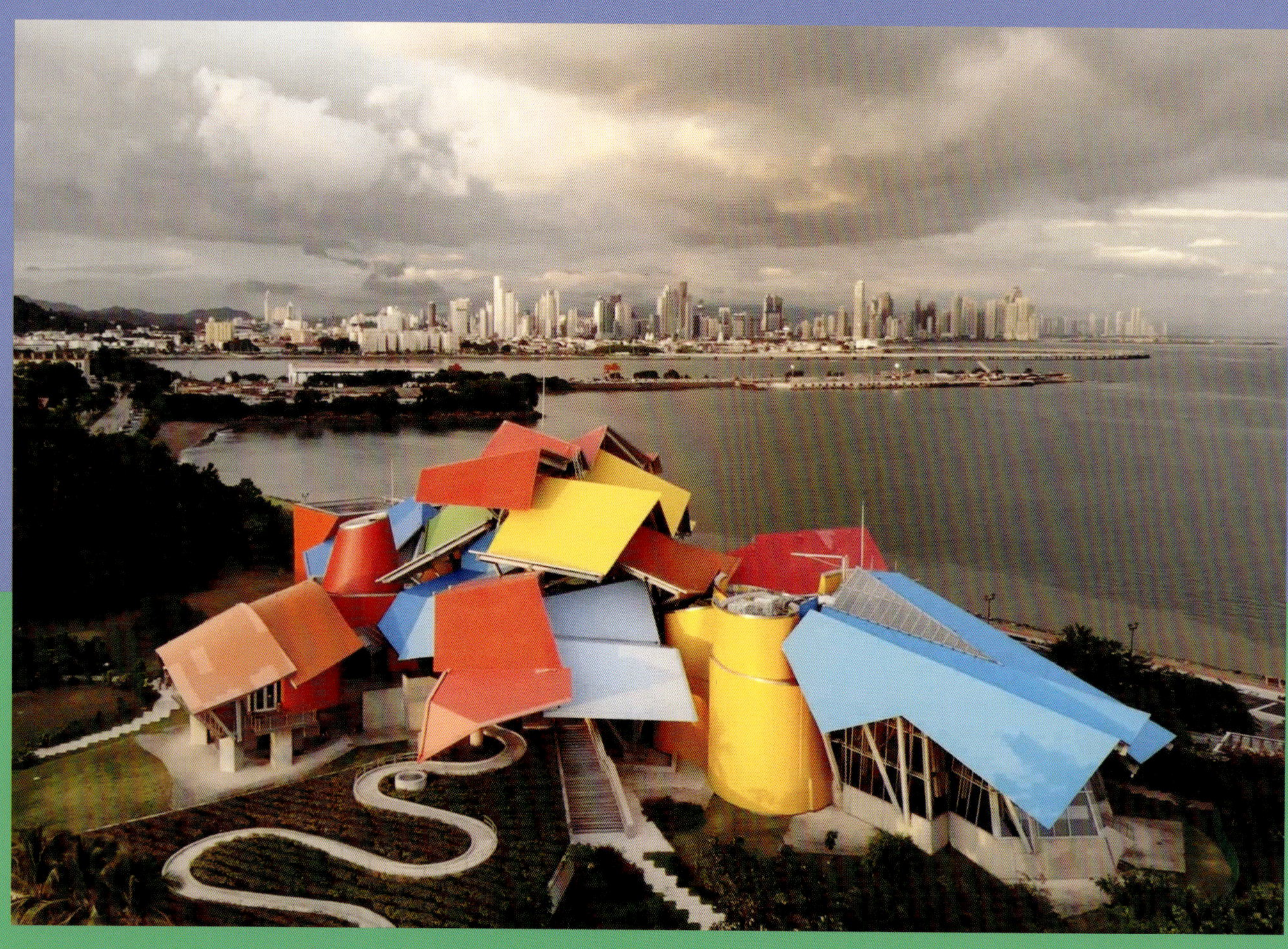

Jeanne Nathan and Robert Tannen worked with and for the Gehry organization to plan the Gehry-designed Biomuseo in Panama City, Panama.

“We’re both interested in a multiplicity of ideas and moving forward as opposed to repetition.”

—Robert Tannen

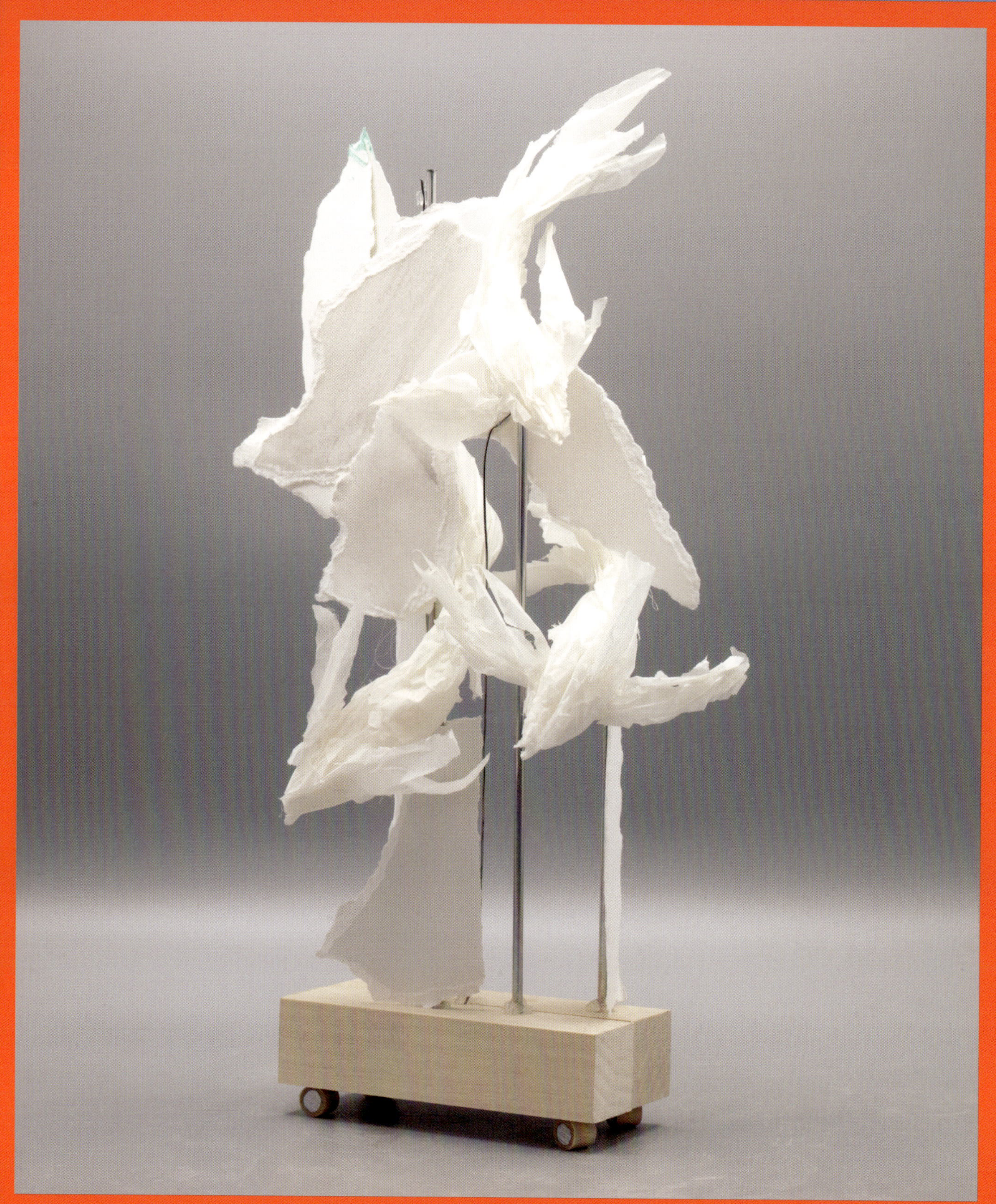

FRANK GEHRY

←

“Very few people have made art based on their being. Duchamp did it, the way he lived his life, playing chess, making objects that were not for sale, blurring the relationship of art and life. We don’t know if Duchamp was Duchamp. Tannen is about living, art, and the world.”

—Frank Gehry

This book accompanies the exhibition

Frank Gehry and Robert Tannen: Art, Architecture, & Ideas
at the Ohr-O'Keefe Museum of Art, Biloxi, Mississippi

April 13 - July 6, 2024

Designed by Virginia Walcott

Museum photography by Bobby R. Harrison
Museum photography assistant Robert C. Harrison
Tannen residence photography by Virginia Walcott

ISBN: 9798991223447

Library of Congress Control Number: 2025936954

Printed in China

This publication is supported by The Ohr-O'Keefe Museum of Art
and funded in part by the Community Foundation of Alabama.

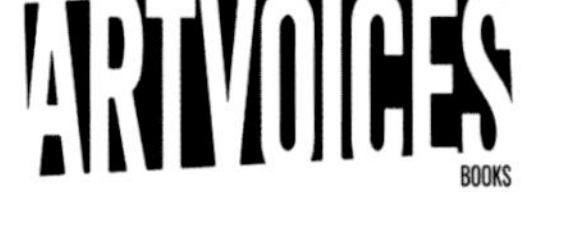

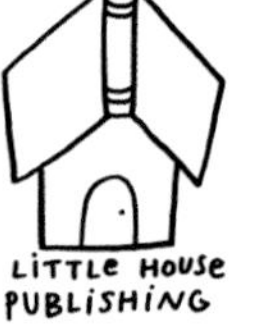

www.artvoicesbooks.com www.littlehousepub.com

Frank Gehry & Robert Tannen: Art, Architecture, & Ideas

Ohr-O'Keefe Museum of Art | April 13 - July 6, 2024

This exhibition was organized by Gehry Partners, LLC
and the Ohr-O'Keefe Museum of Art

Curators: Samuel Gehry and David Houston

Texts by

D. Eric Bookhardt
Frank Gehry
David Houston
Robert Ivy
Shawn Kennedy
Susan Lengen Henning
Kristine McKenna
Jeanne Nathan
Adolfo Nodal
Terrence Sanders-Smith
Robert Tannen

Designed by Virginia Walcott
Museum photography by Bobby R. Harrison
Museum photography assistant Robert C. Harrison
Tannen residence photography by Virginia Walcott

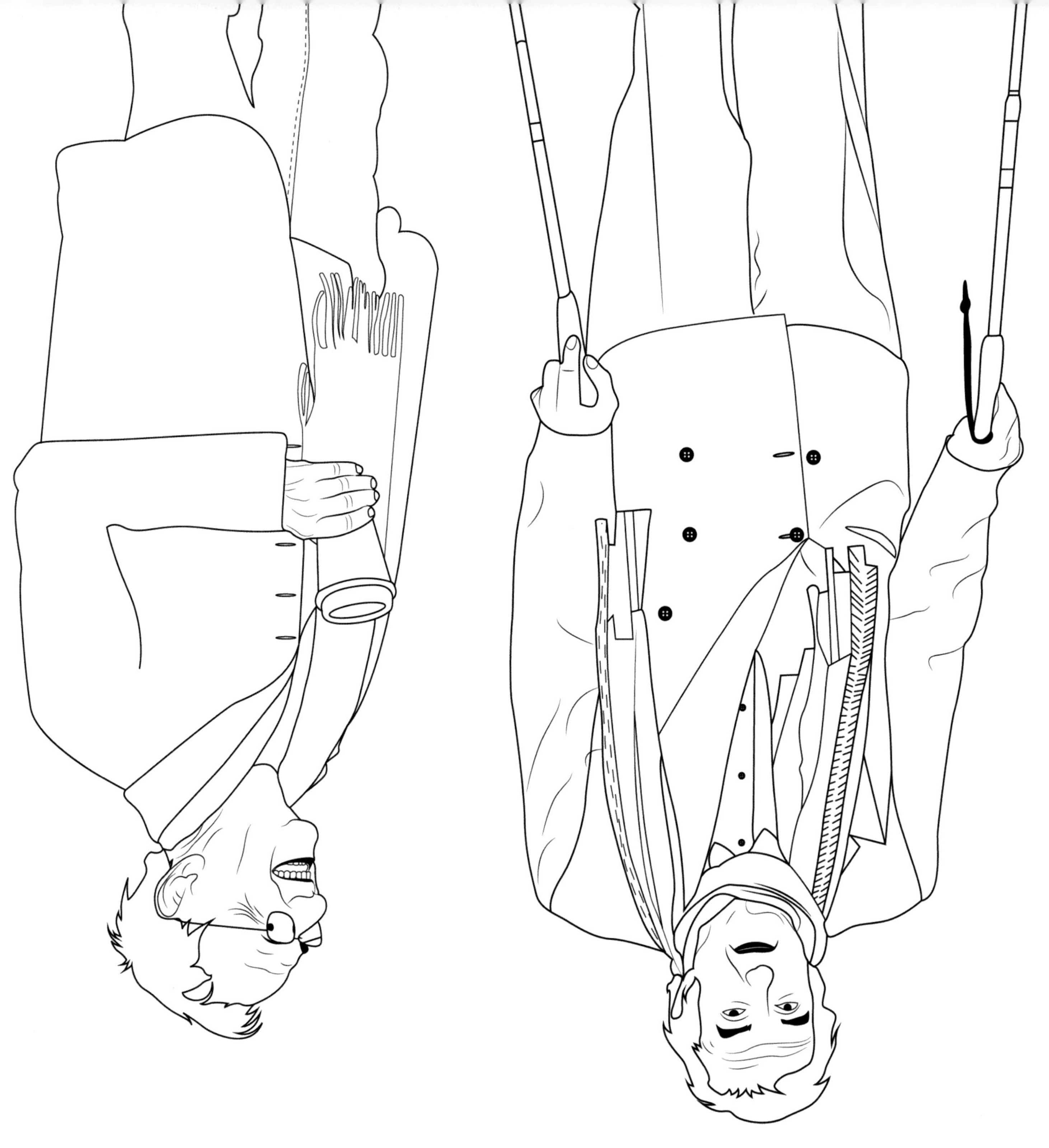

Frank Gehry & Robert Tannen: Art, Architecture, & Ideas

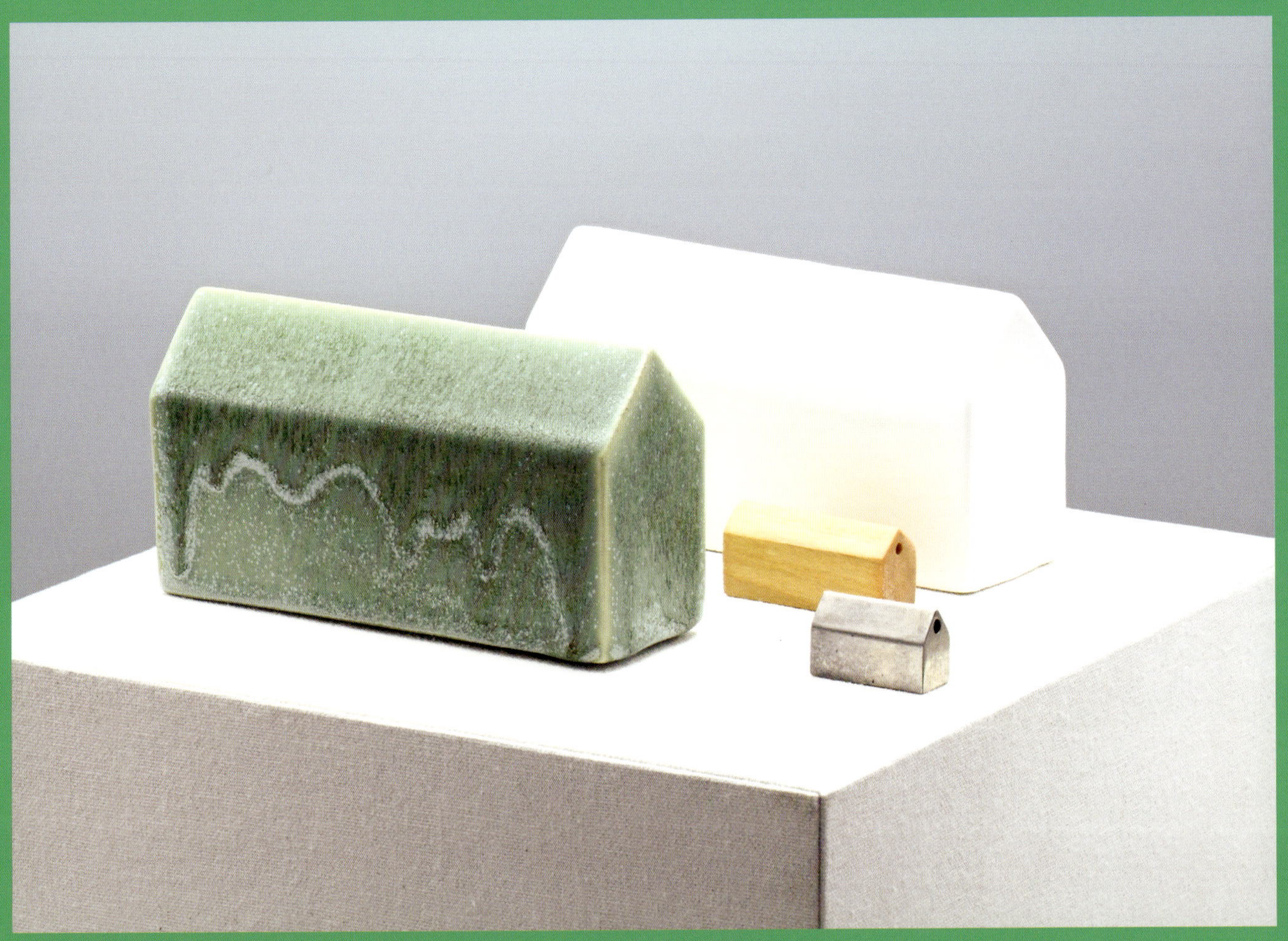

SHOTGUN HOUSES AND JEWELRY DESIGNED BY ROBERT TANNEN
HOUSES MADE BY JOHN HODGE, JEWELRY MADE BY MIGNON FAGET

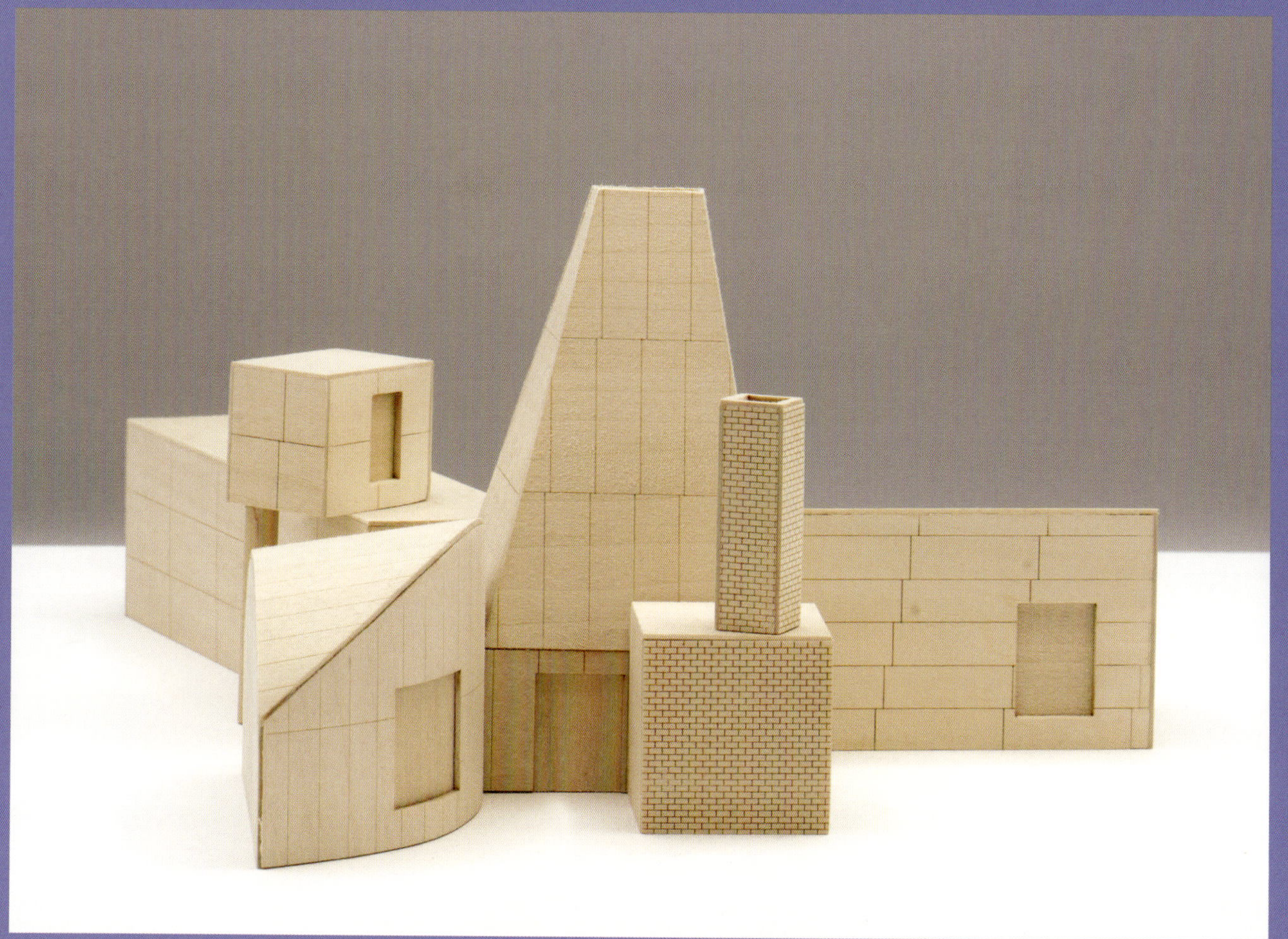

WINTON GUEST HOUSE (1982)
FRANK GEHRY

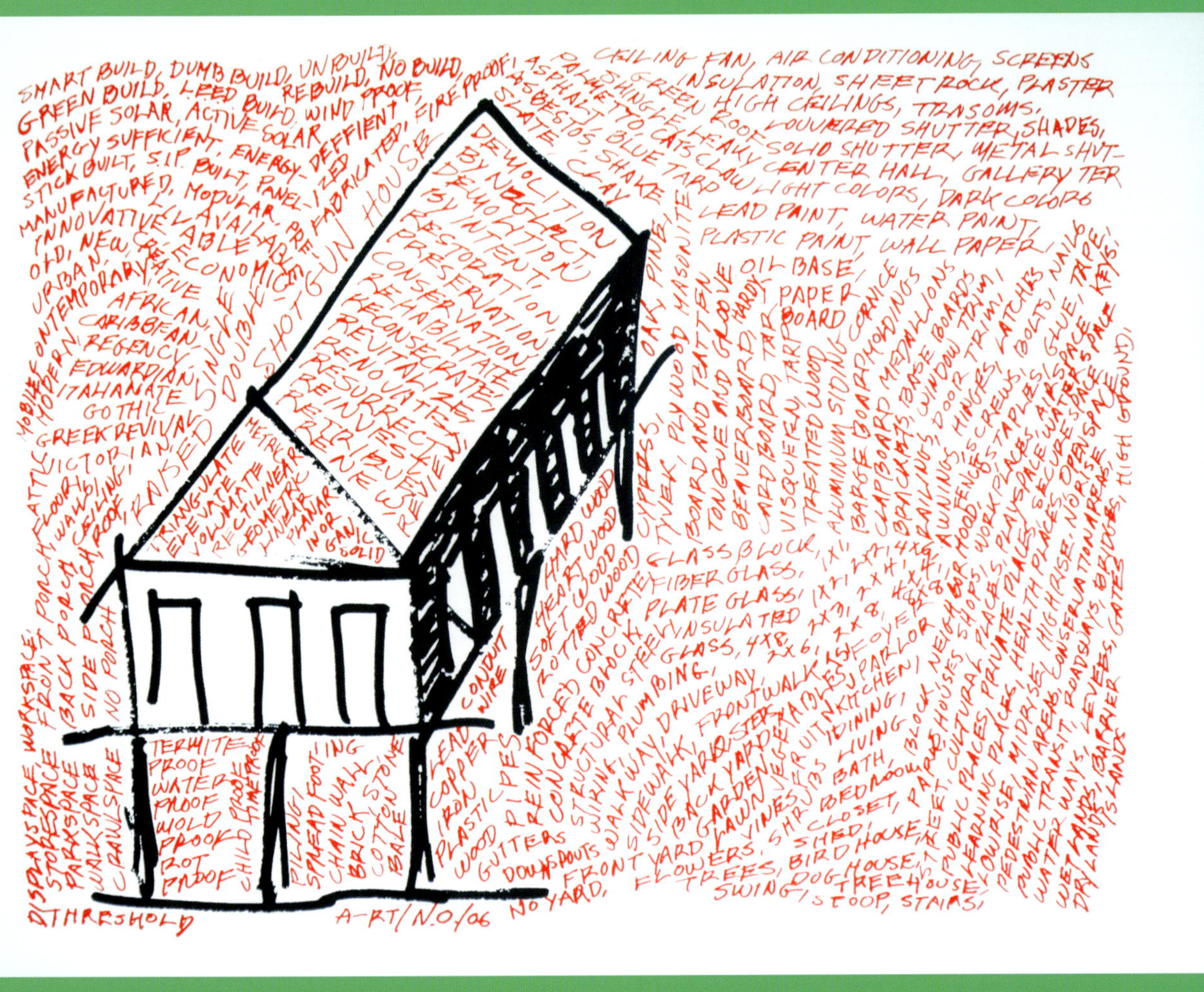

POST-HURRICANE KATRINA RAISED SHOTGUN PRINT & PROPOSAL (2006)
ROBERT TANNEN

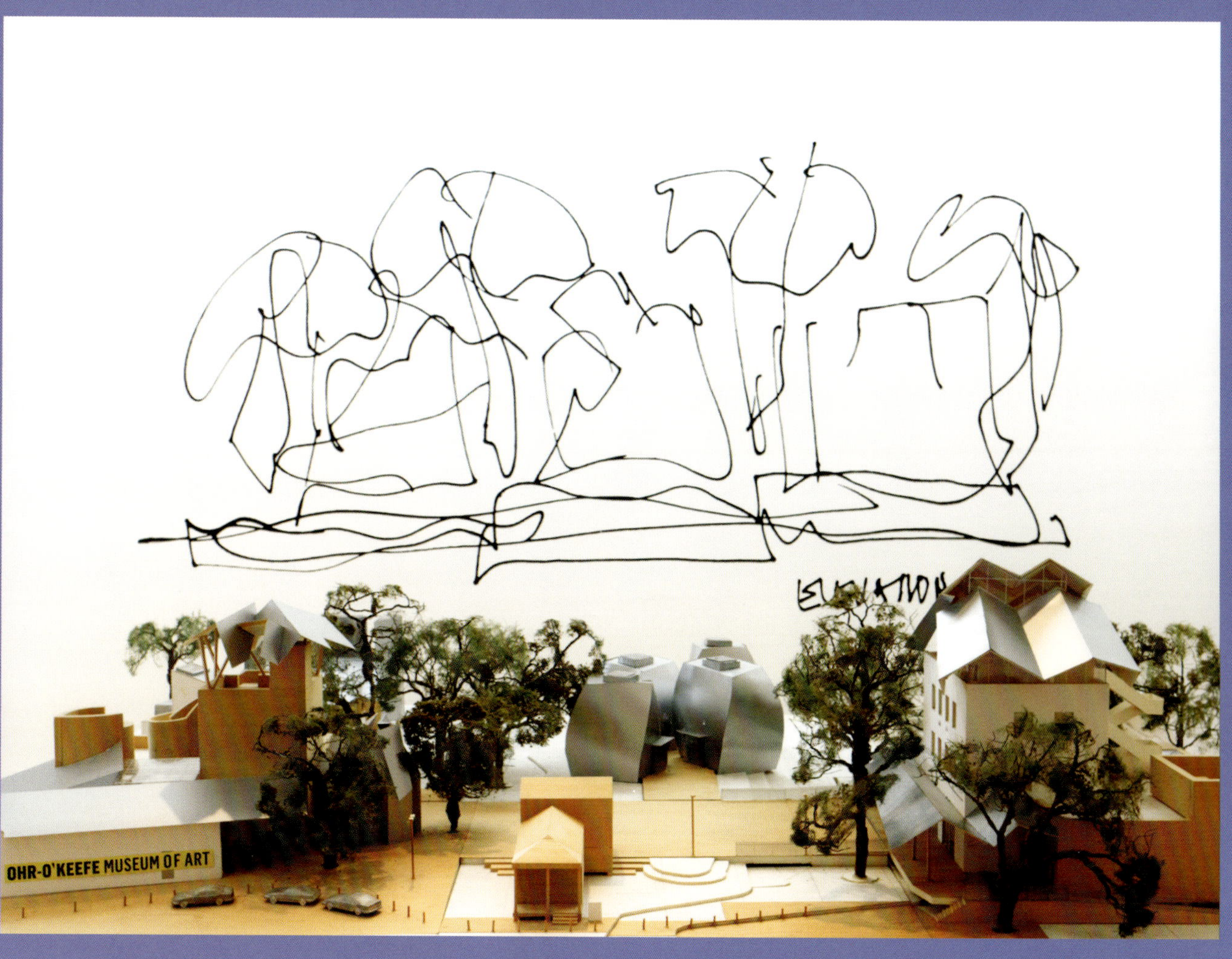

THE OHR-O'KEEFE MUSEUM OF ART
FRANK GEHRY

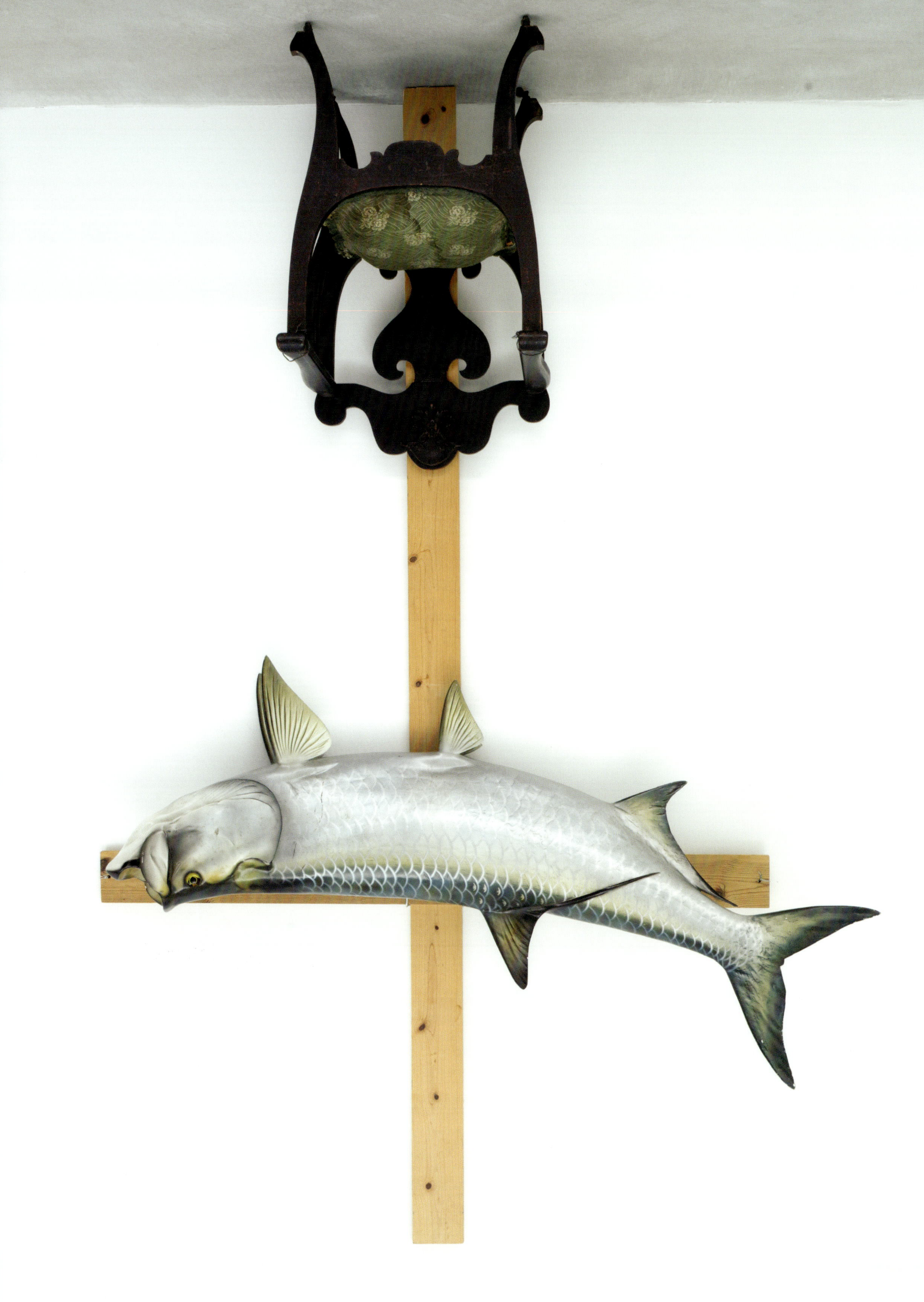

Table of Contents

LEFT: *CRUCIFISH*, ROBERT TANNEN (1975)

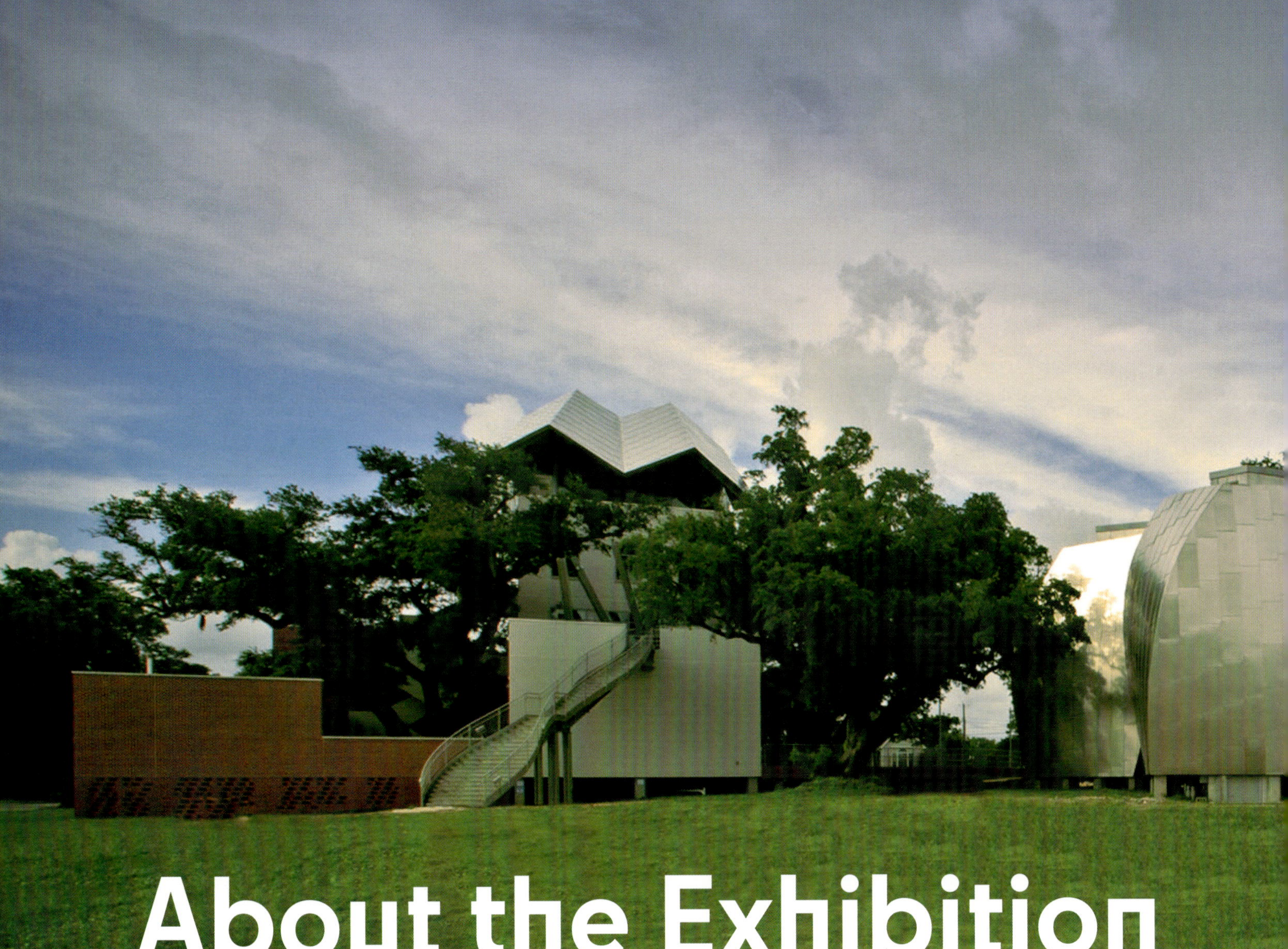

About the Exhibition

Text by David Houston
Executive Director, Ohr-O'Keefe Museum of Art

Art, Architecture, & Ideas: Frank Gehry and Robert Tannen

brings together over five decades of work in a range of media, including architectural models, sculpture, painting, printmaking, urban planning, and product design. Recognized as the defining architect of our times, Frank Gehry changed the cultural landscape with his designs for the Walt Disney Concert Hall in Los Angeles and the Guggenheim Museum in Bilbao, Spain. At ninety-six years old, his architectural and art practices continue to evolve through the exploration of energy and dynamic movement.

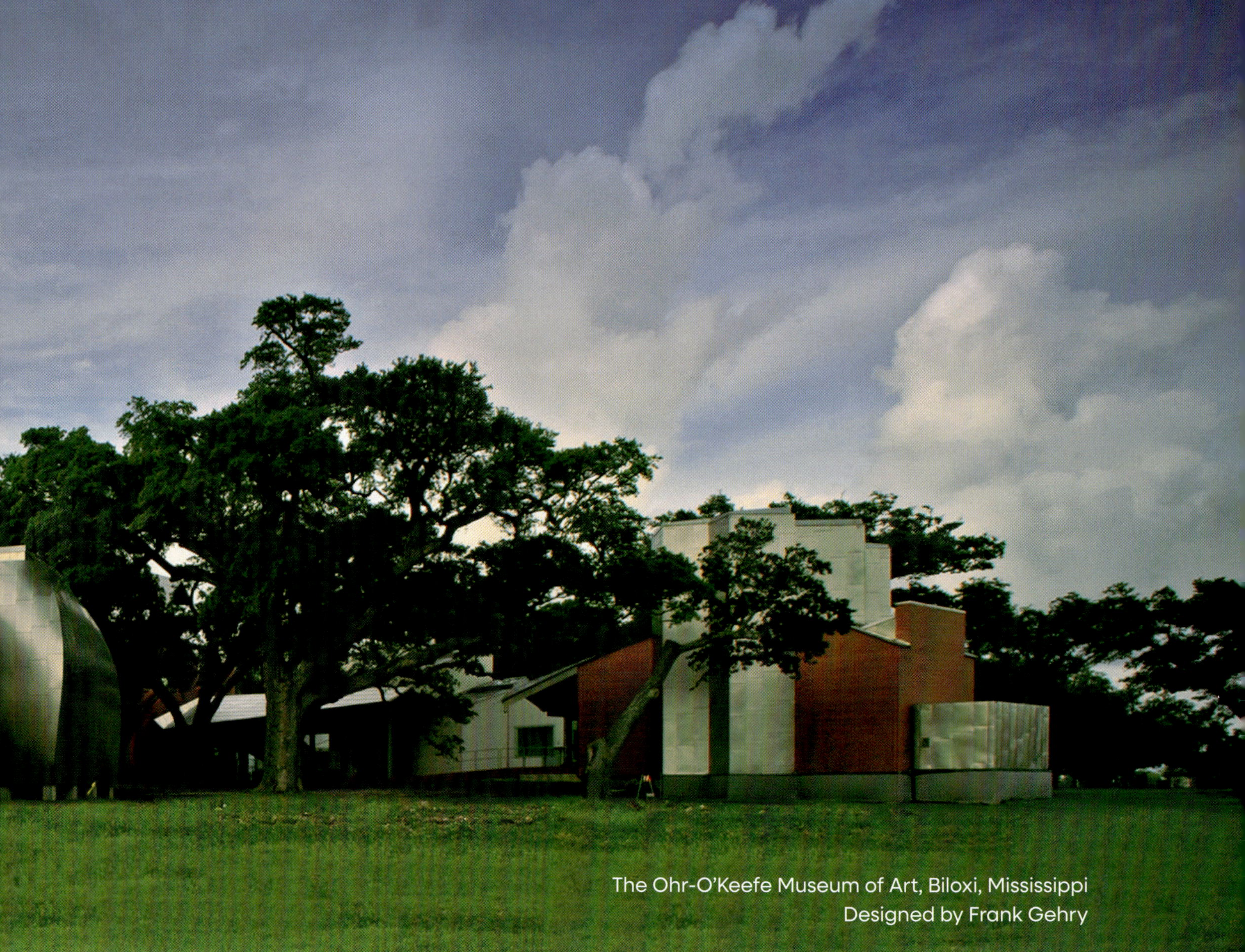
The Ohr-O'Keefe Museum of Art, Biloxi, Mississippi
Designed by Frank Gehry

Robert Tannen's career includes sculpture, painting, conceptual art, and urban planning. After coming to Biloxi, Mississippi to create a masterplan for the Gulf Coast post-Hurricane Camille, he relocated to New Orleans where he master planned the second span of the Mississippi River Bridge, was a founder of the Contemporary Arts Center, and continues his distinctive practice of urbanism, art, and community activism.

Frank Gehry and Robert Tannen's work have intersected with major projects, built and unbuilt, in New Orleans, the Biomuseo in Panama, and the Freeman house in Pass Christian, Mississippi. Tannen, and his partner, Jeanne Nathan, were also instrumental in the choice of Frank Gehry as the architect of the Ohr-O'Keefe Museum in Biloxi, Mississippi, Gehry's only museum in the Southeast.

My friend, Robert

INTERVIEW BY JEANNE NATHAN (1990)

JEANNE NATHAN: How did you meet Robert Tannen?

FRANK GEHRY: I came to New Orleans, to work on the plan I was doing for the restoration and rehabilitation of Lafayette Square in the late 1970s. Tannen had called me to meet with me about the work. People had told me he was very involved in the city, and very interesting. So we met at the Hilton. In thirty seconds we were good friends.

NATHAN: Why?

GEHRY: I didn't threaten him, and he didn't threaten me. We just started talking about what we wanted to do. We disarmed each other, though what we tried to do ultimately did not work in New Orleans at that time. There was opposition in City Hall and in the neighborhood. We did not have the opportunity to reach an agreement on the work with those interested in Lafayette Square. He invited me to a dinner of crawfish at his place. Tannen showed me some of his art, and I related to it, and to him. He was himself, instead of trying to be someone else. I've always liked that about him. People are often looking over their shoulders, worried about their status, their place in the pecking order. Tannen didn't do that. Approval doesn't seem to be important to him. His "stuff"—his boxes, shotguns, the fish and environmental kind of things—felt like home to me. He just never pretends to be anything he isn't. I think he probably cares, but he doesn't wait for what you say, he assumes it's OK. You can just kind of savor it. You never understand where he's going to go. You're always surprised. Just like his latest thing... putting clothes in bottles. That took me off. It's about naturalness... making it easy. You don't have to do anything about it. He doesn't appear interested in putting work in art galleries, museums, or in the media.

NATHAN: You too?

GEHRY: There's maybe a little more edge to me. He's got that New Orleans cool, laid back stance that I don't have. I'm more on the make, more ambitious. Though I'm not that bad anymore.

NATHAN: Tell me more about that quality of surprise you mentioned.

GEHRY: We can't predict ourselves. Like the little cat with the ball of twine. Its curiosity leads it to push it till it falls off the table. It's a surprise to everyone, yet it was always going to fall. I feel that way about my architecture. Why didn't someone else think of that? Or, like my paper furniture, I always wonder why no one else thought of that. When people see manifestations of my work, it is like a weird object or new place to them. I feel that way about Tannen putting possessions and clothes in a bottle or can or bag. It's an obvious thing to do in a way. But why didn't someone else do it? Our work is similar in that we're not doing giant things. We focus on people through a humanist approach. We're interested in a certain scale, in accessibility. Right now, I'm working on a concert hall, and an important thing to me is how people will relate to the orchestra. I'm going to great lengths to move an organ two feet back, so it will be placed next to people in the audience. People will say it was an obvious thing to do. But another architect would put the organ,

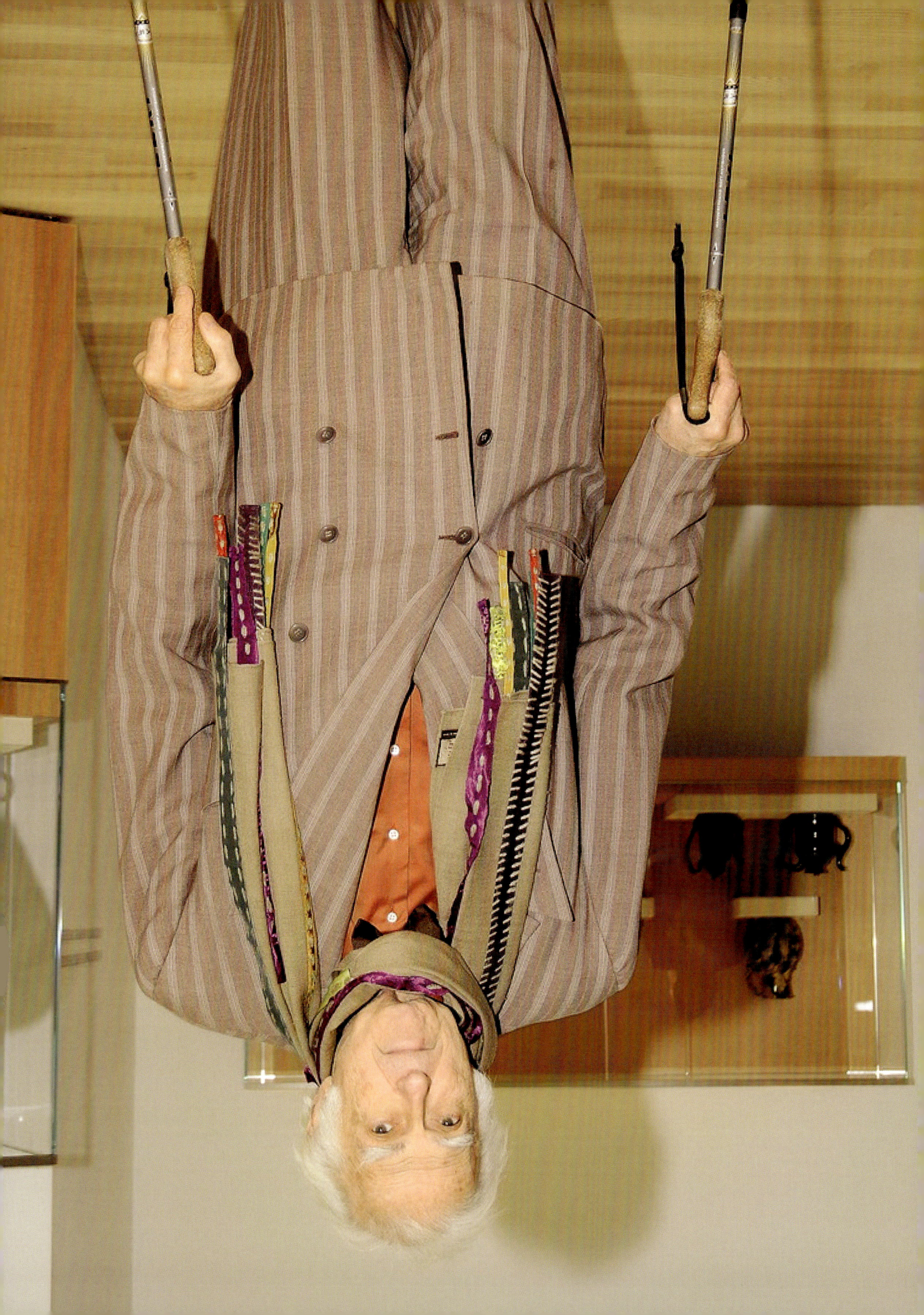

like the sculpture, on a pedestal way up in the hall, up in heaven. A person would have to die to get there. Tannen shares that with me. He's driven by that humanism. I don't know, maybe it's that Judeo-Christian guilt trip. Whatever it is in our background, it is that kind of thing that moves us forward to new sacrifices or to produce work that requires confession. I can't imagine anything Tannen did that was made to be on a pedestal. His work is emotional, accessible, and to be utilized. I know he feels that way about my work too. When he sees what I do, he gets that shit-eating grin on his face. He really loves it. He's saying, "Oh my god, look what he's done."

NATHAN: Tell me about your use of common, everyday materials in your work, which seems related to Tannen's use of common materials in his.

GEHRY: I'm interested in materials that people use extensively in life that are often at the same time unacknowledged. Chain-link fencing, for example. It's used in such great quantities, yet there's so much denial about it. Interestingly, if I recommend a material like this to a client, it would be hard for them to accept it. But if a client tells me that is all we can afford, then it's OK to use it. Materials like chain link represent such a legalistic, moralistic indictment of our culture. It recalls prisons and death camps. So I decided to try to see if it had inherent qualities about it that would transcend its typical use and symbolism. When I emphasize the raw qualities of wood framing, for example, I'm dealing with the question of details, of perfectionism, of how things meet properly. In the real world, builders and contractors are always accepting certain conditions of reality. The joints might not be perfectly fitted. I have a certain optimism about what is generally considered negative. Some architects and artists gain acceptance for their buildings because of craftmanship. But their buildings are not interesting. They put all this money into perfecting a joint. The result is putting a Brâncuși in a room that is devastating to the art work. The values behind the choice of architectural perfectionism are wrong. Yet the world, the marketplace tends to endorse those values. I'm always rubbing materials and people against each other and sometimes against the grain. I'm looking at human nature... human frailty is beautiful. A beautiful woman with her slip showing is beautiful. Can't people see that perfection is uninteresting? It's the collision of thought that's interesting. A meeting of people all being nice is boring. It's also about allowing a kind of intimacy. I don't care if someone comes in my office and there are models all over the place. It's still perfect. Letting things fall where they might. Letting your intuition drive. It's not about a preconceived, orderly perfection that you jam. One move leads to the next move, and takes with it the accidents that happen and the opportunities that come with the accidents. I know Tannen has a similar attitude. He must say, "I could make the beautiful choice, but I'll put the concrete block down here, in a different way... I'll hang the clothes as art." We both play off that note. Always testing ourselves. I'll always put the car just a foot away from where it's expected to be.

NATHAN: What about the relationship between art and architecture, in your work as well as Tannen's?

GEHRY: I've never focused on the difference between them. Historically, the architect was involved in both the outer design of the building, as well as the art that filled it. The master builders of the Parthenon had a coterie of people who worked with them

on both the building and the sculptures in them. Stone and brick are the same, inseparable. Painting is different. I always put painting on a pedestal. It's a mystery I don't understand. Tannen has used architectural themes in art in ways nobody else has. His shotgun houses, for example. His tower of shotgun houses has remained a very powerful image for me. In his planning work, his attitude of opening up, clearing the path, parting the waters, is key to what makes him unique. It's also the surprises of his fish stuff, the red fish Cadillac suspended on the wall at the World's Fair, that leave powerful images that linger. The shotguns, the galvanized metal stuff, the stuff in bottles, all linger for me.

NATHAN:: How would you describe the ways in which your and Tannen's approach is related?

GEHRY: Though I've produced art such as the fish lamps, I don't feel art is a part of my real life. I'm not interested in producing work for galleries. I started out studying art, but floundered. It wasn't until I got into architecture that I did well. My liberal instinct pushed me towards planning. But at Harvard, the writing, statistics, and presentations that go with planning convinced me planning wouldn't be my primary calling. Throughout the years of working in architecture, I've enjoyed the big projects that involved planning. Like Tannen, I still take a major interest in planning issues, including, for example, planning for Los Angeles' downtown. And I can tell you that my attitude on this matter again works off the reality of this city, and not some of the ideas I've heard that would attempt to Europeanize this city, or make it like some other place. Tannen really is an artist. But like me, he's really a hybrid, dancing between realms. I often ask myself how he makes a living. The world doesn't really know how to deal with hybrids. How do I explain why I love these things Tannen makes? They really spin me out. I picture his work doing gyrations, floating down the Mississippi River. It's very clear in my head, very powerful. Dealing with his work is dealing with his life. It's coming into his house... how you go into it, how you get there, how you leave. He's not at all conventional. His whole being is so hybrid, so related to where he lives, his environment, how he feels, even his health. His art doesn't edit his feelings out. And his art isn't about going into a gallery, about whether someone is going to buy it. He's not a Stella or a Gehry. It's about his life as he lives it and how he experiences his surroundings. People get to see his art who get to know him, others may not get it. There are very few people in the world like that. I think of the poet Carl Sandburg. Very few people who have made art based on their being. Duchamp did it, the way he lived his life, playing chess, making objects that were not for sale, blurring the relationship of art and life. We don't know if Duchamp was Duchamp. Tannen is about living, art and the world.

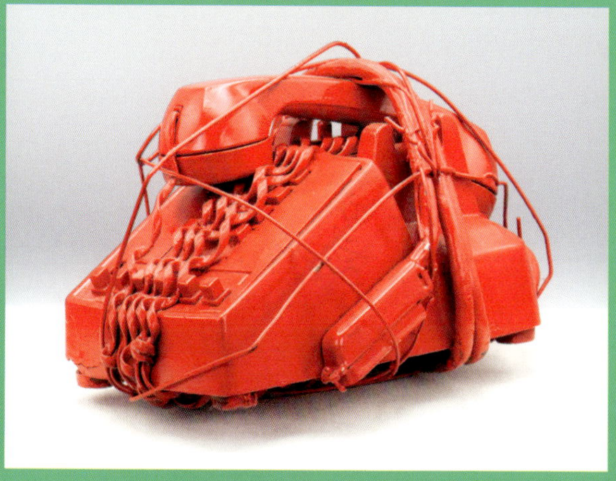

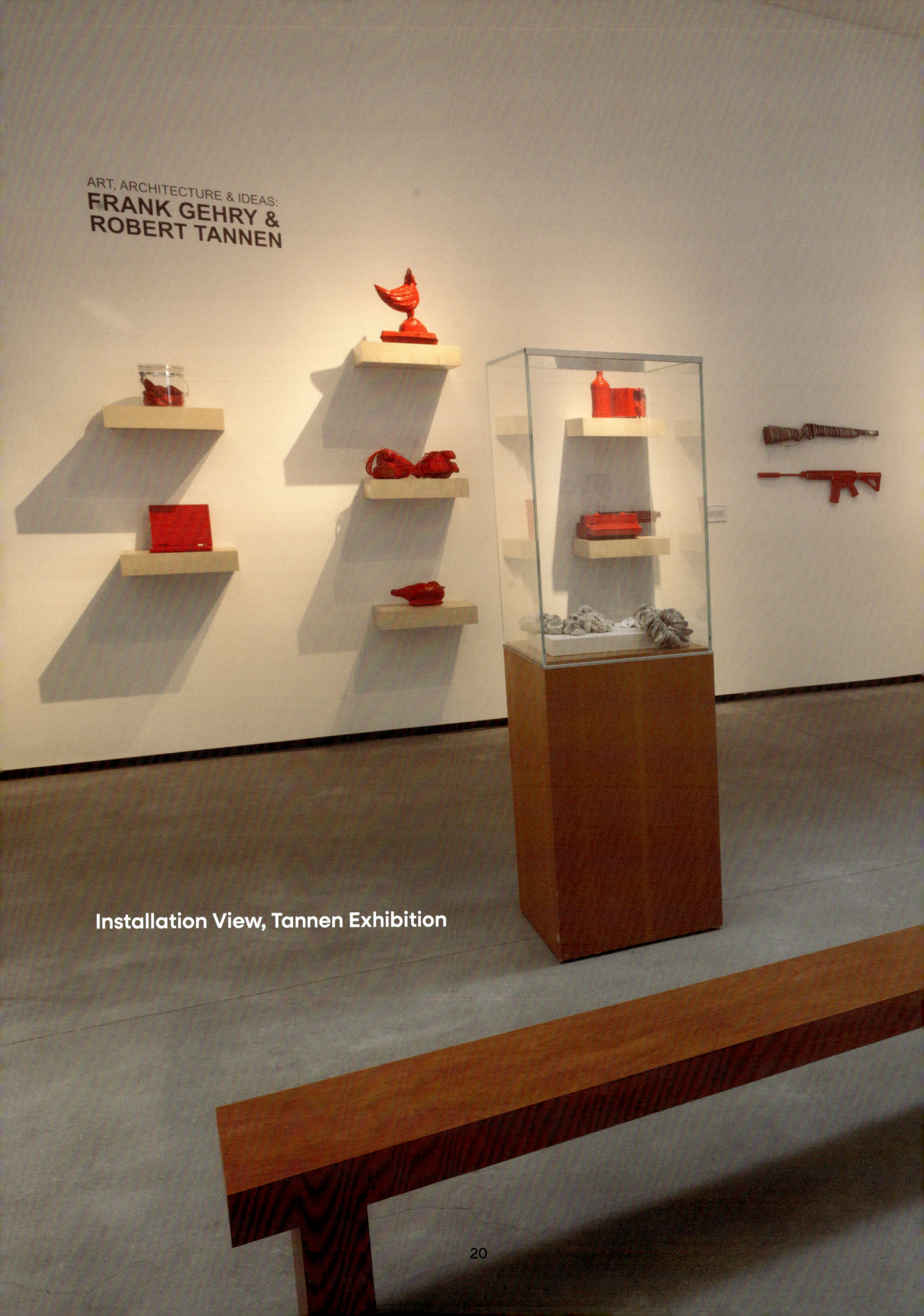

Installation View, Tannen Exhibition

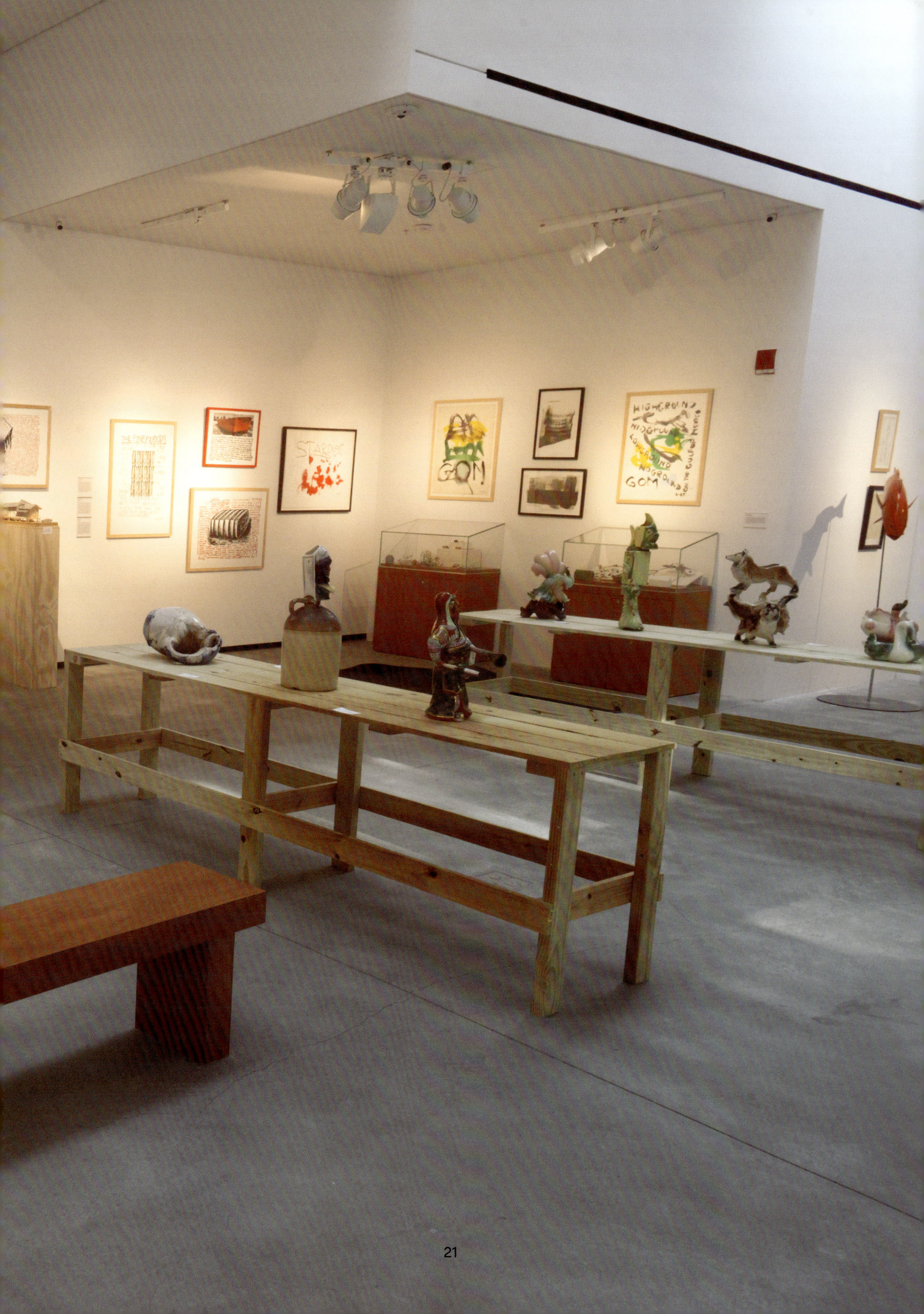
GOM

POST-KATRINA RAISED SHOTGUN (2006)
ROBERT TANNEN

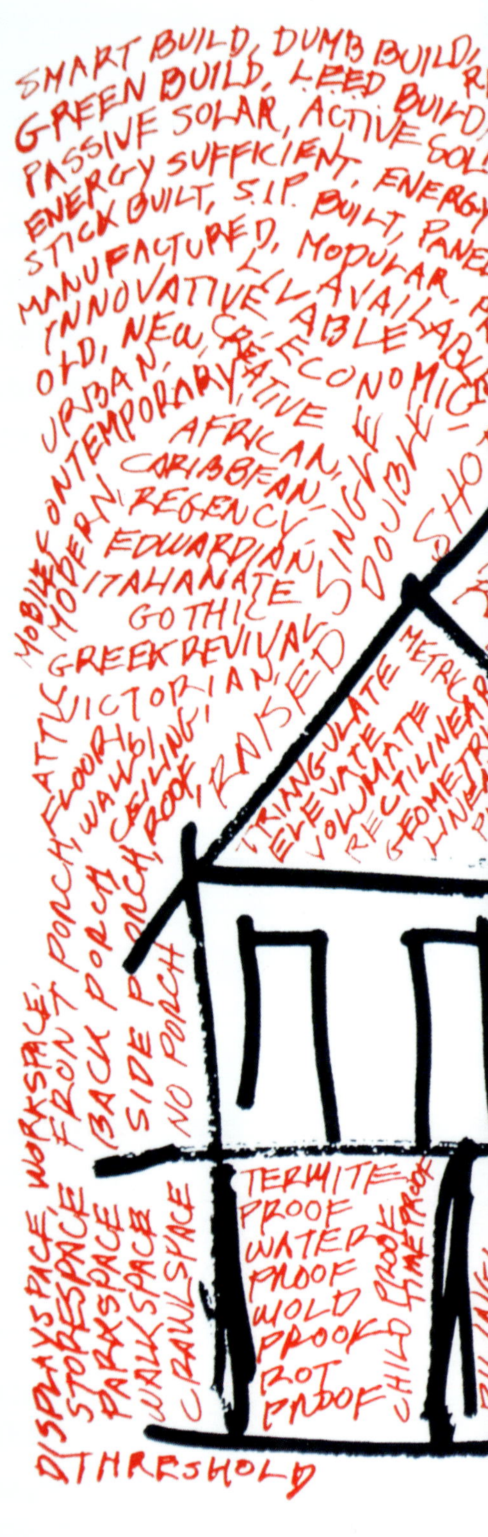

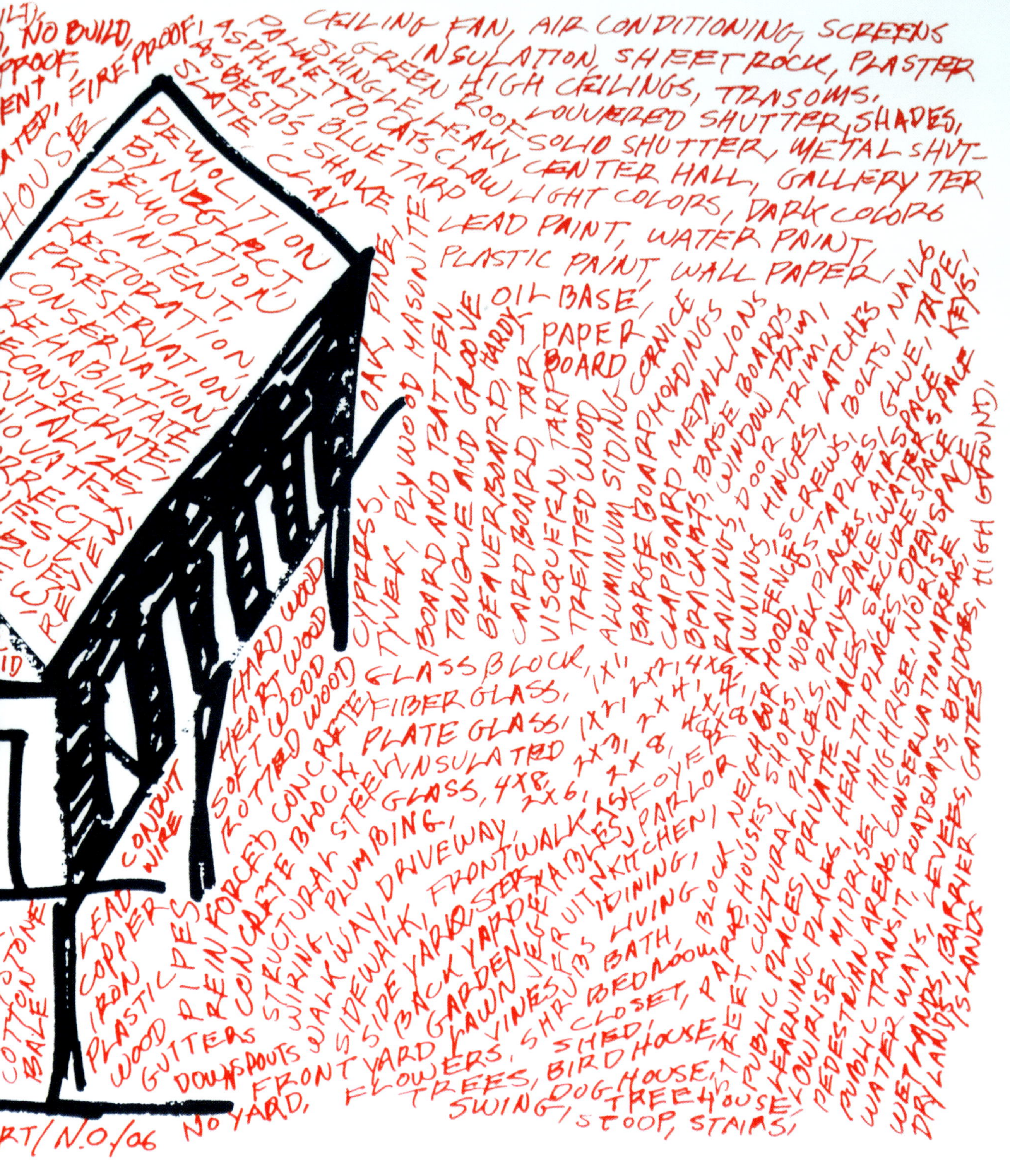

NO BUILD,
CEILING FAN, AIR CONDITIONING, SCREENS
INSULATION, SHEET ROCK, PLASTER
HIGH CEILINGS, TRANSOMS,
LOUVERED SHUTTER, SHADES,
SOLID SHUTTER, METAL SHUT-
CENTER HALL, GALLERY TER
LIGHT COLORS, DARK COLORS
LEAD PAINT, WATER PAINT,
PLASTIC PAINT, WALL PAPER,
OIL BASE,
PAPER
BOARD
DEMOLITION
BY NEGLECT,
DEMOLITION
BY INTENT,
RESTORATION,
PRESERVATION,
CONSERVATION,
REHABILITATE
CONDUIT
WIRE
HARD WOOD
HEART WOOD
SOFT WOOD
ROTTED WOOD
GLASS BLOCK,
FIBER GLASS,
PLATE GLASS,
INSULATED
GLASS,
GUTTERS
DOWNSPOUTS
FRONT YARD
NO YARD,
FLOWERS,
TREES, BIRD HOUSE,
SWING, STOOP, STAIRS,
RT/N.O./06

The Cotton Bale (1983)

Robert Tannen

The Cotton Bale ties a direct relationship to the South in that "cotton was king," especially in New Orleans, which was at the center of cotton exportation. Here, Tannen has taken what was the major export that created tremendous wealth for the region and infused commentary on the underlying taboo themes of slavery and poverty.

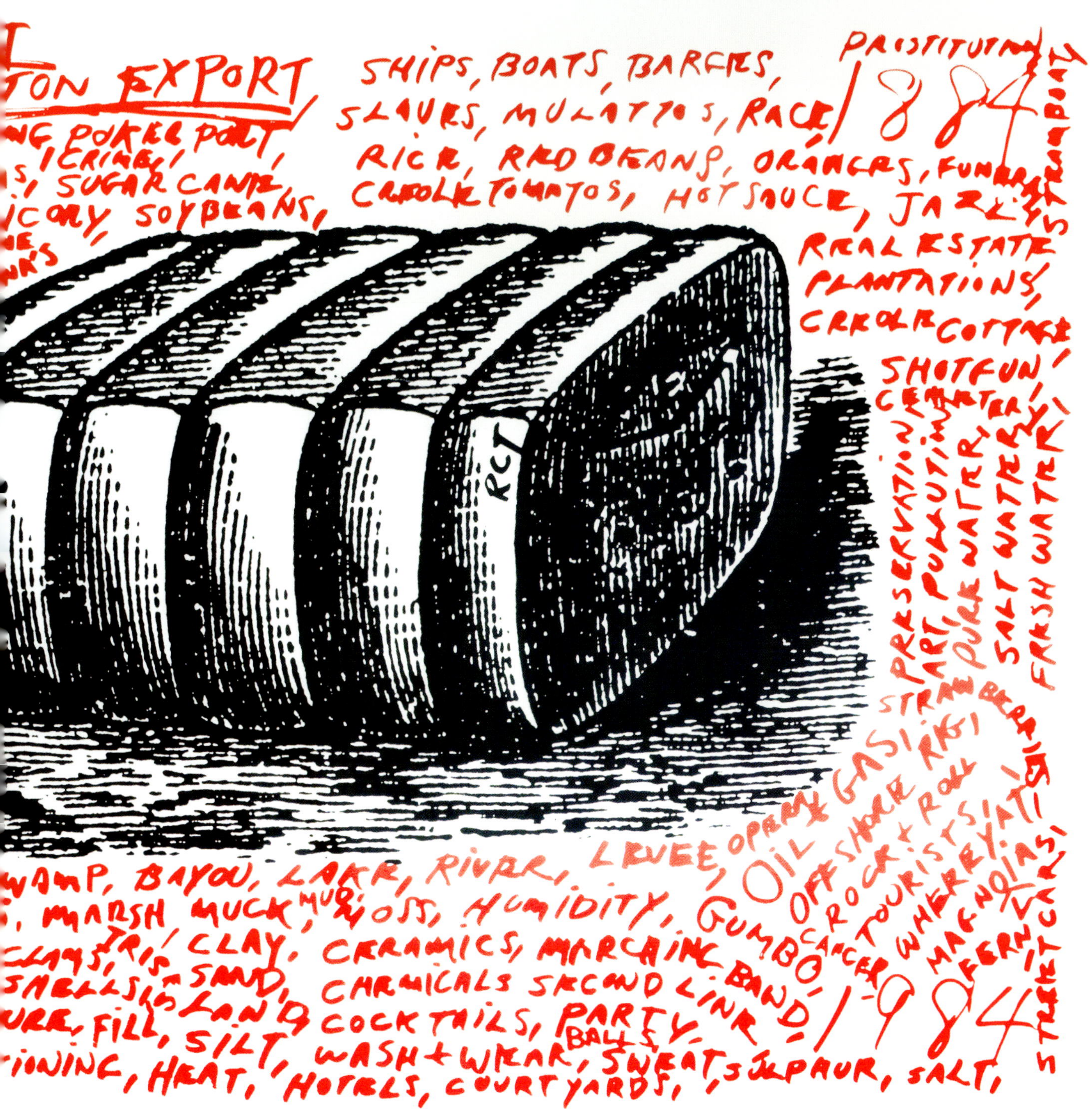

TON EXPORT
SHIPS, BOATS, BARGES,
SLAVES, MULATTOS, RACE,
RICE, RED BEANS, ORANGES,
CREOLE TOMATOS, HOT SAUCE, JAZZ,
1884
PROSTITUTION
STEAMBOAT
REAL ESTATE
PLANTATIONS,
CREOLE COTTAGE,
SHOTGUN,
PRESERVATION,
ART, POLLUTION,
PURE WATER,
SALT WATER,
FRESH WATER,
STRAWBERRIES,
SUGAR CANE,
SOYBEANS,
BAYOU, LAKE, RIVER, LEVEE,
OPERA,
OIL & GAS,
OFFSHORE RIGS,
ROCK & ROLL,
TOURISTS,
MARSH MUCK, MUD, MOSS, HUMIDITY, GUMBO,
CLAY, CERAMICS, MARCHING BAND,
SAND, CHEMICALS SECOND LINE,
LAND, COCKTAILS, PARTY,
FILL, SILT, WASH+WEAR, SWEAT,
HEAT, HOTELS, COURTYARDS,
SALT,
1984
MAGNOLIAS,
STREETCARS,
RCT

Stardust (2018)

Robert Tannen

Stardust is debris from dead stars, which scientists theorize combined to form the universe. Thus, "dust to dust" becomes a proverb that Tannen uses to address both spiritual and secular concerns. His body of work titled "Stardust", which was originally exhibited at the Ogden Museum of Art in New Orleans in 2008, warns of the world's end and refers to the recent discovery that our solar system was formed from the particles and debris thrown off by other dying stars. This series explores his commentary on the theories that this stardust helped in the creation of humanity. His sculptural installation on the grounds of Ohr-O'Keefe Museum of Art use boulders as a metaphor for the earth and our "our dying planet." These large boulders are reminders that the earth will soon be nothing but rock given the present rate of global warming, consumption, and mismanagement of its natural resources by humans.

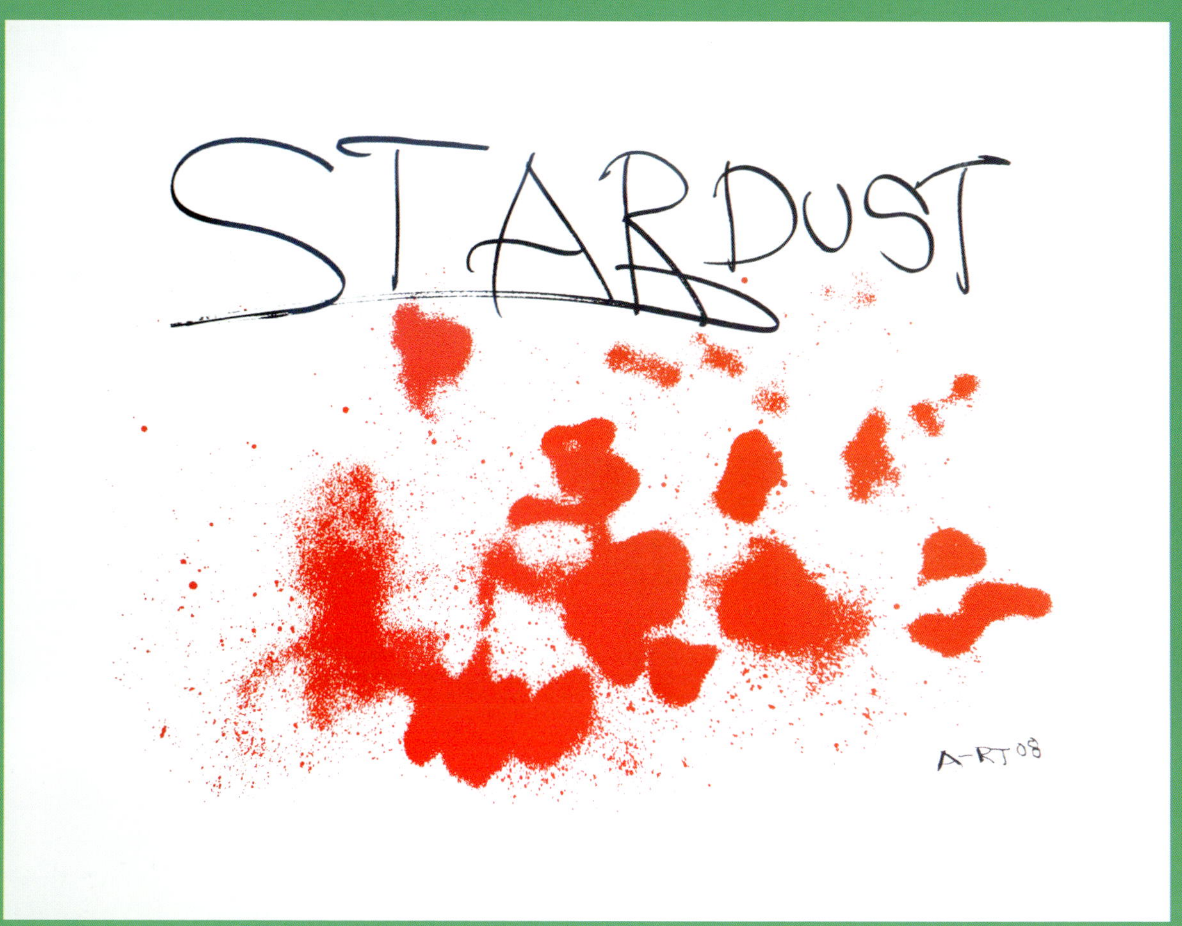
STARDUST
A-RT 08

ART PAPERS

January/February 1991

L O U I S I A N A

Robert Cary Tannen
REPROspective
Contemporary Arts Center
New Orleans, Louisiana

Stereo Toyotas
Res Nova

Floorlamp
Leitmotif
October - November

Robert Tannen is a hard guy to get a read on, at least in terms of most people's expectations. A sculptor, architect, and urban transportation planner, he purposely takes an oblique route to and through these things. High-profile, connected with developers and politicians, he turns up all over the place, but in roles often subject to speculation. Well established, however, are his roles with two city landmarks—the Contemporary Arts Center, which he co-founded, and the massive Greater Mississippi River Bridge, for which he designed the arterial flow.

He churns out schemes and concepts with machine-like prolificacy, many of which seem too far-fetched to fly: for instance a proposed off-ramp from the bridge ceremoniously spiraling around the Virlane sculpture plaza, or his elaborate proposal to turn the entire Mississippi River and adjacent lands into a vast U.S. National Park. (These were both summarily rejected, but the latter proposal is being reconsidered in Washington.)

Such schemes engender confusion—is he serious, and if so, about what? The artist seemed to bait such questioners with neo-dada spinoff shows at Res Nova and Leitmotif. The former featured *Stereo Toyotas*, two identical showroom-new Toyotas functioning as enormous stereo speakers in the otherwise empty space, while the latter—a '50s vintage wood motorboat on its trailer, titled *Floorlamp*—was installed in the middle of Leitmotif's usual selection of high-tech designer lamps, prompting irate customer commentary. ("Horrible—you said you only carried *contemporary* lamps!" Or, more cryptically, "Disgusting. Some dogs only sniff at the strongest scent....")

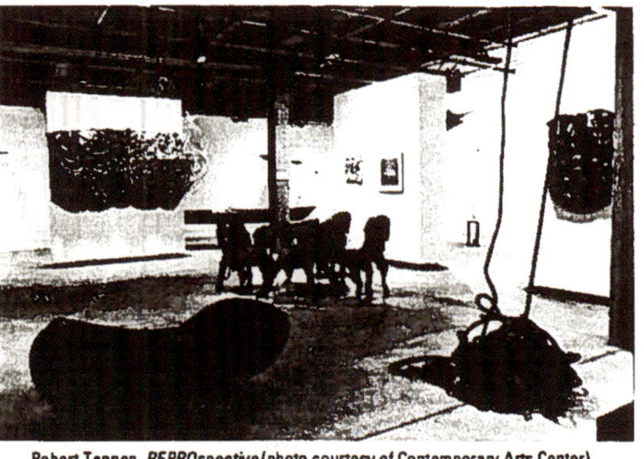

Robert Tannen, *REPROspective* (photo courtesy of Contemporary Arts Center).

Tannen is viewed by some as a mad purveyor of stunts foisted off on the public, and for this reason his REPROspective at the CAC was born in an atmosphere of some controversy. This is partly because New Orleans is steeped in a tradition of meticulously crafted art objects since the 18th century, reinforced by the Parisian academic technique dominant here through the 19th century. Tannen by contrast deigns to truck in objects, regarding them only as evidence, incidental ephemera left behind as markers delineating the structure of a concept, which was never visible, except within the neon concourse of his imagination. This bothers some people.

But his show at the CAC was largely successful because, for once, his processes and methodology were somewhat accessible. At first glance it is all very sketchy, a big room filled with weird, often regional, junk. A large, stuffed and mounted fish on a cross (*Crucifish*), a giant wall-mounted sailfish in lurid day-glo color, inexplicable tangles of anchor rope or industrial cable affixed to the ceiling, tethered pirogues (cypress swamp boats) float through space near numerous giant-sized monopoly pieces arranged strategically on the floor, while two grand pianos, keyboard-to-keyboard, are autonomously playing. Often things appearing more like art turn out to be art by other artists incorporated by Tannen.

What Tannen is up to is a purposeful blurring of boundaries between art and non-art, a provocative fragmenting of expectation. Objects that might be art are presented somewhat like art, but one is never sure, the system of contexts is ever-shifting, seemingly random constructs of zen-junk materializing like wayward koans.

I think Tannen views the entire regional environment in this way, a welter of objects disjoined from their original function, taking on surreal configurations of visual bebop. Tannen takes a macro view—it is all art, you just have to adjust your perspective. So this is art about the idea of art, but in a special way that reflects back on this environment as an evolving organic entity. The random physics of objects in motion/repose becomes metaphysical, a metaphor, a time-lapse ballet.

All of which reflects Tannen's background with the Experimentalist tradition, and his early work with Buckminster Fuller (as well as growing up on Coney Island and in the East Village of the abstract expressionists, where his father had a bookstore). In or near New Orleans since 1969, he seems to view this area, with its adjacent Mississippi Gulf Coast, as analogous to Coney Island, a surreal urban jive enclave adjacent to international waters. But with a special twist, the aura of mystery provided by a surfeit of disjunctives, human and material, with no apparent reason to be as they are, but which simply are, and pointedly remain so: a place of perverse willfulness. Robert Tannen's art explores these mysteries.

So Tannen's art is not always understood because it is veiled, contained within the processes of his investigation, and is then—in the last analysis—simply his vision and its residual effluence, an ecology of iconography that lingers like an afterimage. This show, for those who were willing to make the leap, elucidated these points as a journey through a mysterious topography, in which the landscape and the map often intersect—finally merging into one, somewhere just around the bend, along vast sweeping arcs swirling through the cloverleafs of cognition.

D. Eric Bookhardt

appearing more like art turn out to be art by other artists incorporated by Tannen.

What Tannen is up to is a purposeful blurring of boundaries between art and non-art, a provocative fragmenting of expectation. Objects that might be art are presented somewhat like art, but one is never sure, the system of contexts is ever-shifting, seemingly random constructs of zen-junk materializing like wayward koans.

I think Tannen views the entire regional environment in this way, a welter of objects disjoined from their original function, taking on surreal configurations of visual bebop. Tannen takes a macro view—it is all art, you just have to adjust your perspective. So this is art about the idea of art, but in a special way that reflects back on this environment as an evolving organic entity. The random physics of objects in motion/repose becomes metaphysical, a metaphor, a time-lapse ballet.

All of which reflects Tannen's background with the Experimentalist tradition, and his early

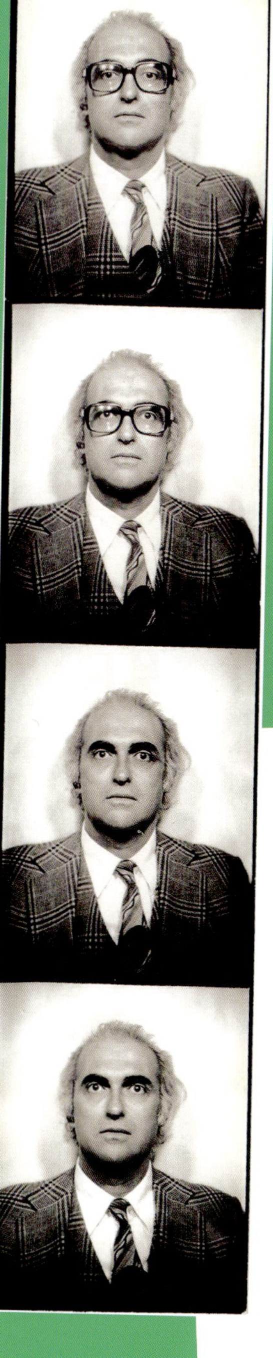

“I’m less interested in repeating an image or idea to become a signature association of myself rather than exploring new ideas on a continuing basis”

— ROBERT TANNEN

Robert Tannen: Citizen Artist

In American civic processes there are extensive opportunities for citizens who have the time, inclination and ability to affect the sytem in fundamental ways. Yet few American artists select to eschew their solitary aesthetic missions in order to involve themselves in the sometimes mundane, and always challenging, business of providing quality-of-life services to a public broader than the denizens of the art circuit. This civic/artistic conscience is manifested, however, in the actions of a small but diverse group of artists who pioneered an urban, global, and environmental aesthetic that is the precursor of what may become a unified cultural approach to making the earth more liveable and providing nuance and surprise to our urban environment.

Art can help the world in many ways, none more important than by just being good art, providing aesthetic integrity as a primary function. In addition, art plays an important role by contributing to the quality of our visual landscape. Consequently, architecture, urban design, and planning become an extended palette for artists like Robert Tannen. Used in combination with discrete art objects, he creates artistic statements that serve as working models for further development.

Tannen's concern for the natural environment, and for rural and urban affairs has fueled thirty year of projects devoted to identifying ecological and cultural issues and proposing solutions that range from formal masterplans to poetic objects. His wish to help the world through his art makes Tannen a citizen artist.

In this role, he has embraced such issues as housing, transportation, land use, waste management, public amenities, water conservation, architecture, and economic and cultural development. These have been impacted through such diverse strategies as consensus planning, sculpture, governmental relations, conceptual art, civil engineering, drawing, real estate development, art activism, disaster recovery, site specific art installation, architecture, and environmental activism.

TEXT BY ADOLFO NODAL
LOS ANGELES DEPARTMENT
OF CULTURAL AFFAIRS

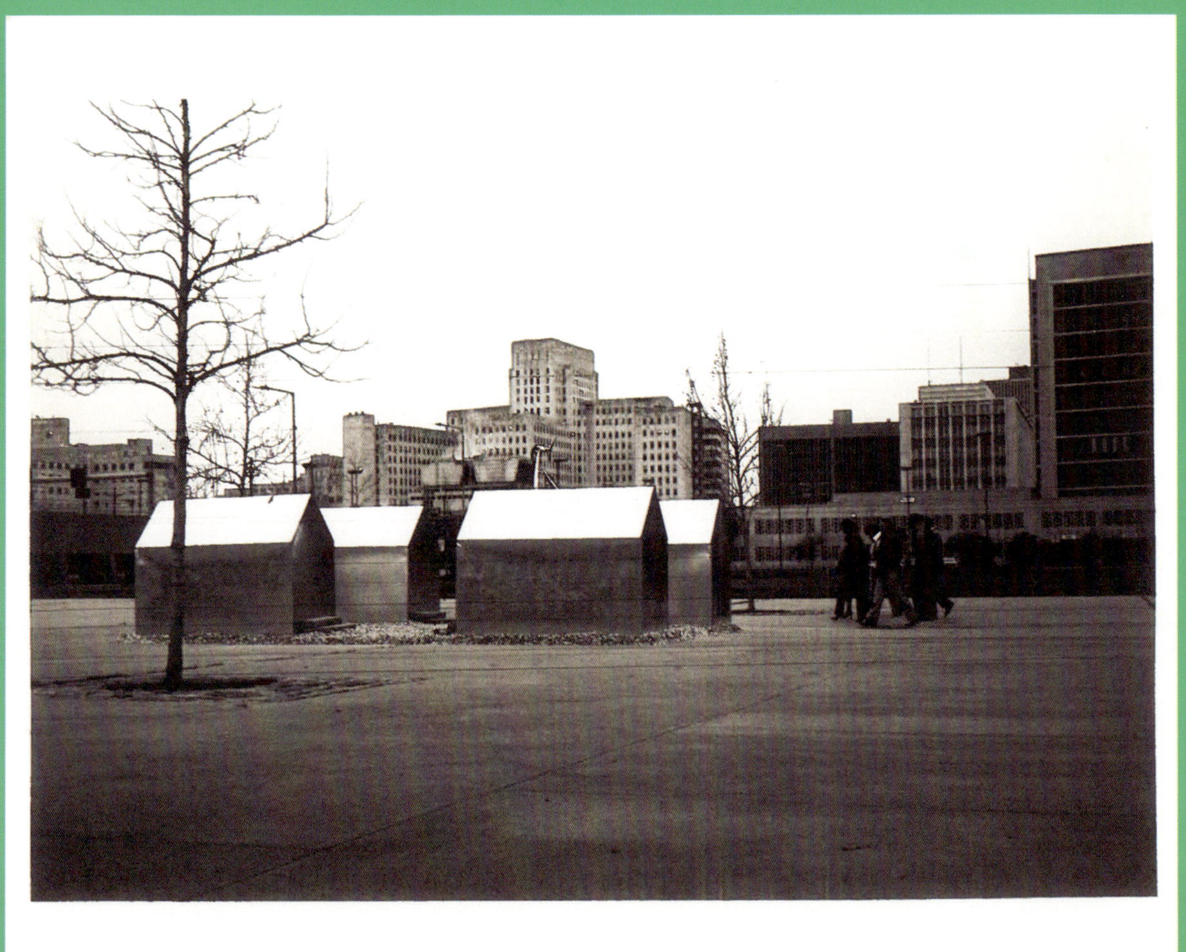

SHOTGUN HOUSE SCULPTURES
INSTALLATION AT THE SUPERDOME

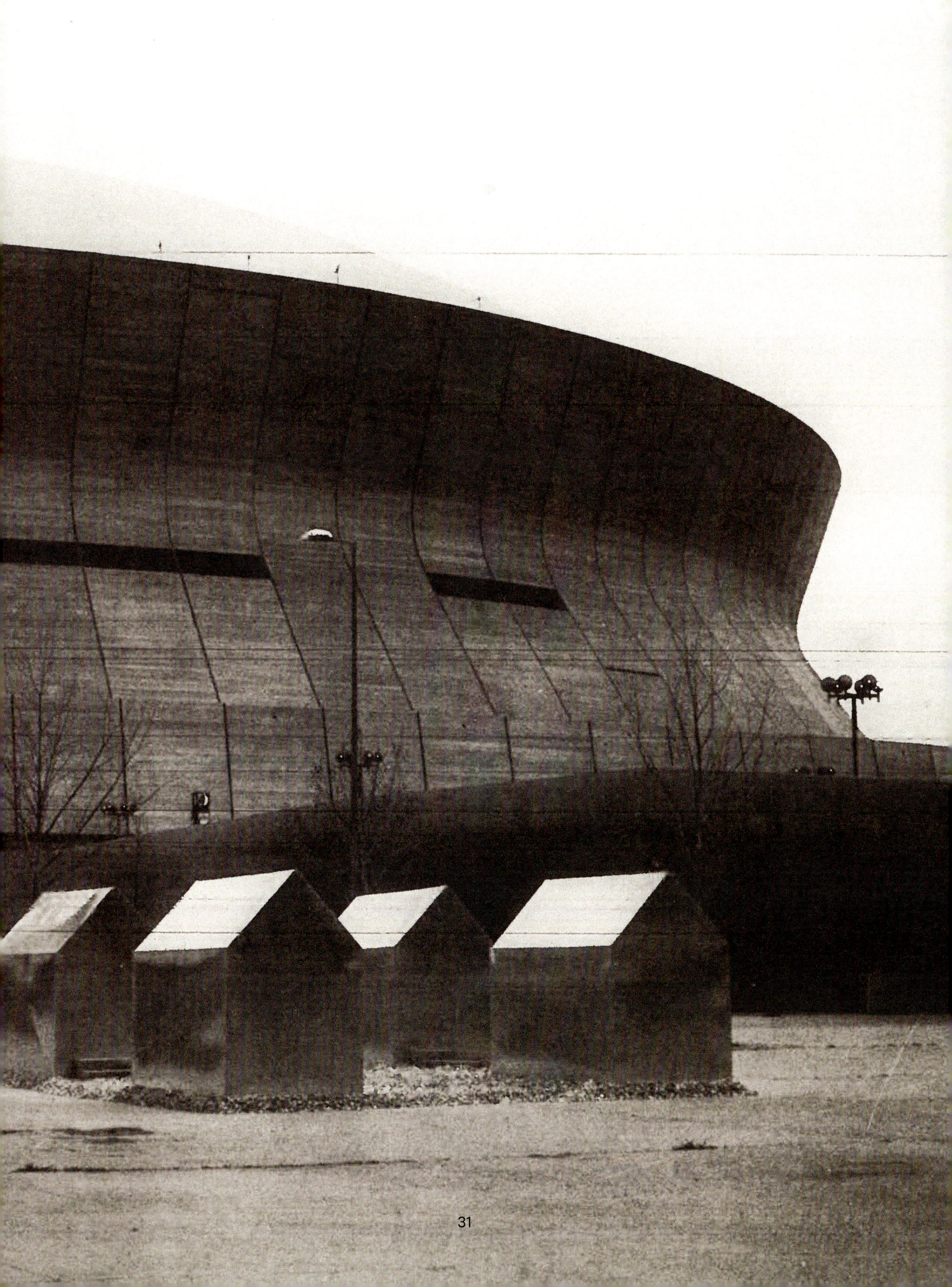

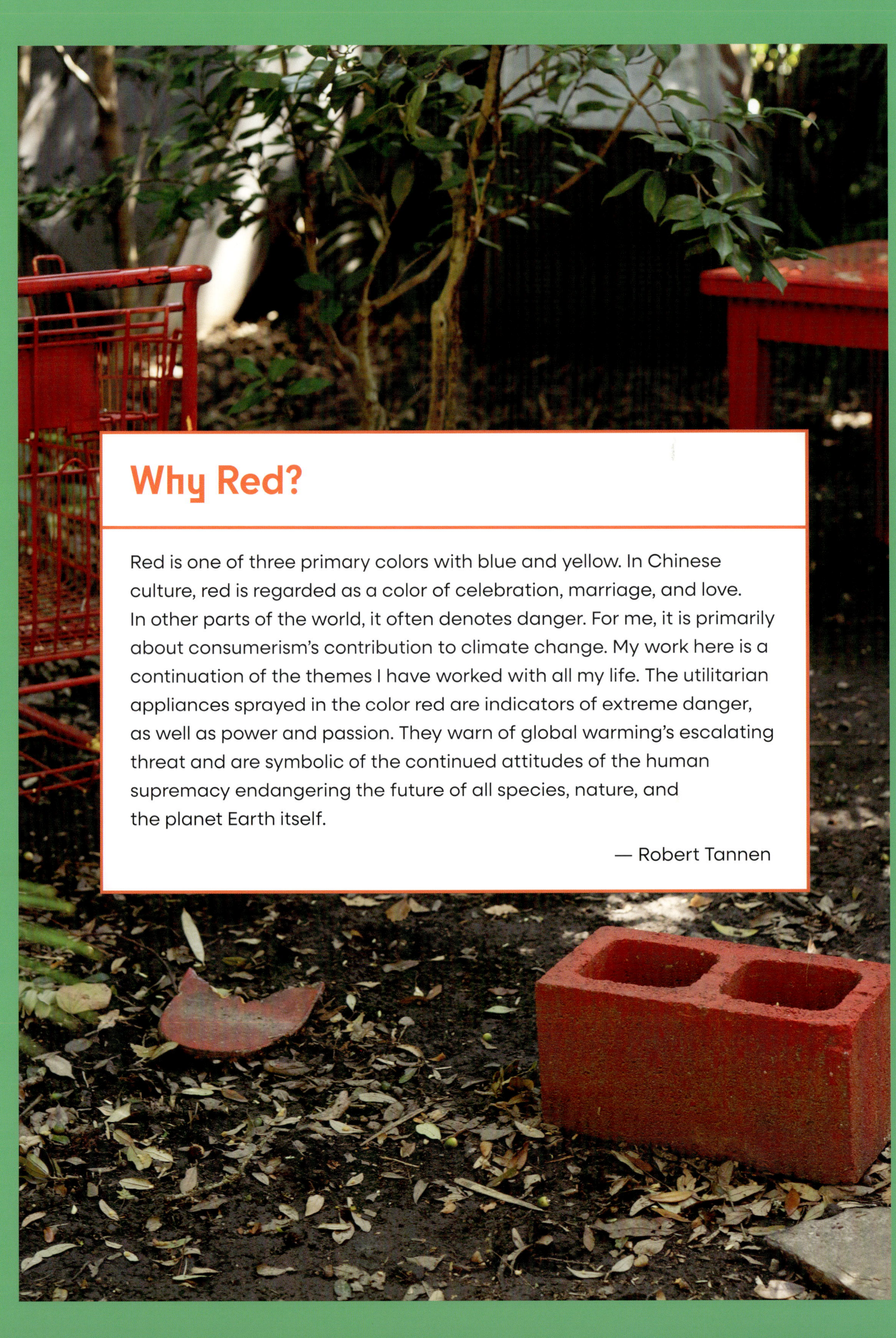

Why Red?

Red is one of three primary colors with blue and yellow. In Chinese culture, red is regarded as a color of celebration, marriage, and love. In other parts of the world, it often denotes danger. For me, it is primarily about consumerism's contribution to climate change. My work here is a continuation of the themes I have worked with all my life. The utilitarian appliances sprayed in the color red are indicators of extreme danger, as well as power and passion. They warn of global warming's escalating threat and are symbolic of the continued attitudes of the human supremacy endangering the future of all species, nature, and the planet Earth itself.

— Robert Tannen

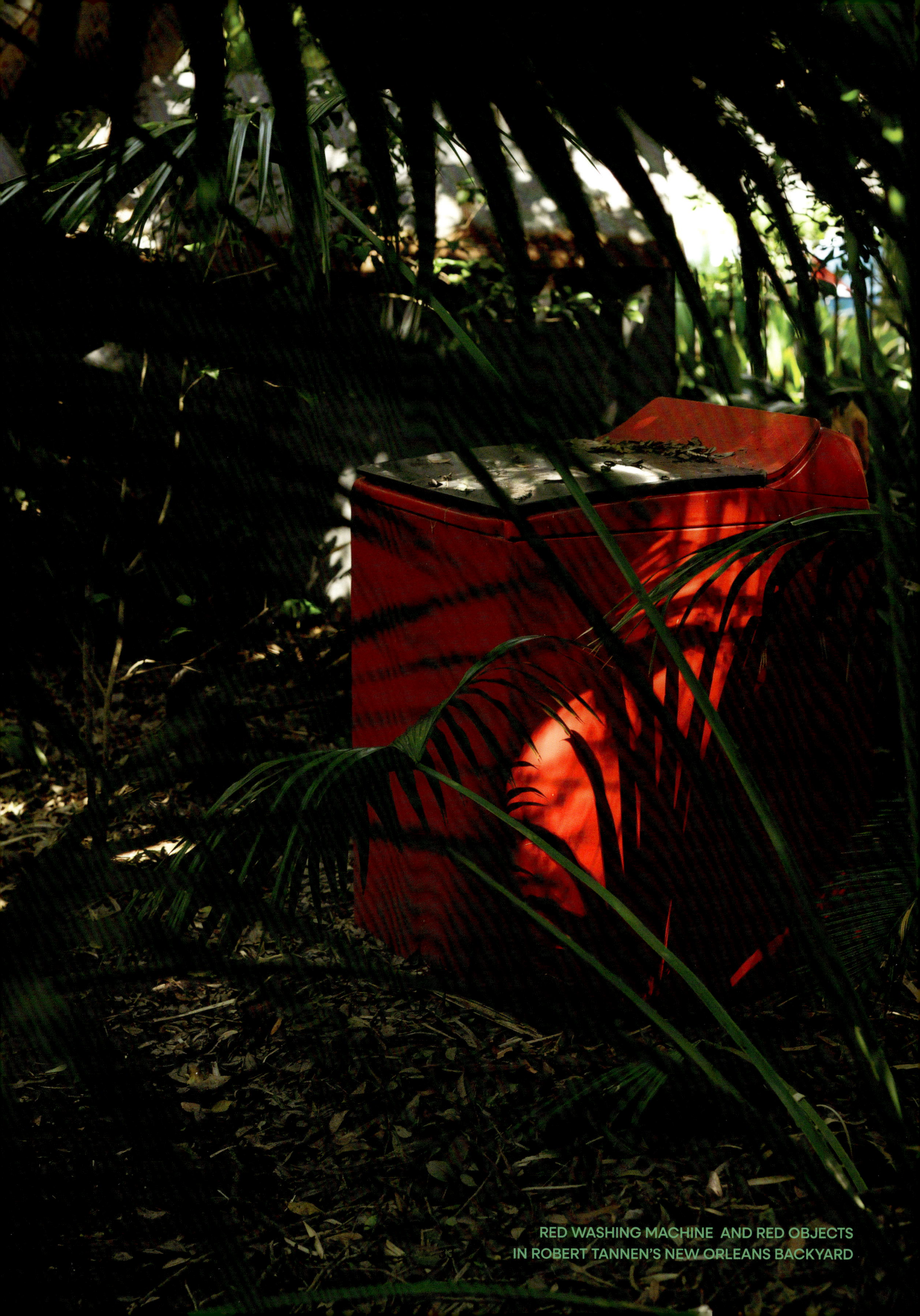

RED WASHING MACHINE AND RED OBJECTS
IN ROBERT TANNEN'S NEW ORLEANS BACKYARD

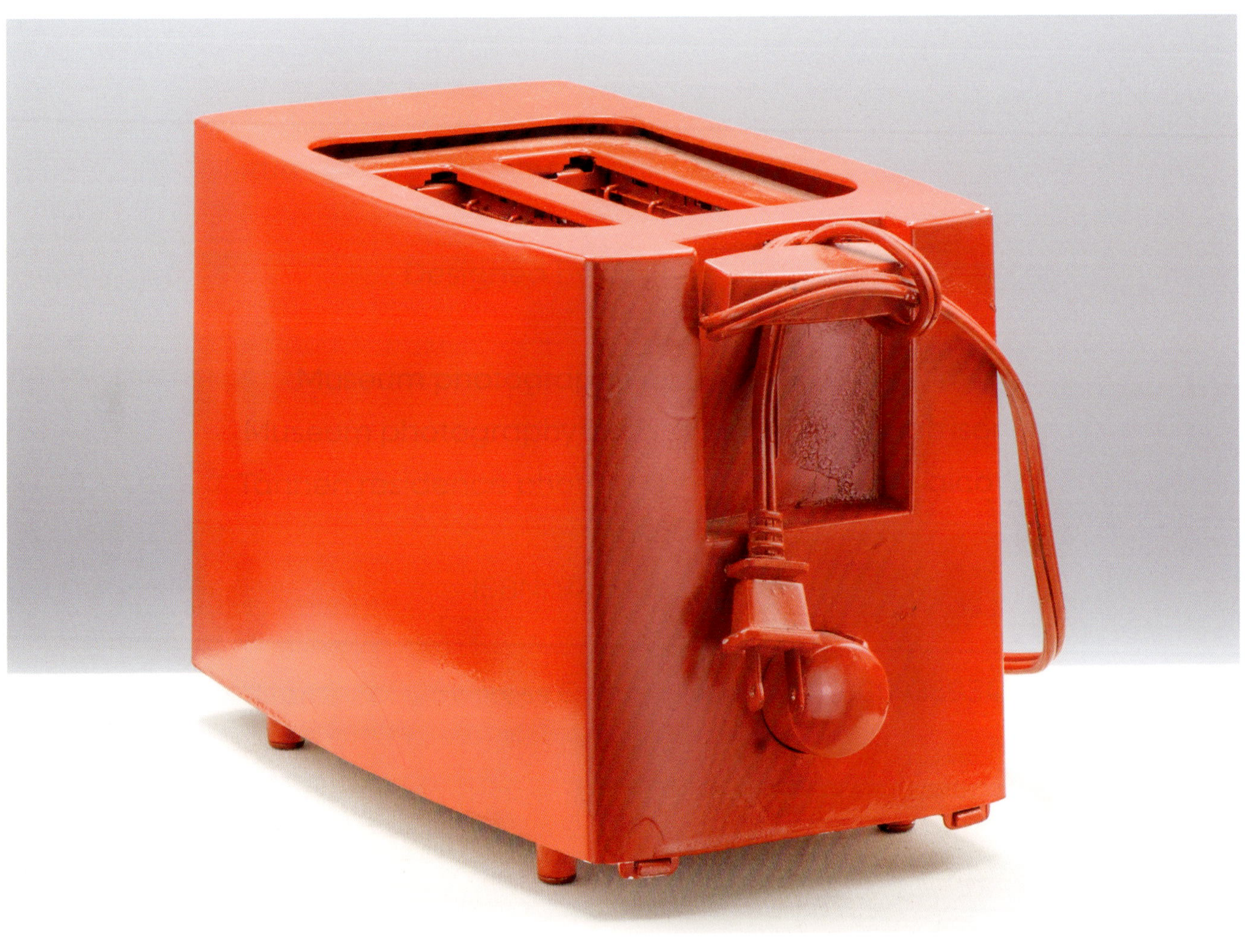

REDART, FORMER ELECTRIC TOASTER
ROBERT TANNEN

RIGHT: REDART, FORMER BOTTLE OF STOLI VODKA
REDART, FORMER OLIVETTI TYPEWRITER

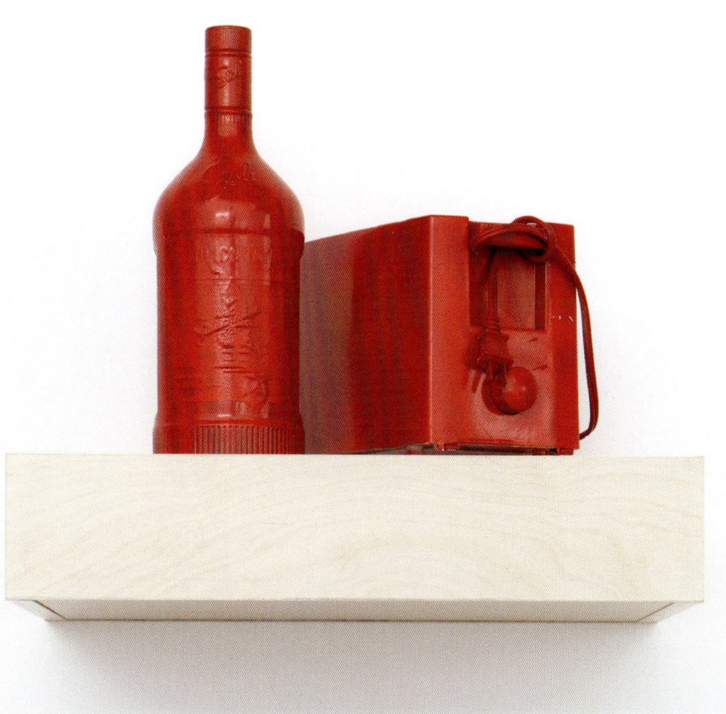

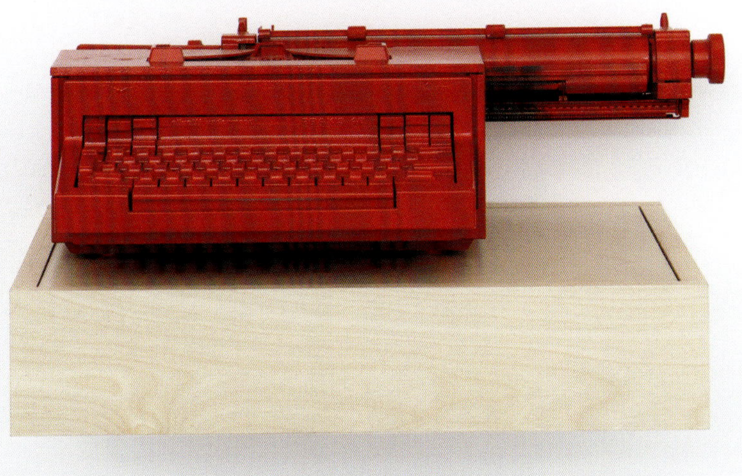

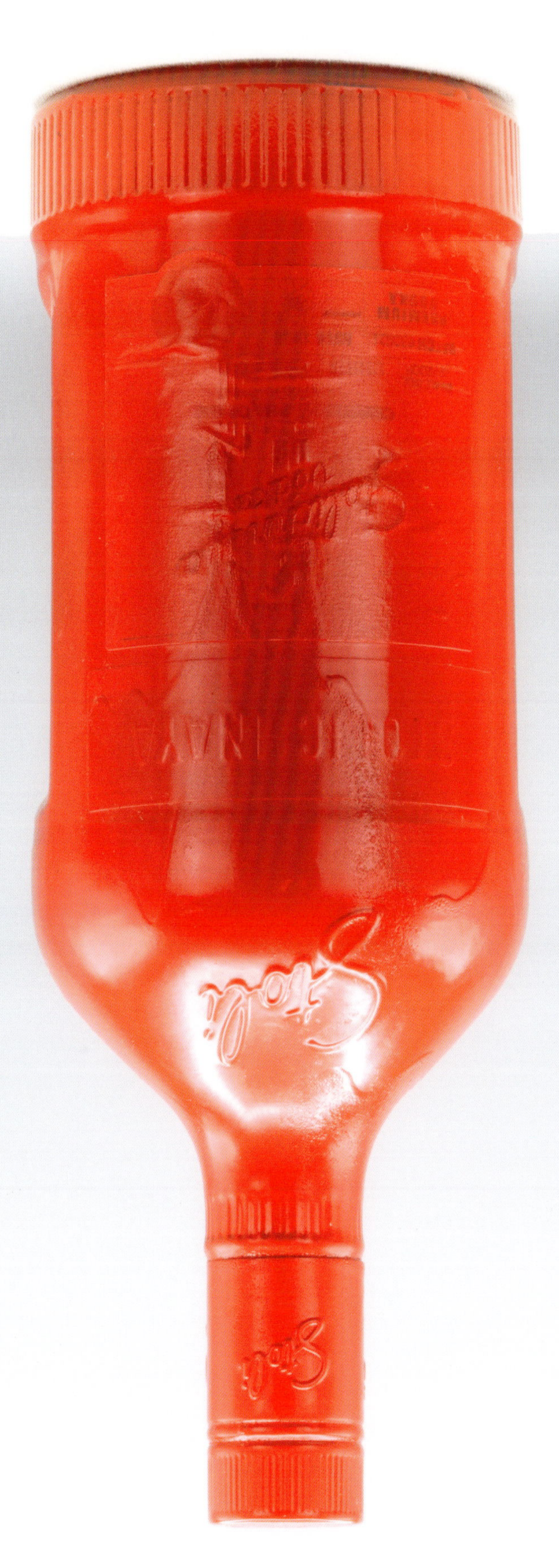

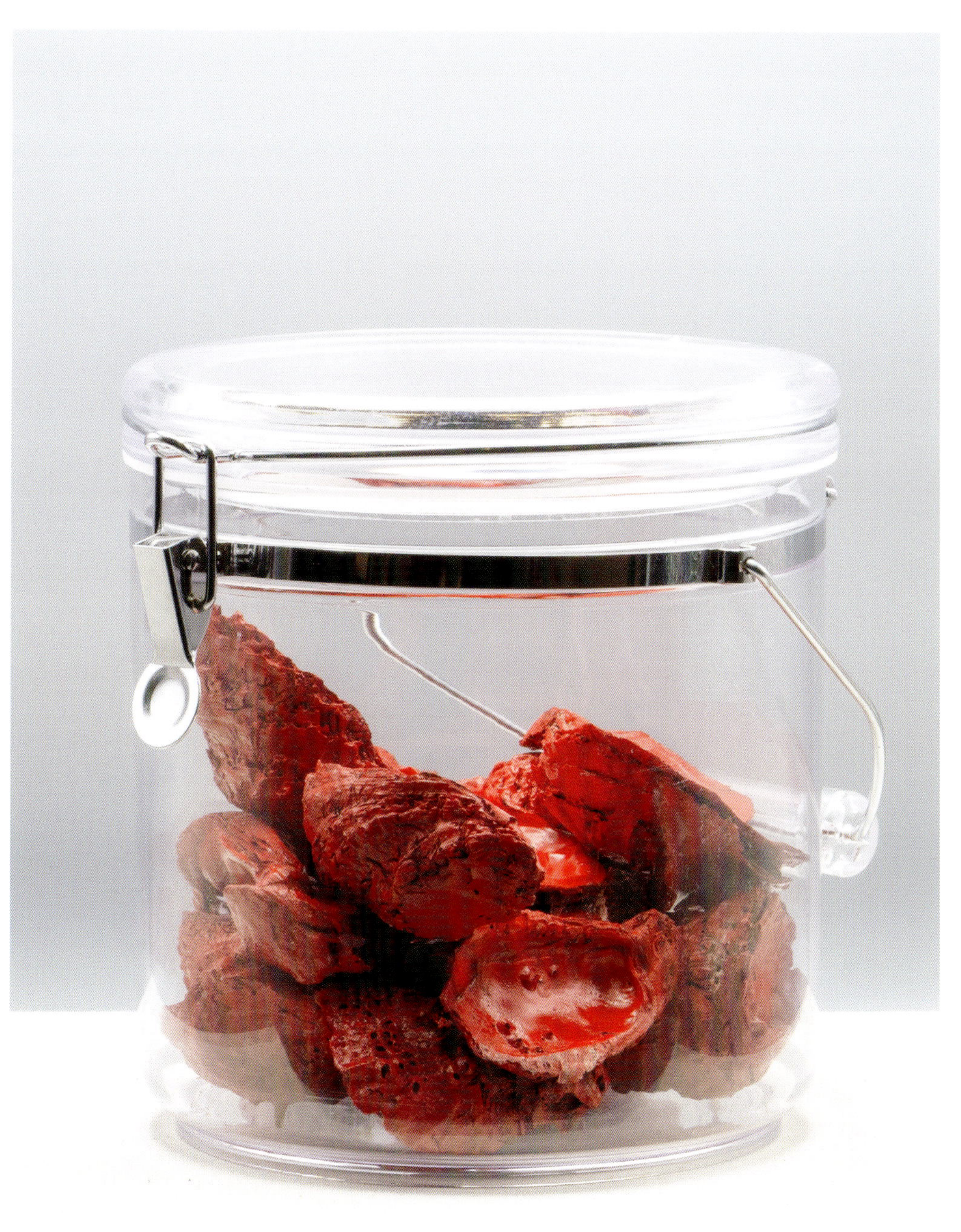

REDART, CONTAINER OF FORMER OYSTER SHELLS
ROBERT TANNEN

LEFT: FORMER BOTTLE OF STOLI VODKA

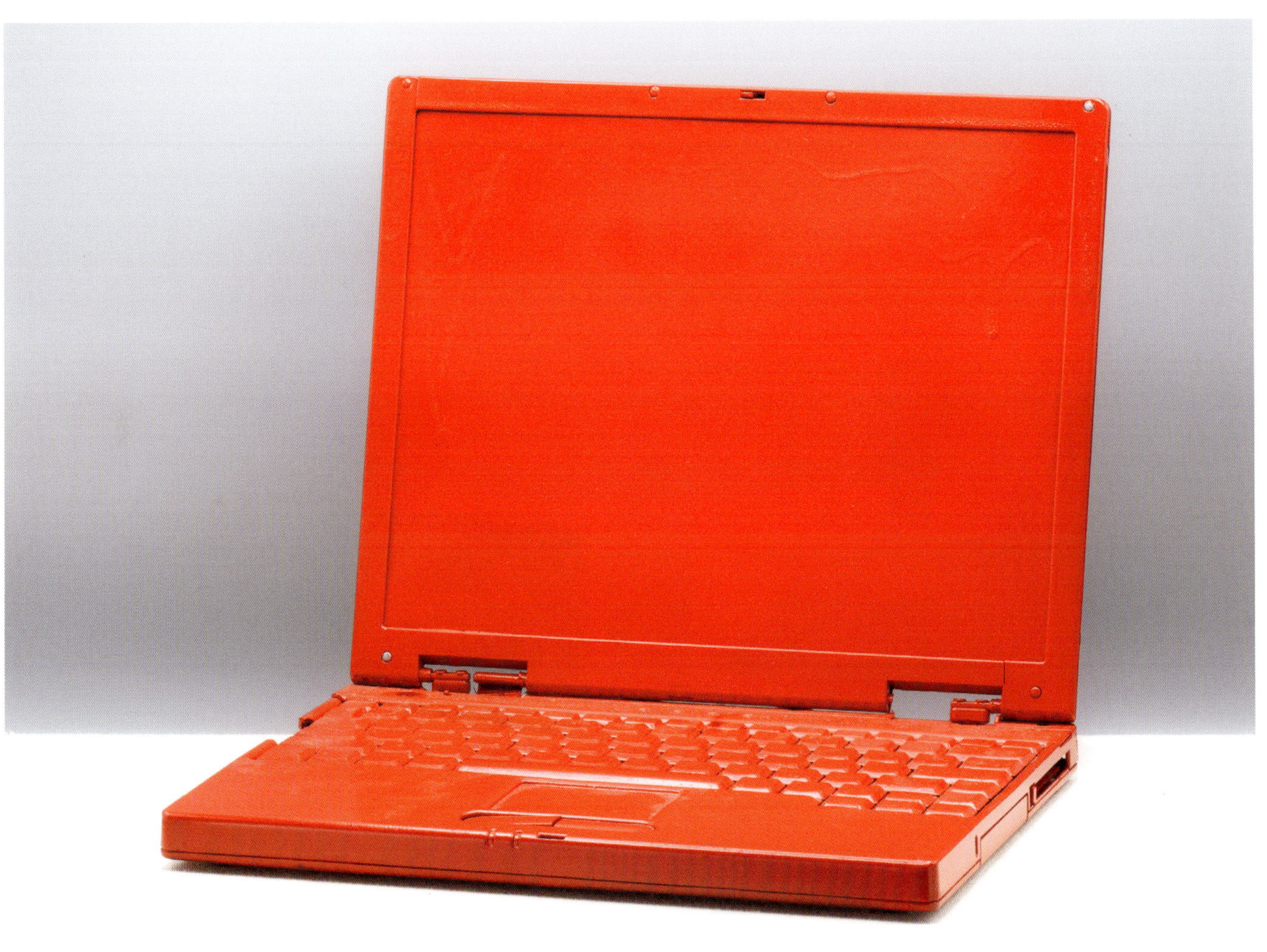

REDART, FORMER LAPTOP COMPUTER
ROBERT TANNEN

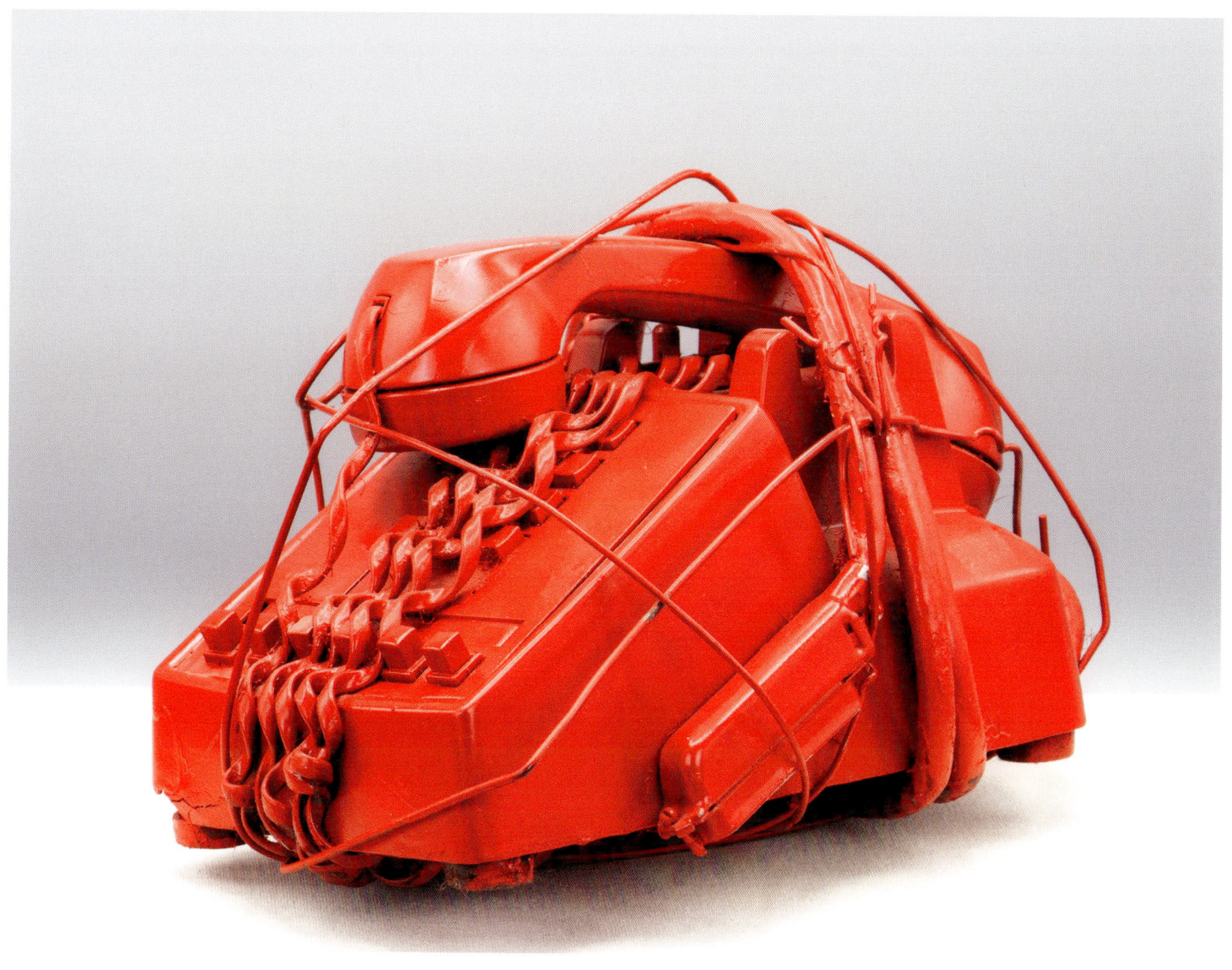

REDART, FORMER PUSH BUTTON PHONE
ROBERT TANNEN

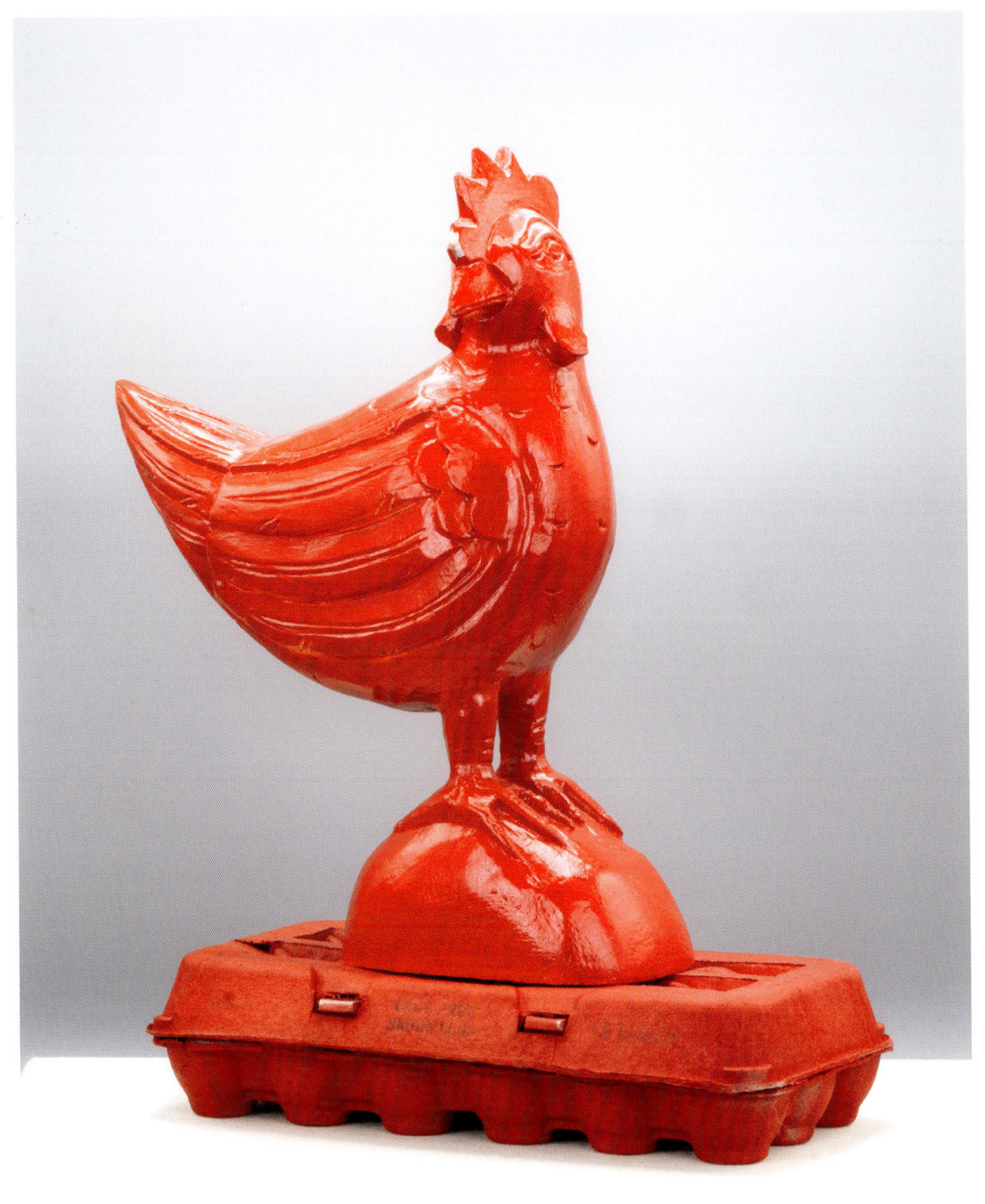

REDART, FORMER CARVED CHICKEN AND FORMER TWELVE EGGS
ROBERT TANNEN

RIGHT: VIEW OF REDART APPLIANCES

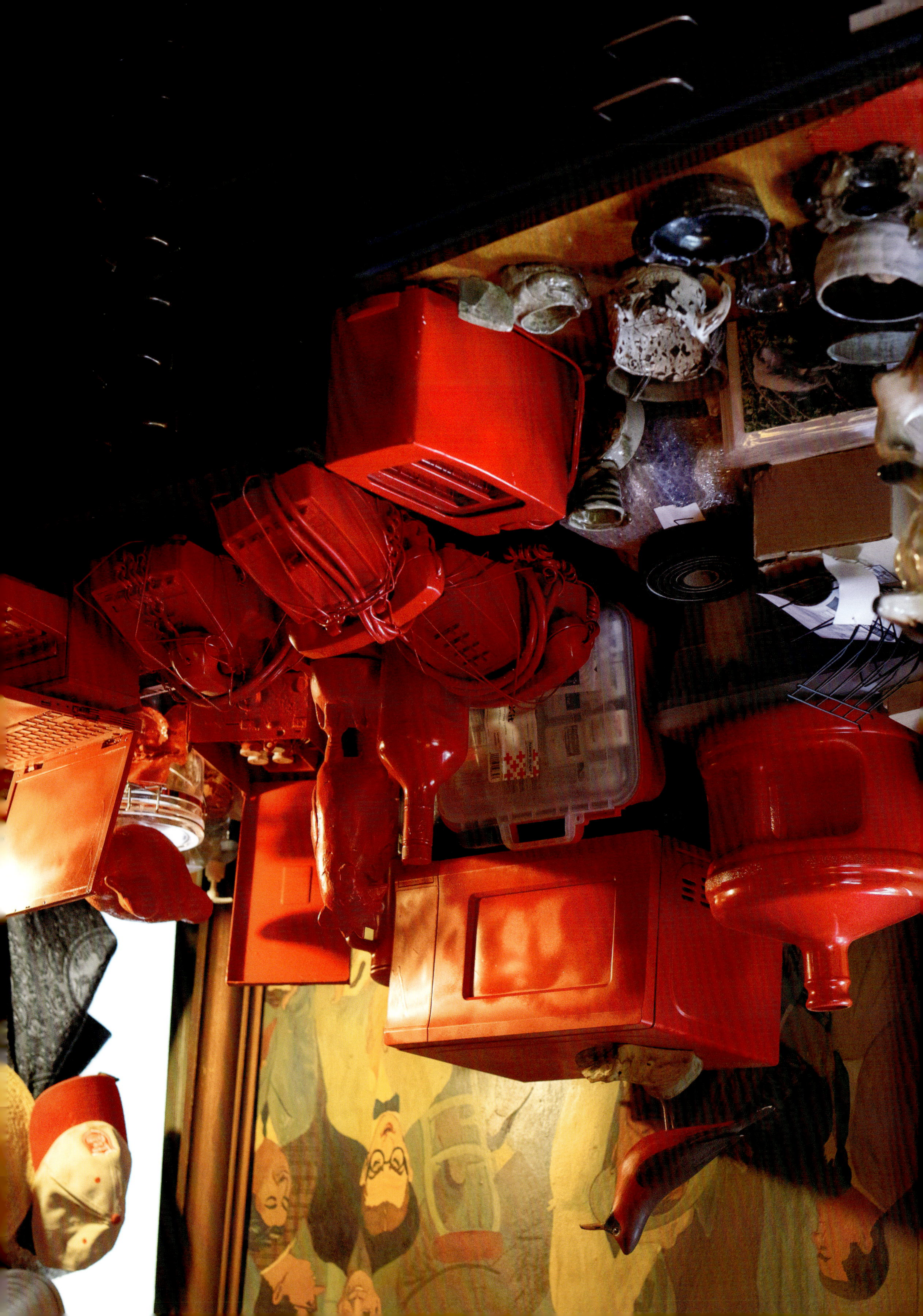

REDART, FORMER WIRED RIFLE, FORMER AK-15
ROBERT TANNEN

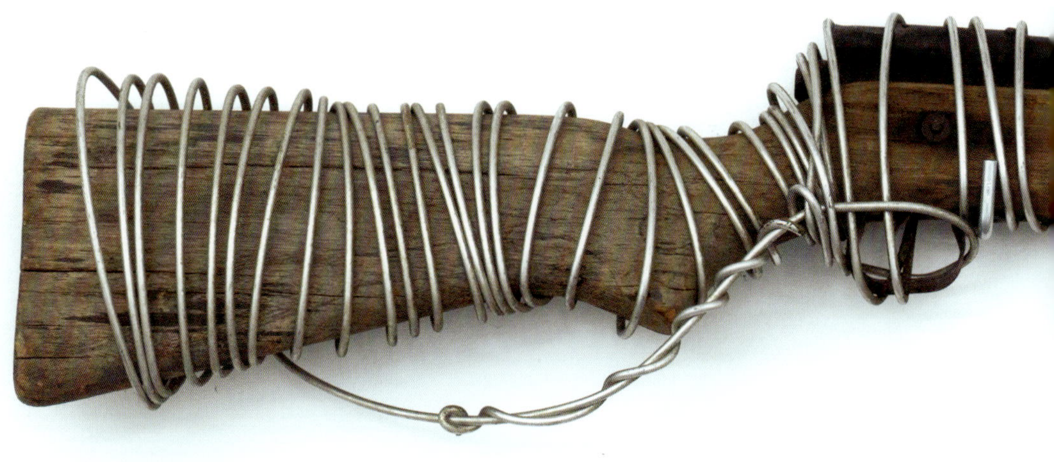

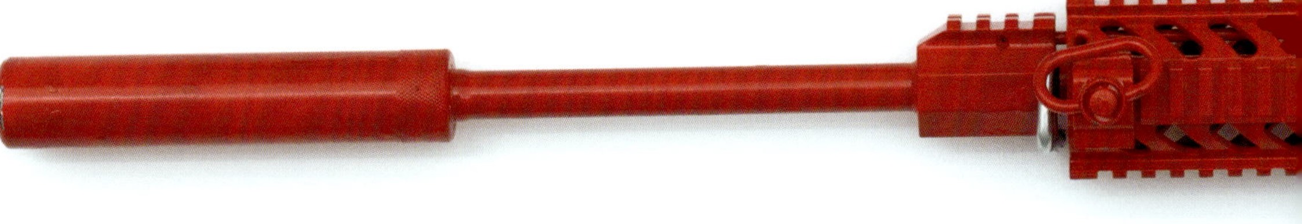

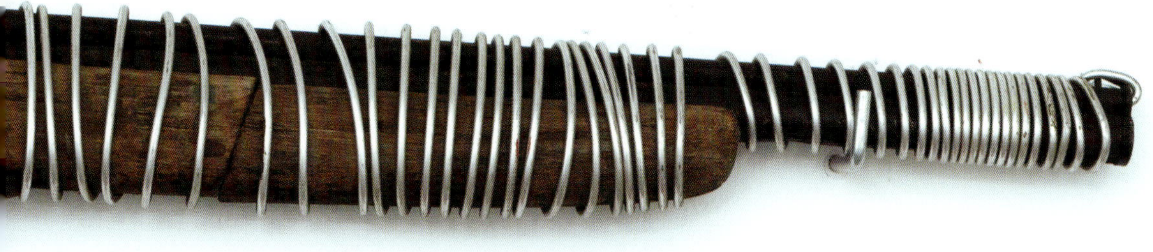

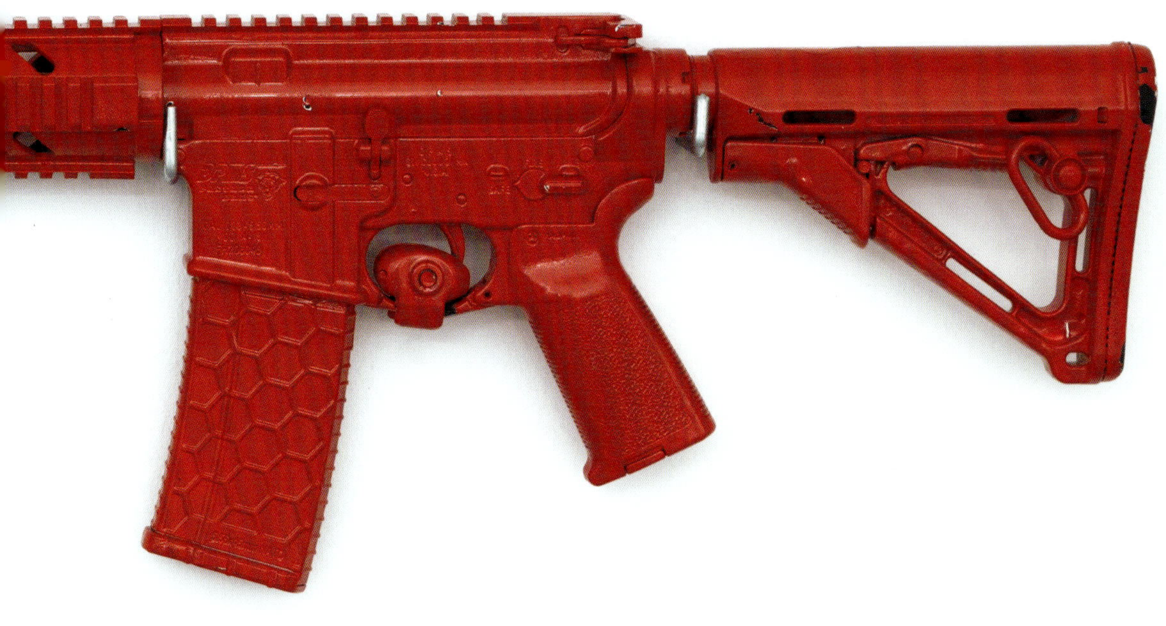

"Coming home from the hospital after femur surgey in 2024, I was struck by the basic idea of working with primary colors and selected patterns. I chose a size and place to make this art that was convenient from a wheelchair. The patterns began to reflect the inherent contrast between the linearity of human design as opposed to natural, organic systems in nature."

— Robert Tannen

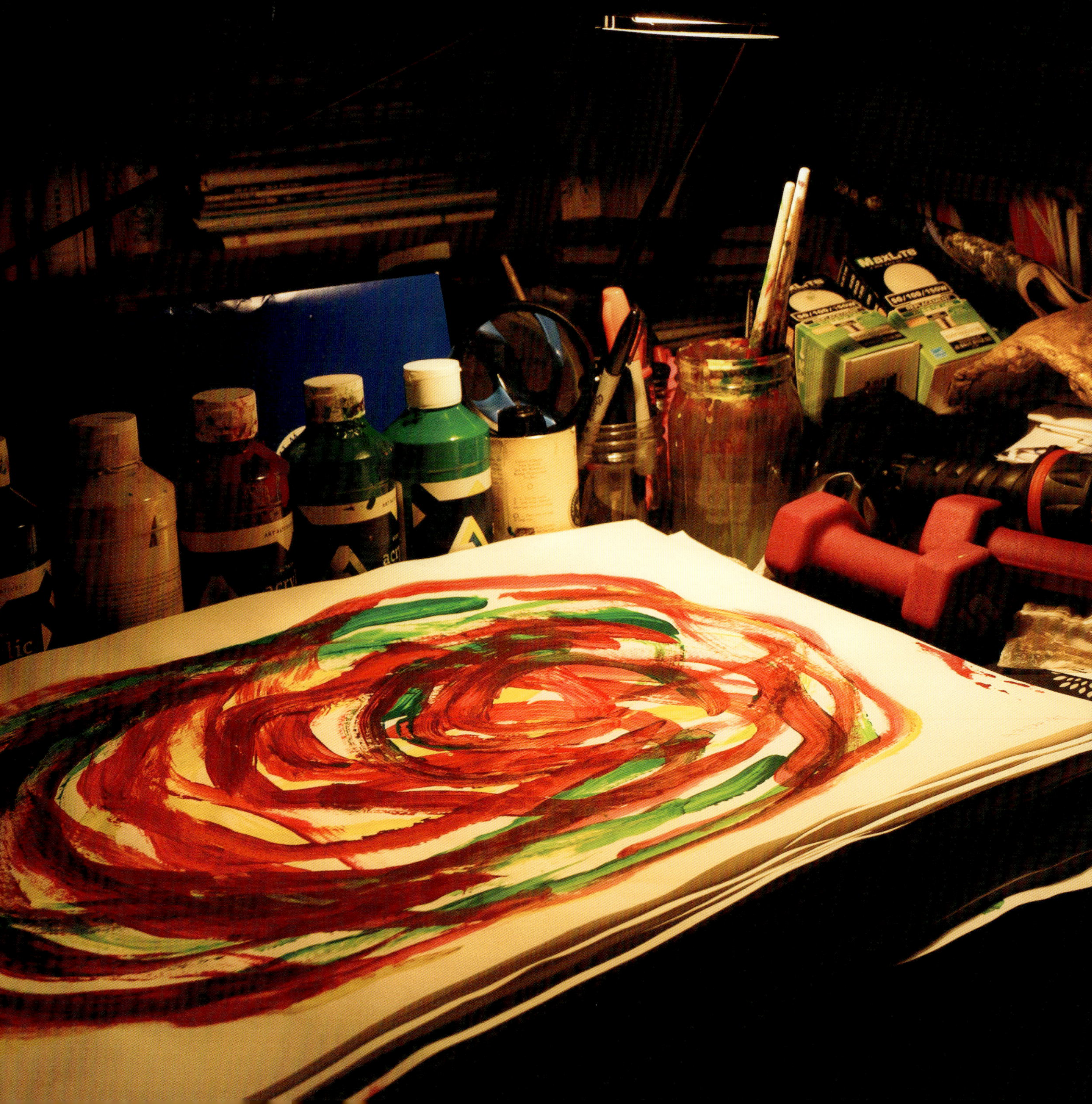

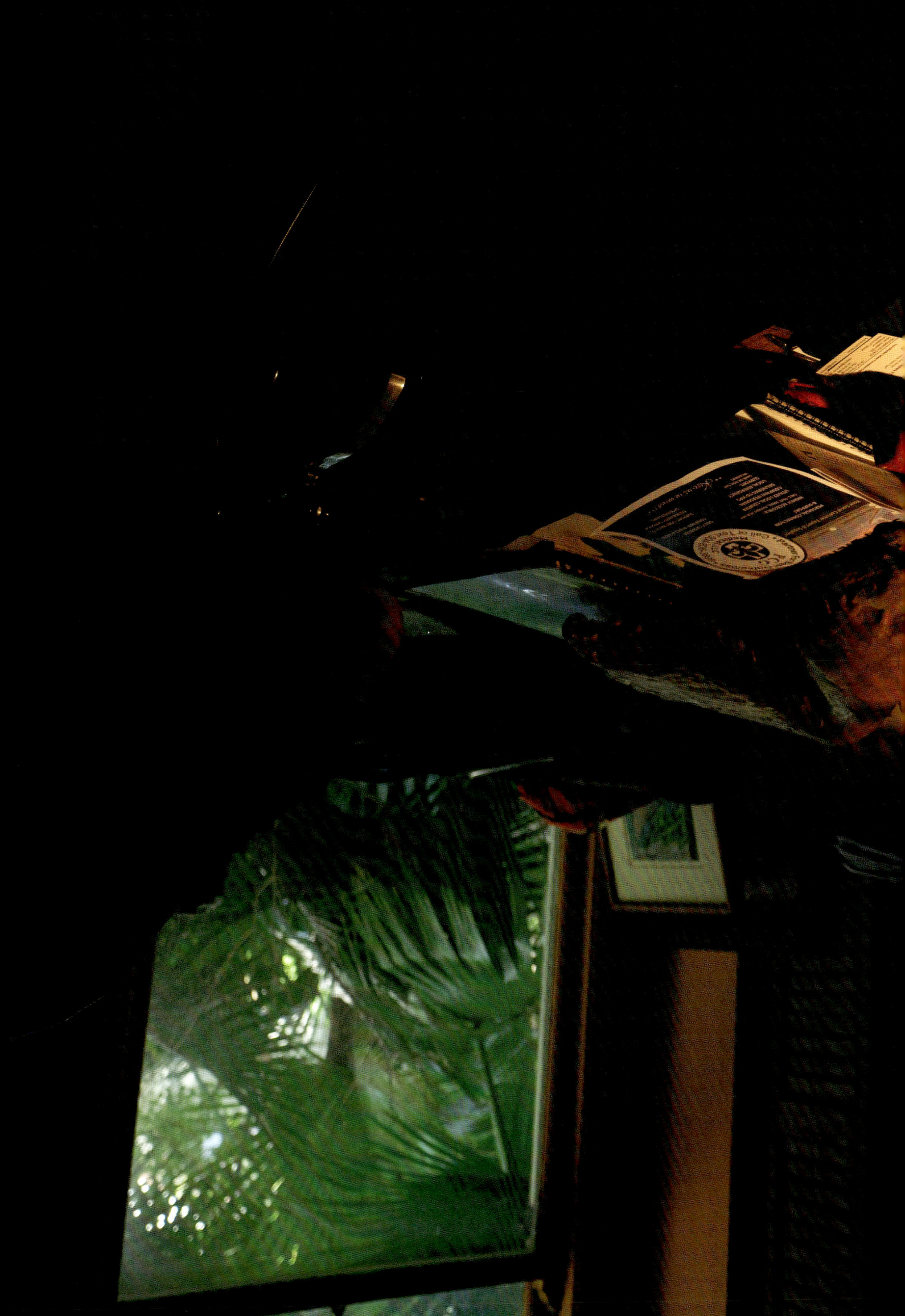

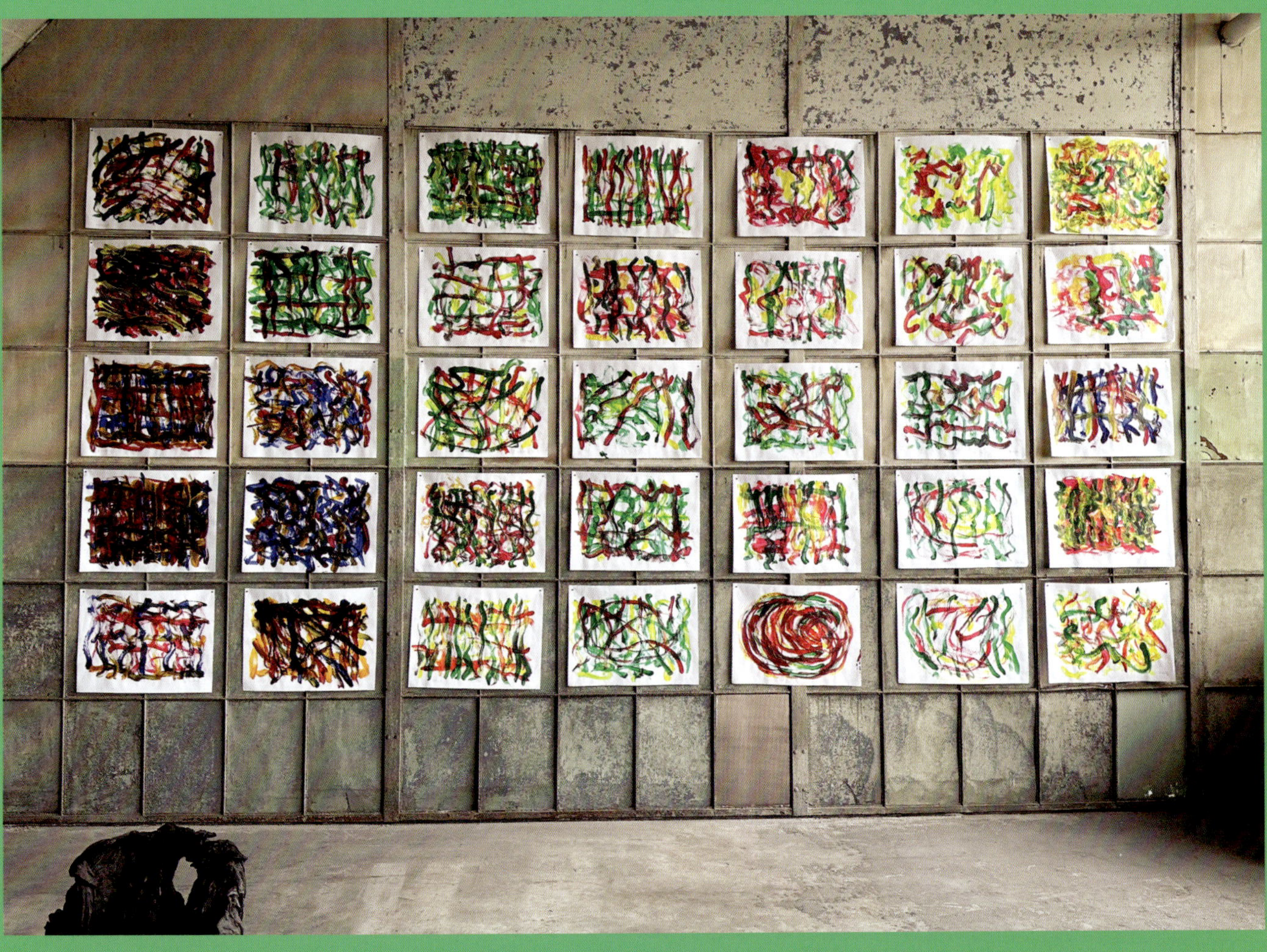

‘War and Peace’ (a selection from 80+ paintings) was installed at the former Ford Motor Assembly Plant in Arabi, Louisiana in association with Prospect.6. It shows the cooperation and conflict between primary colors and patterns, calling attention to the threats to our earth.

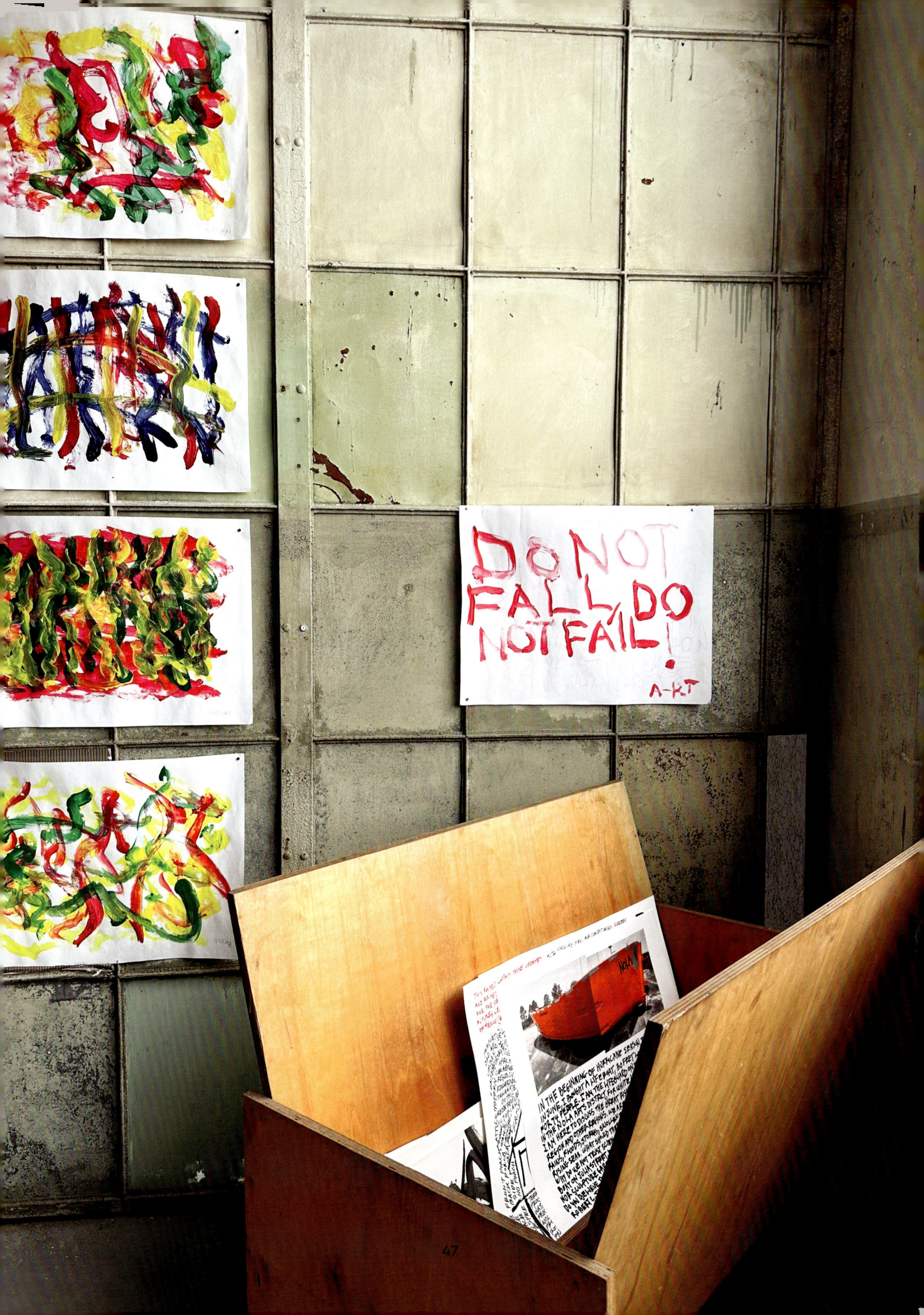
DO NOT FALL DO NOT FAIL!
A-KT
NOLA

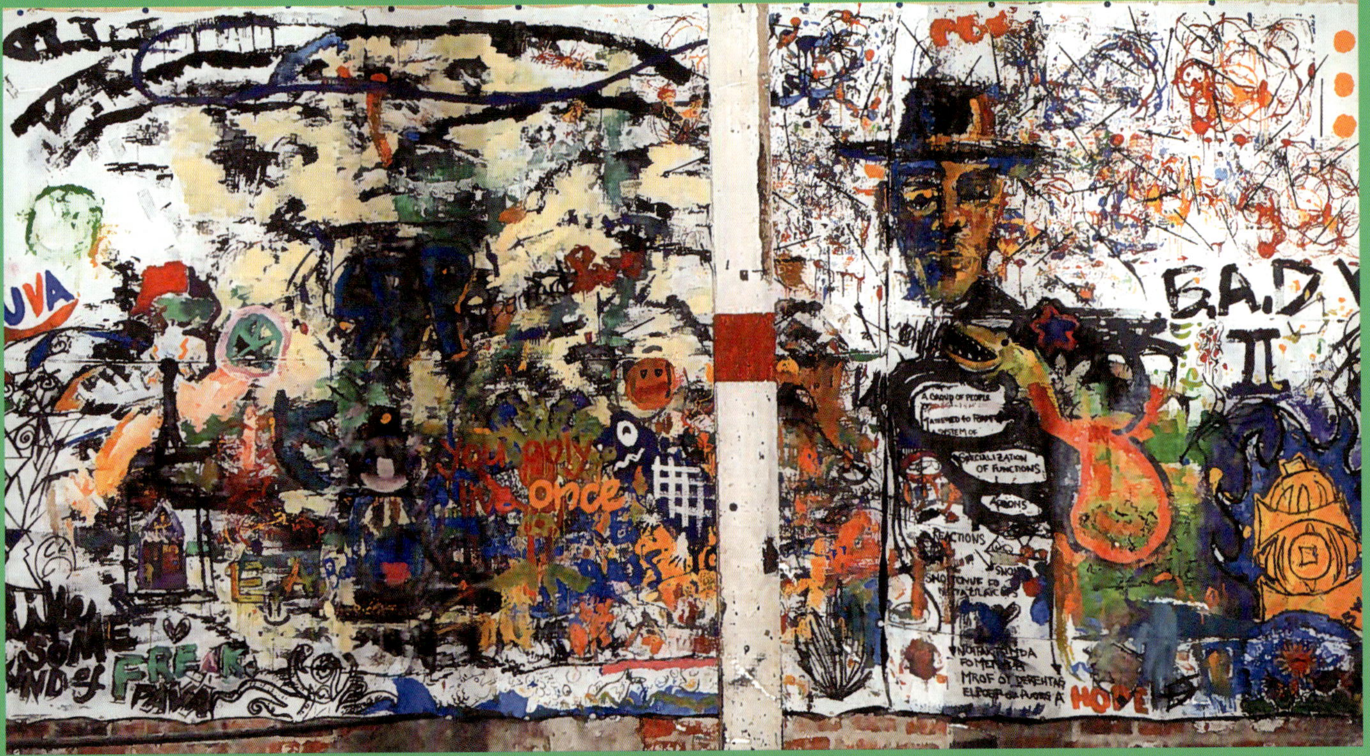
B.A.D
you only
live once
HOME

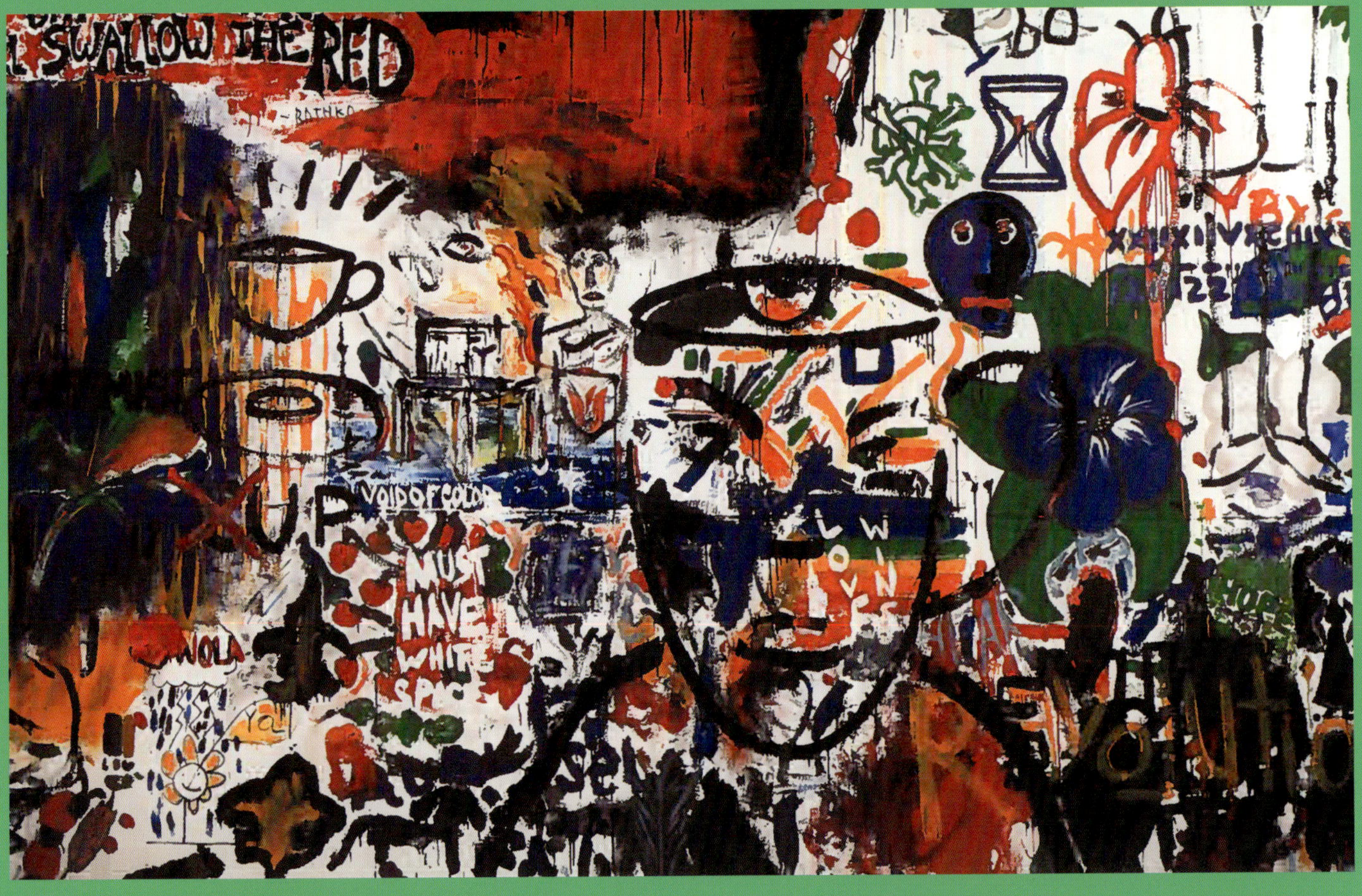
SWALLOW THE RED
VOID OF COLOR
MUST
HAVE
WHITE
UP

"I generally involve other people in my work. My Prospect.2 idea was art by committee, because committee is the basic organization of human communication. I feel more comfortable working in community versus as an independent artist alone in the studio."

—Robert Tannen

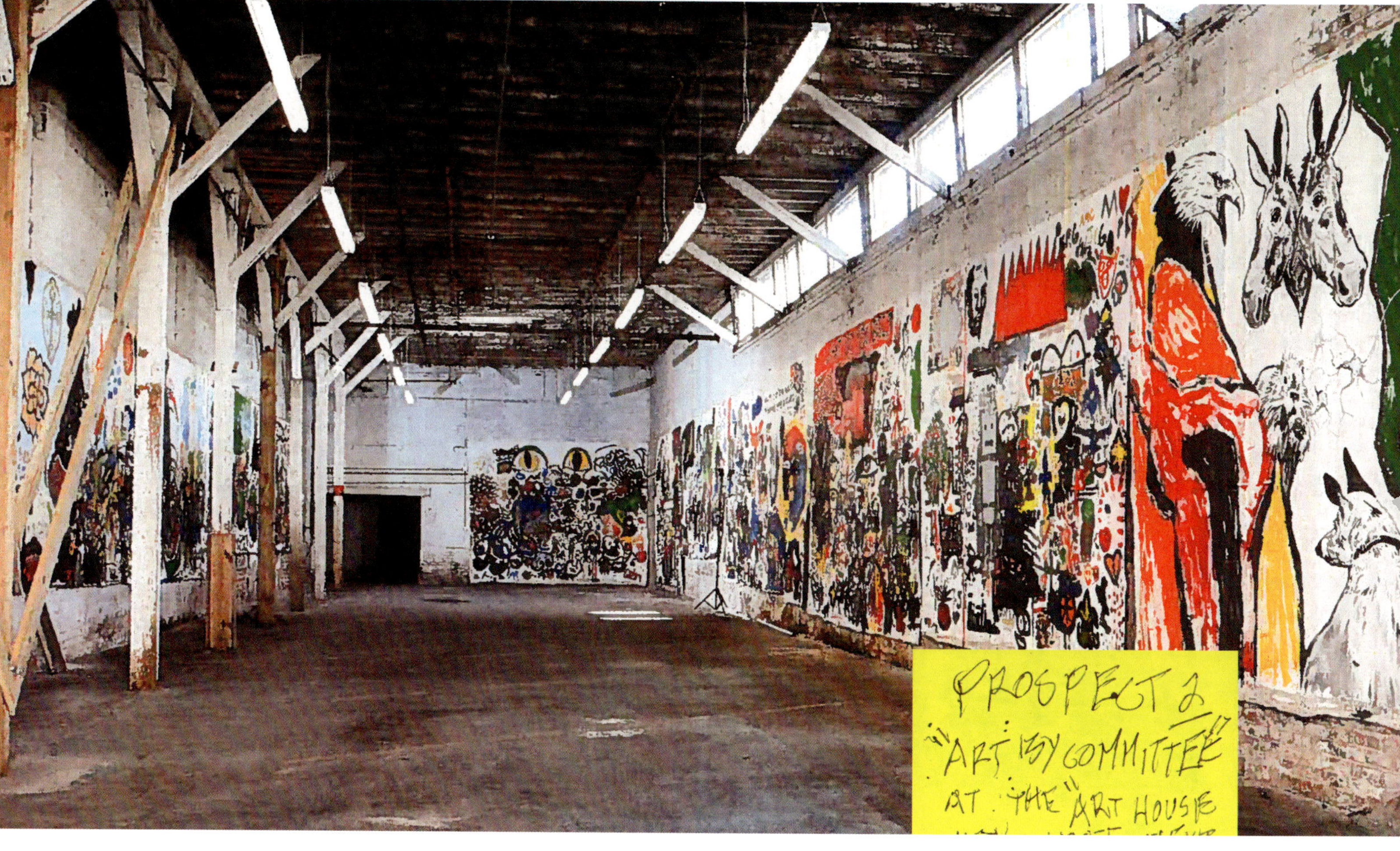

THE TIMES-PICAYUNE | DECEMBER 3, 2015 | TEXT BY SUSAN LANGEN HENNIG

The Artist's Folly: Robert Tannen and Jeanne Nathan turn a double shotgun into a creative hub

"Tannen provided the paint and stood back. He offered guidance, if asked, but no rules. Graffiti artists worked alongside folks with art school educations and kids using finger paints. One woman brought her infant daughter, dipped the child's feet in the colors and painted with them..."

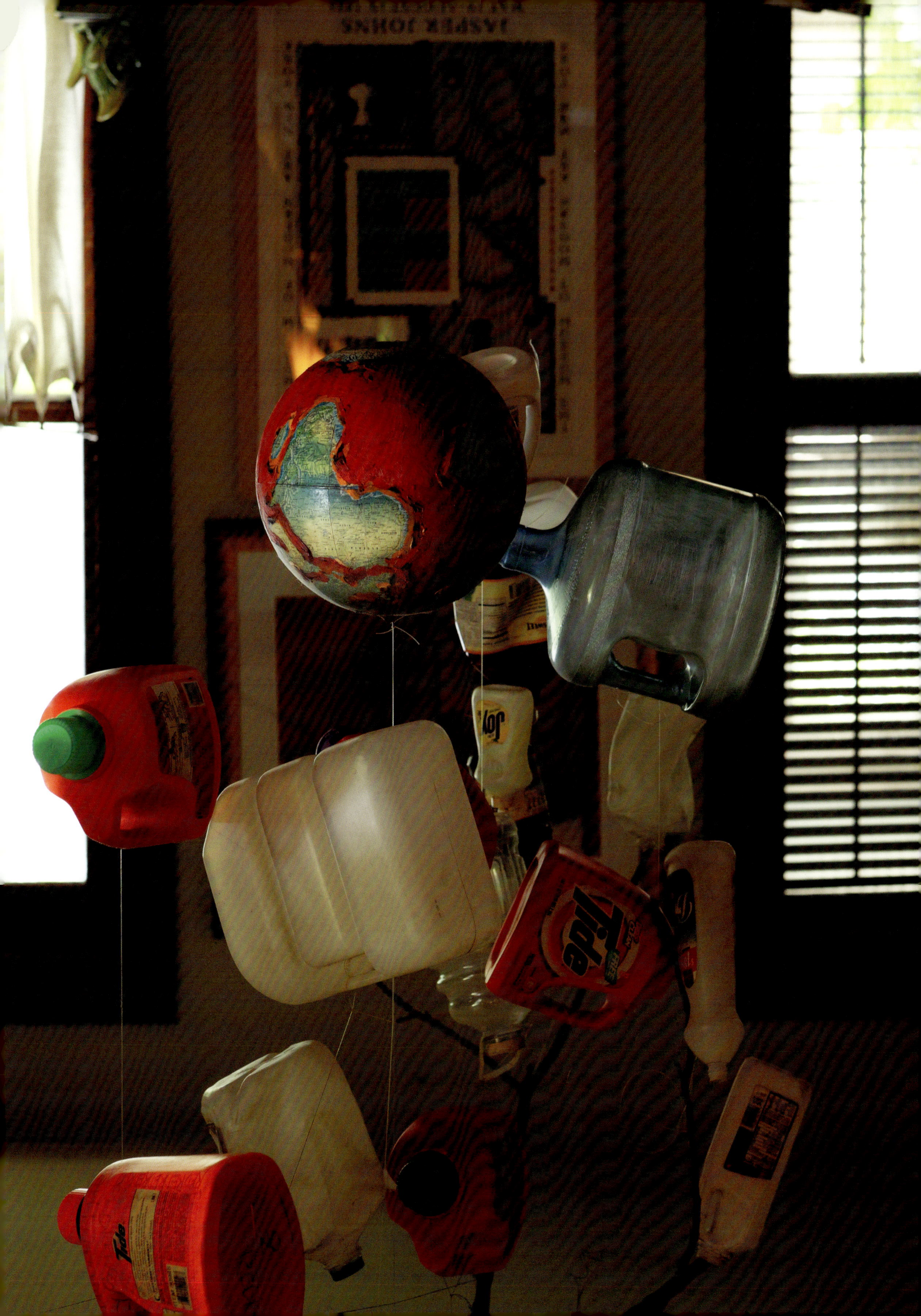
JASPER JOHNS
Tide
Joy
Tide

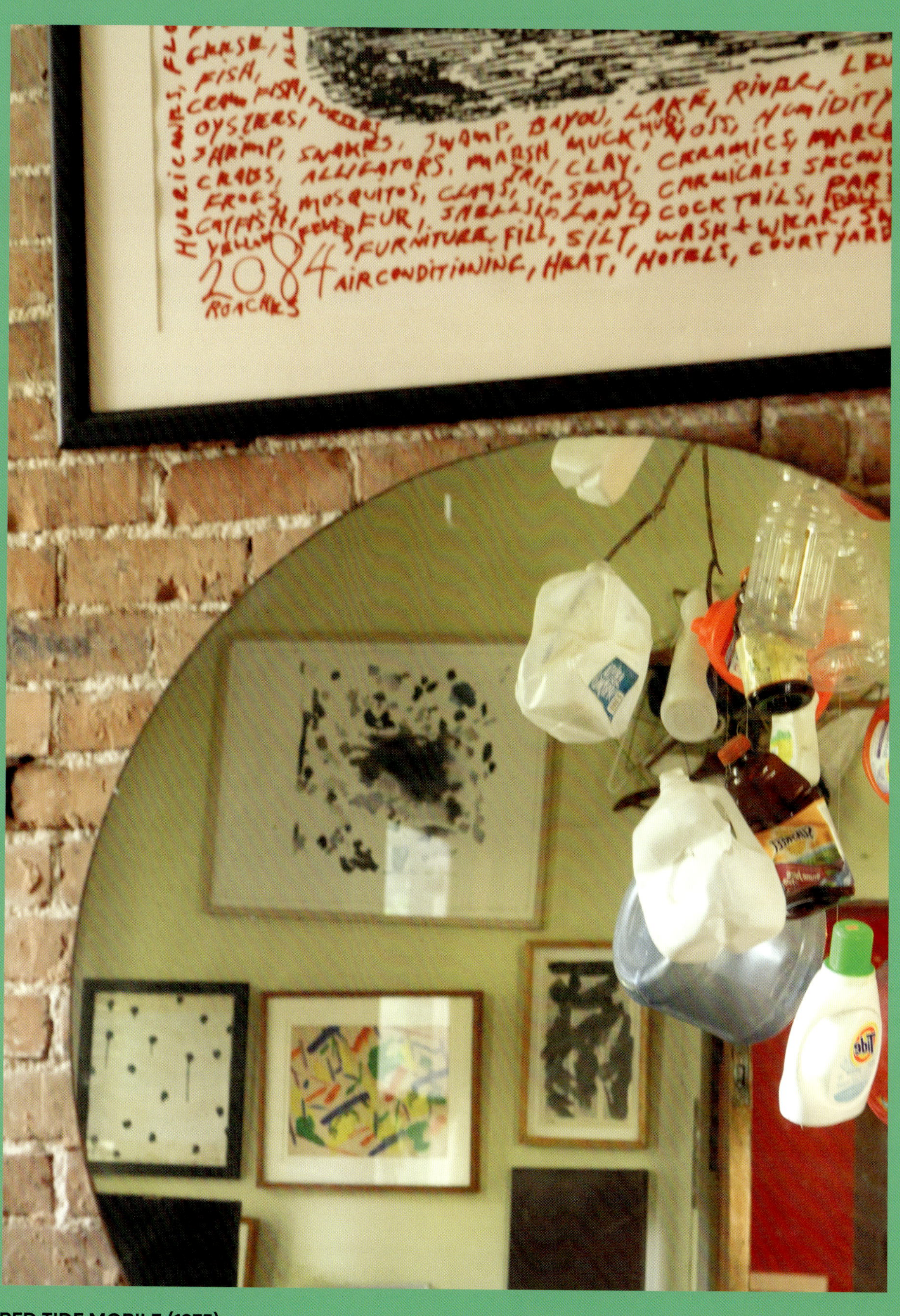

RED TIDE MOBILE (1975)
DISCARDED PLASTIC CONTAINERS SUSPENDED FROM A TREE BRANCH

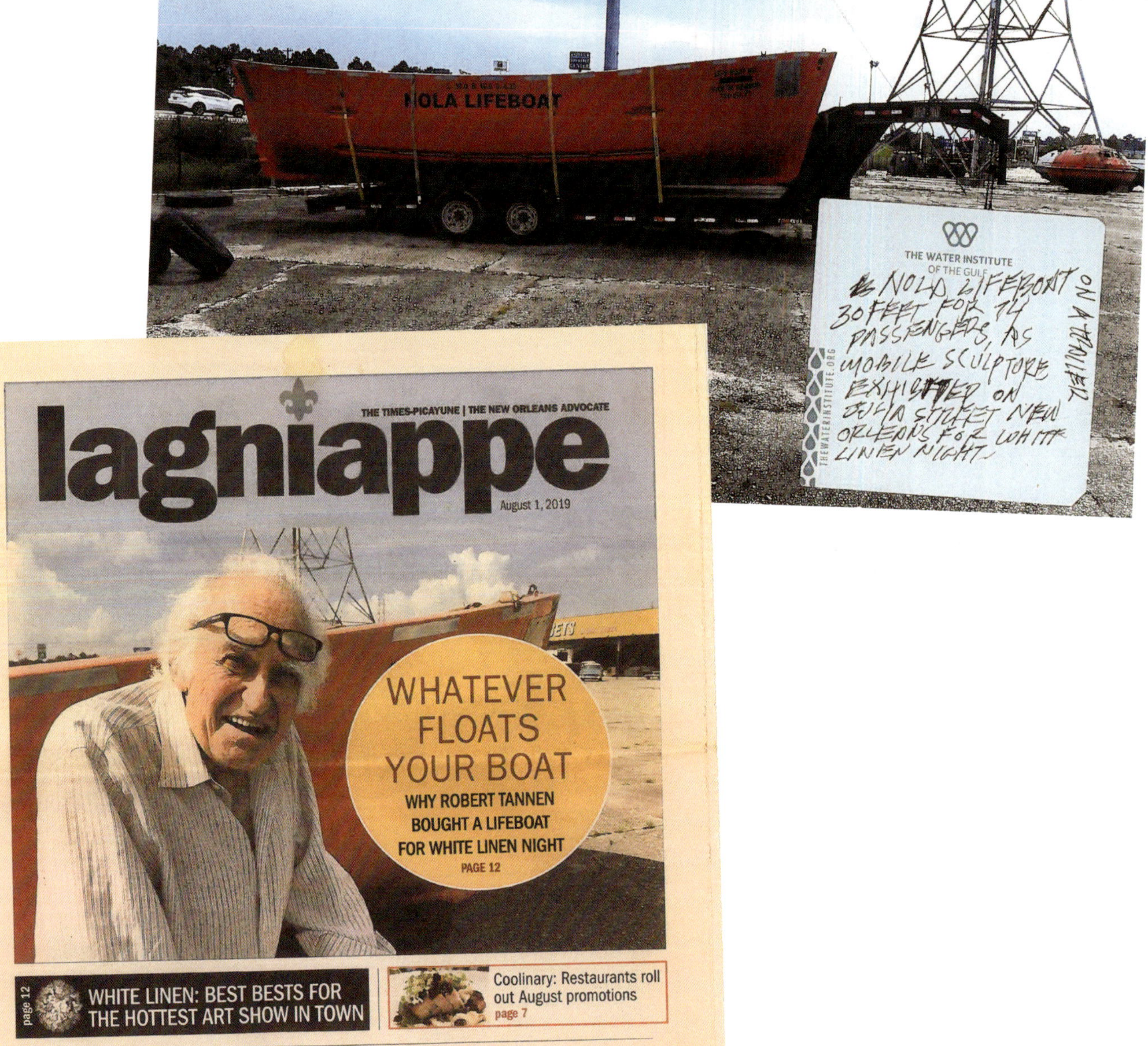

NOLA Life Boat (2019)

Robert Tannen

In June of 2019, Tannen spent $6,000 to purchase a retired thirty foot lifeboat from a movie industry prop shop in Slidell. The boat, rather than serving as an emergency vessel intended to hold seventy-four people, now symbolized crisis. The bright orange vessel was intended to remind the city of New Orleans that they were facing imminent sea encroachment and shore loss. By extension, it served as a symbol of the crisis faced by the large percentage of the world's population that lives precariously close to coastlines, and as a symbol of a limited ability to survive. In conjunction with New Orleans' White Linen Night, Tannen set up the boat on Julia Street, which is in Gallery Row, the city's arts district. Here, dressed in a life-guard's outfit, the artist and lifeguard Valery Besthoff used the boat as an artistic sculpture and a platform to discuss the threat of water, weather, and hurricanes.

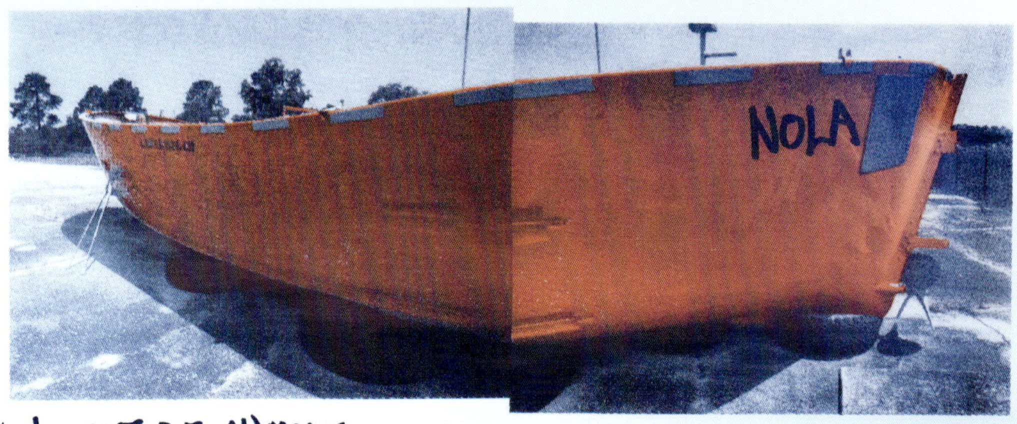

IN THE BEGINNING OF HURRICANE SEASON, THIS YEAR 2019, IN JUNE, I BOUGHT A LIFEBOAT, 30 FEET LONG WITH CAPACITY FOR 74 PEOPLE. I AM THE LIFEGUARD ON DUTY, ON JULIA STREET, IN THE NOLA ARTS DISTRICT, FOR WHITE LINEN NIGHT, AUGUST 3/19 I AM HERE TO DISCUSS THE GREAT RISKS WE ARE FACING IN THIS REGION AND OTHER REGIONS. WE ARE EXPERIENCING MORE FREQUENT RAINS, FLOODS, STORMS, SWOLLEN RIVERS, RISING TEMPERATURES AND RISING SEAS. WHAT SHOULD THESE EXPERIENCES INDICATE TO US?. AND, WHY DO WE NOT TRUST SCIENCE IN THESE MATTERS?. AND, WHY PUT A LIFEBOAT ON JULIA STREET, FOR WHITE LINEN NIGHT, AND NOT IN A ART GALLERY NOR SCULPTURE GARDEN. THIS LIFEBOAT AND SCULPTURE IS NAMED NOLA. DO YOU BELIEVE THIS LIFEBOAT IS ART?

ROBERT C. TANNEN, A-RT, AUGUST 2019.

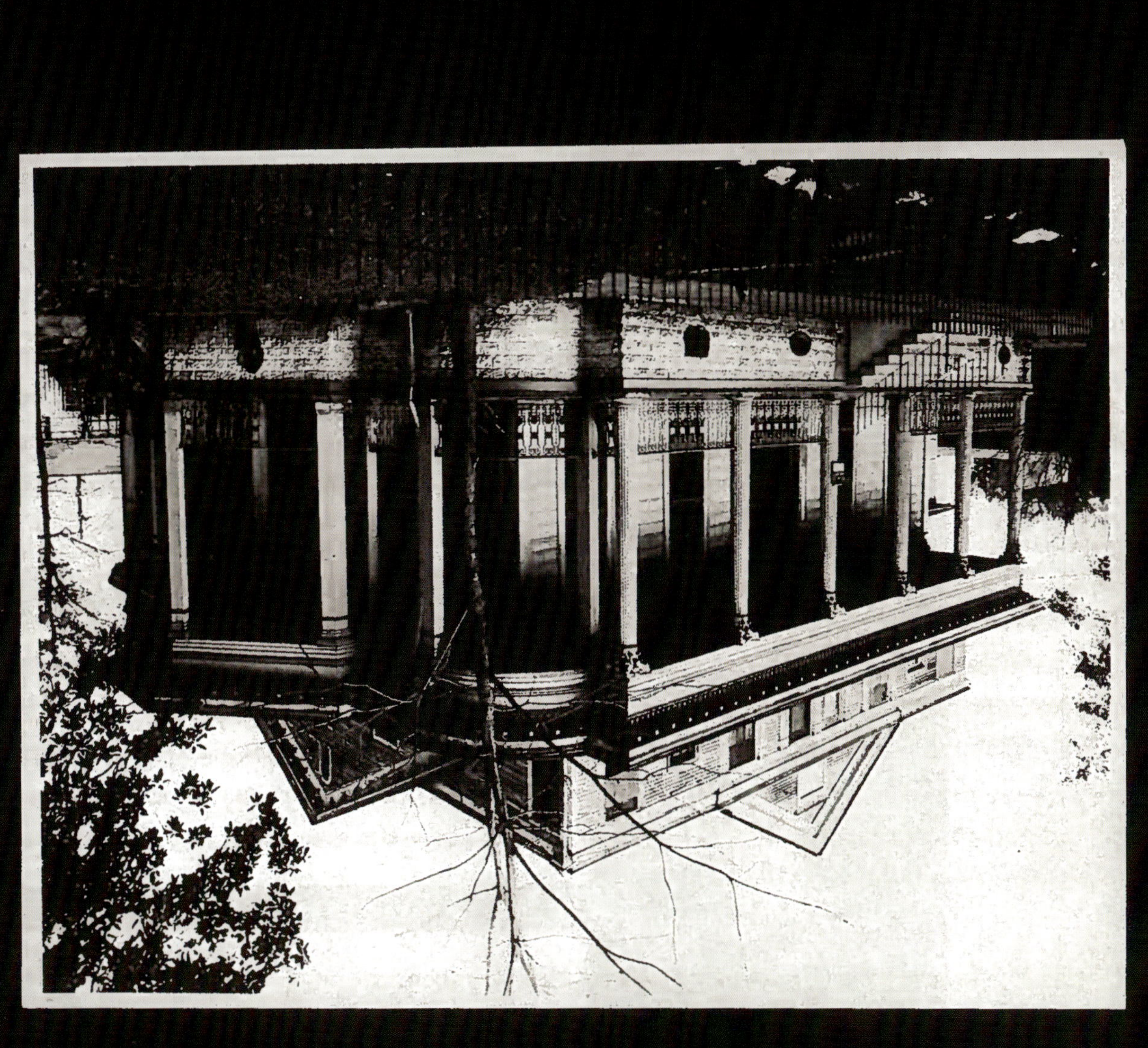

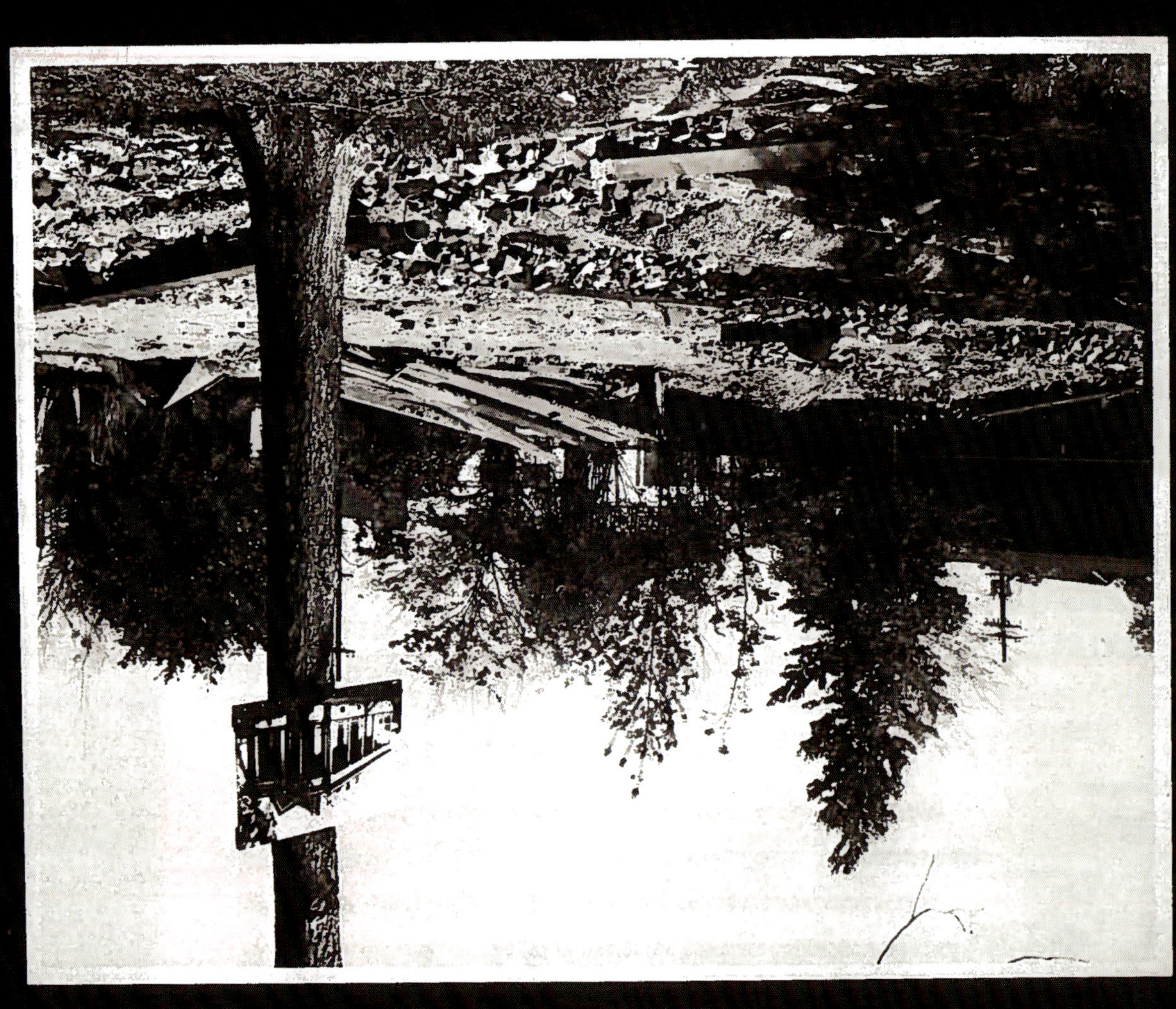

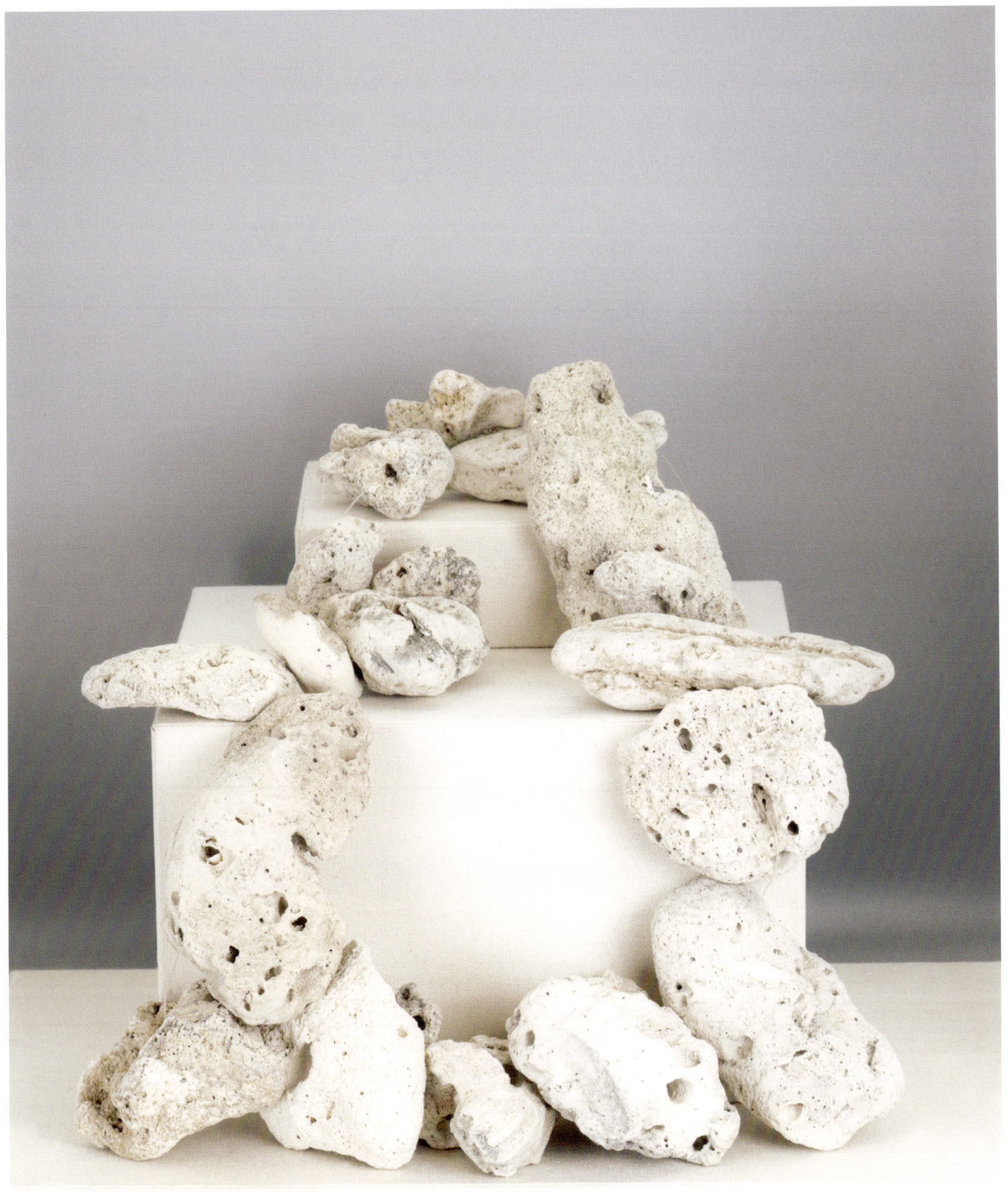

CORAL NECKLACE
FROM MIAMI BEACH COLLECTING
ROBERT TANNEN

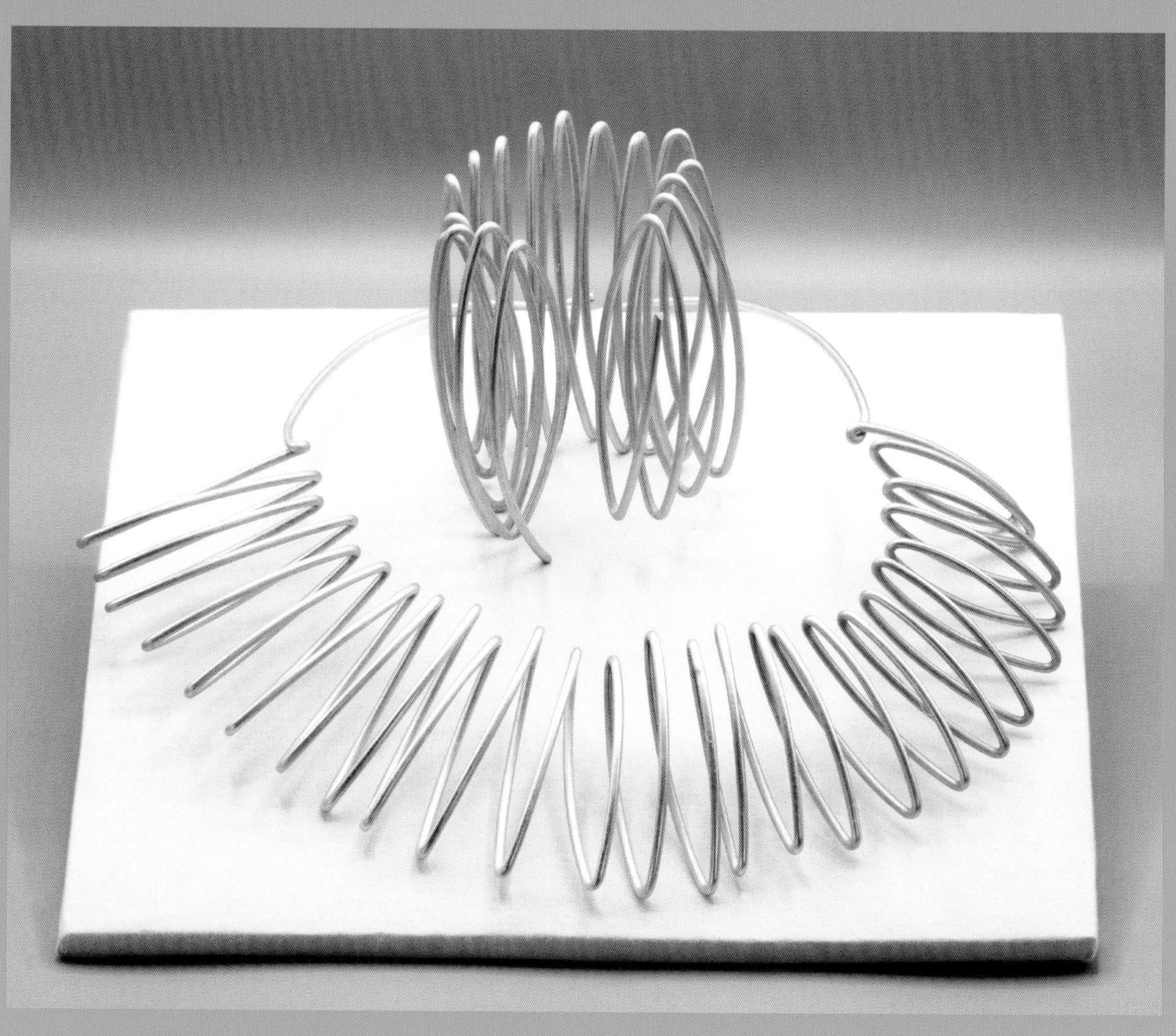

ALUMINUM WIRE NECKLACE AND BRACELET
ROBERT TANNEN

OYSTER SHELL AND SILVER WIRE TIARA
ROBERT TANNEN

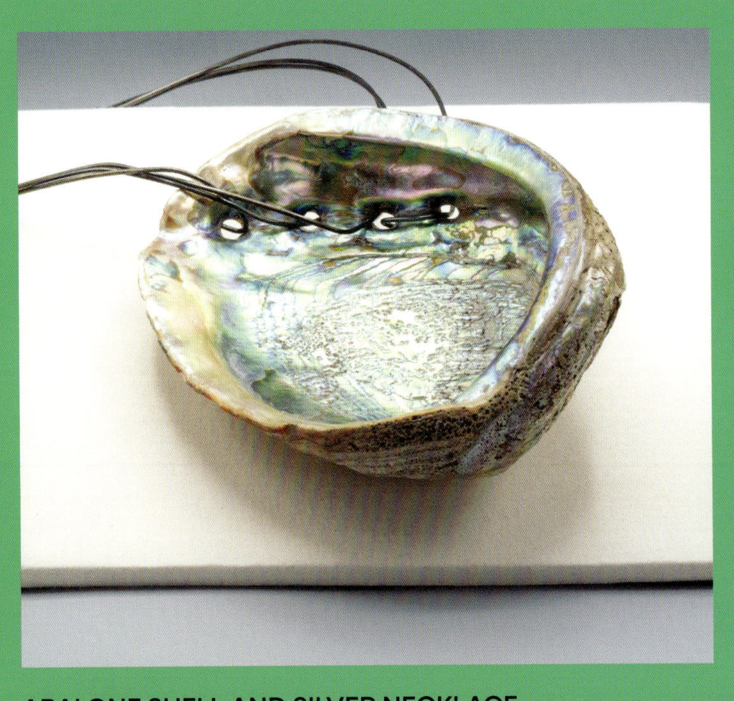

ABALONE SHELL AND SILVER NECKLACE
ROBERT TANNEN

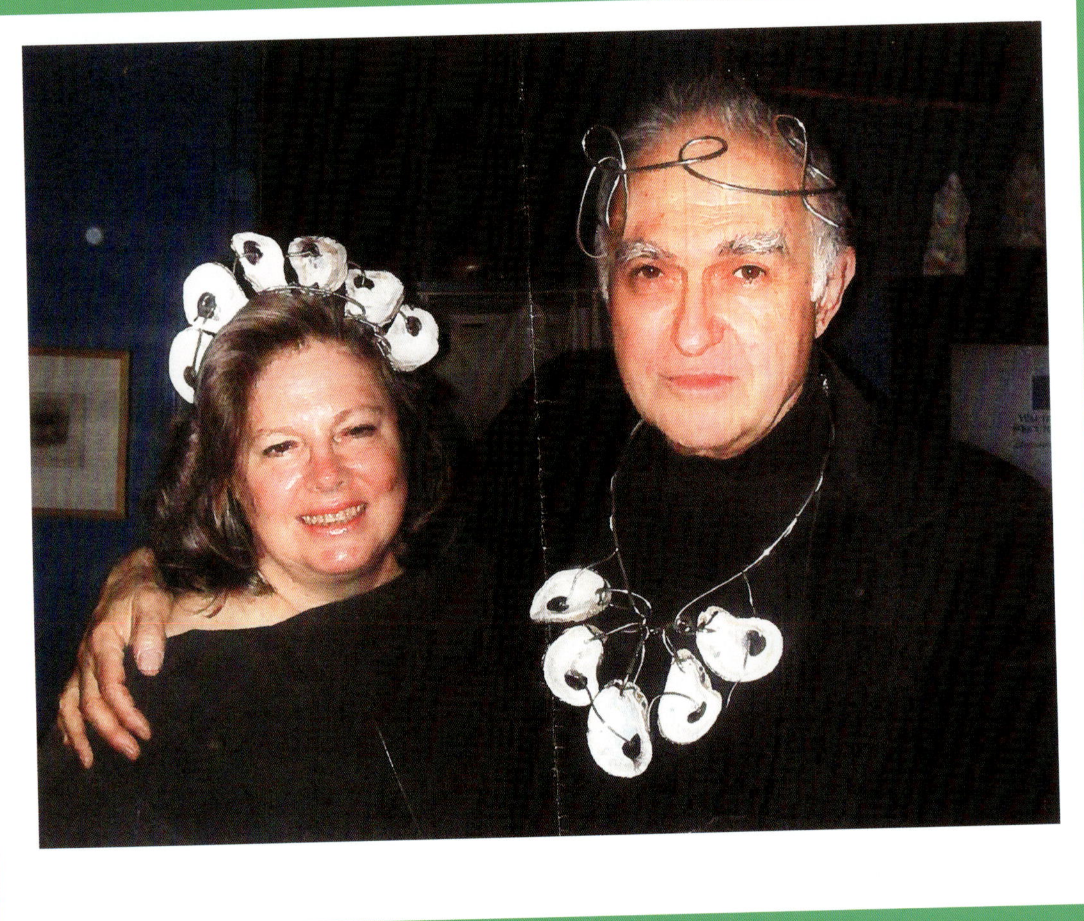

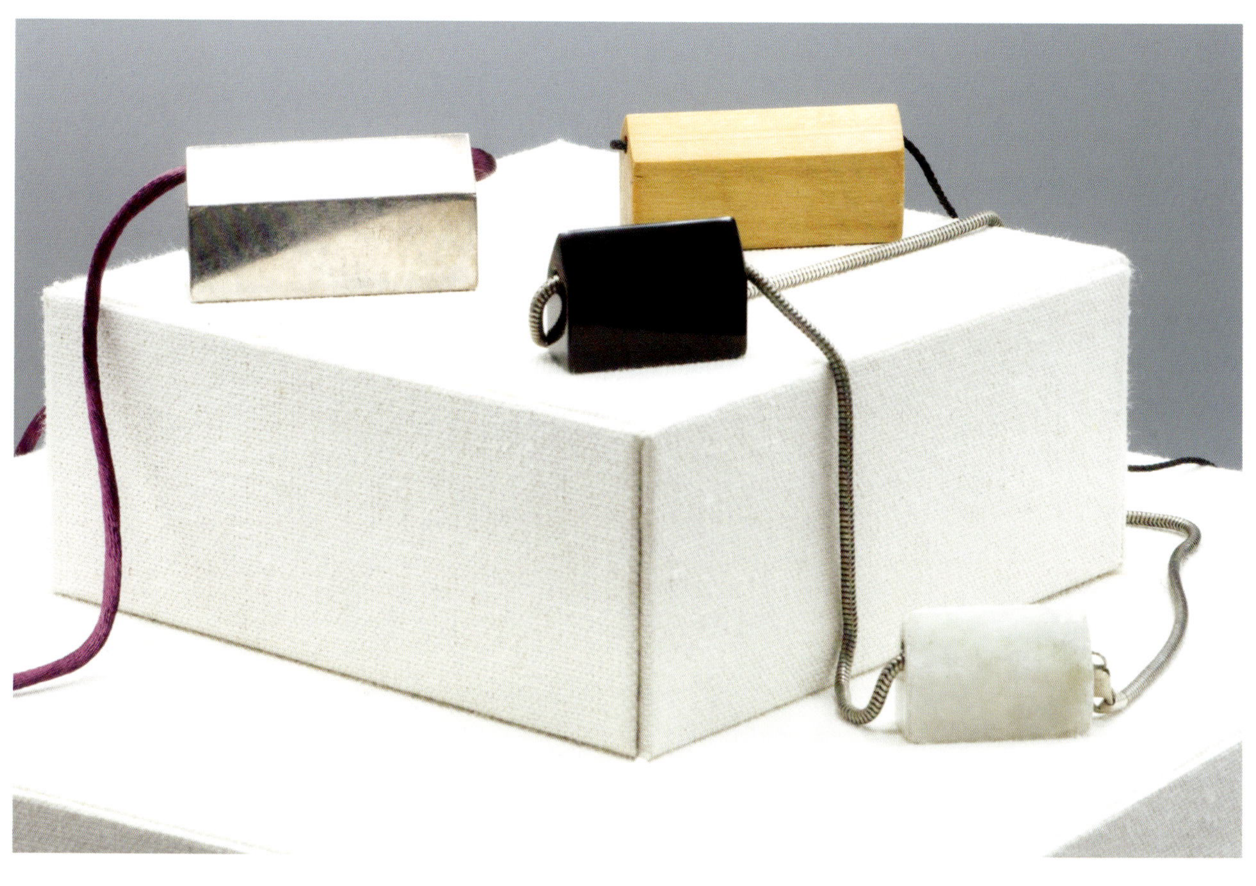

ROBERT TANNEN'S SHOTGUN HOUSE JEWELRY DESIGNED IN STONE, SILVER, AND GOLD MANUFACTURED BY MIGNON FAGET

LEFT: ROBERT TANNEN AND PARTNER JEANNE NATHAN WEARING TANNEN'S JEWELRY

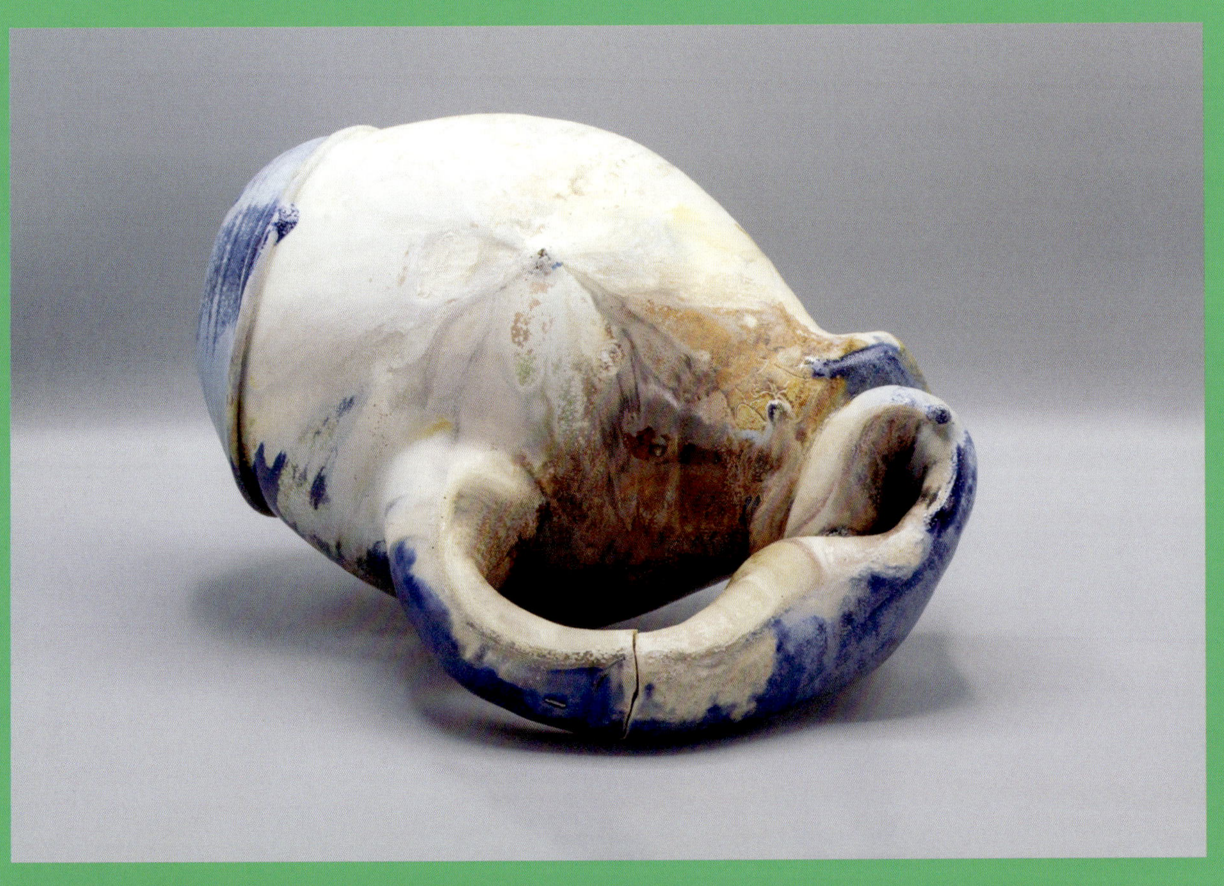

TANNEN COMMISSIONED MISSISSIPPI ARTIST KEVIN O'KEEFE TO CREATE A CERAMIC KLEIN BOTTLE (AN OBJECT WITH NO INDEPENDENT EXTERIOR OR INTERIOR, BUT ONE CONTINOUS SURFACE) (2019)

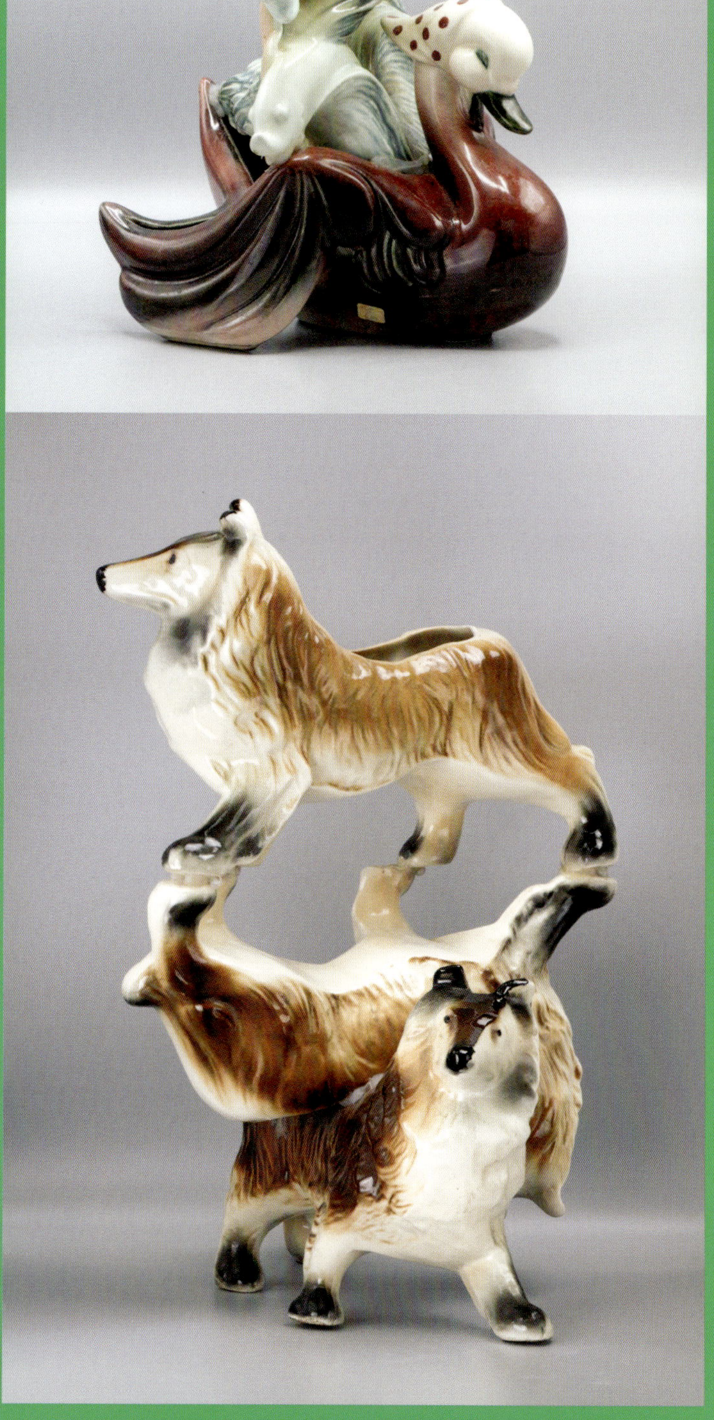

ASSEMBLAGE,
FOUND CERAMIC OBJECTS
ROBERT TANNEN

HERE LASSIE, LASSIE, LASSIE
FORMER CERAMIC DOGS
ROBERT TANNEN

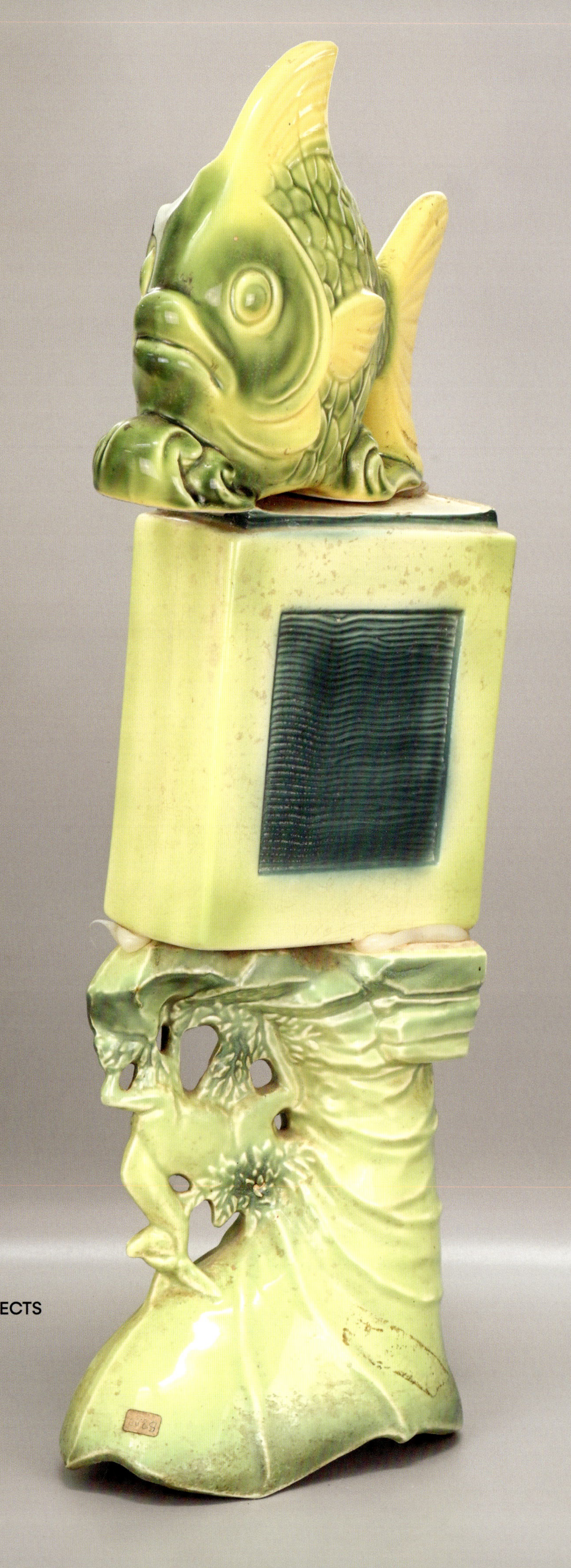

ASSEMBLAGE,
FOUND CERAMIC OBJECTS
ROBERT TANNEN

"I can't imagine Tannen ever making anything intended to be seen on a pedestal—his work is emotional, accessible, and meant to be used," says architect Frank O. Gehry, who is also a Tannen friend.

TEXT BY KRISTINE MCKENNA | LOS ANGELES TIMES | FEBRUARY 21, 1993

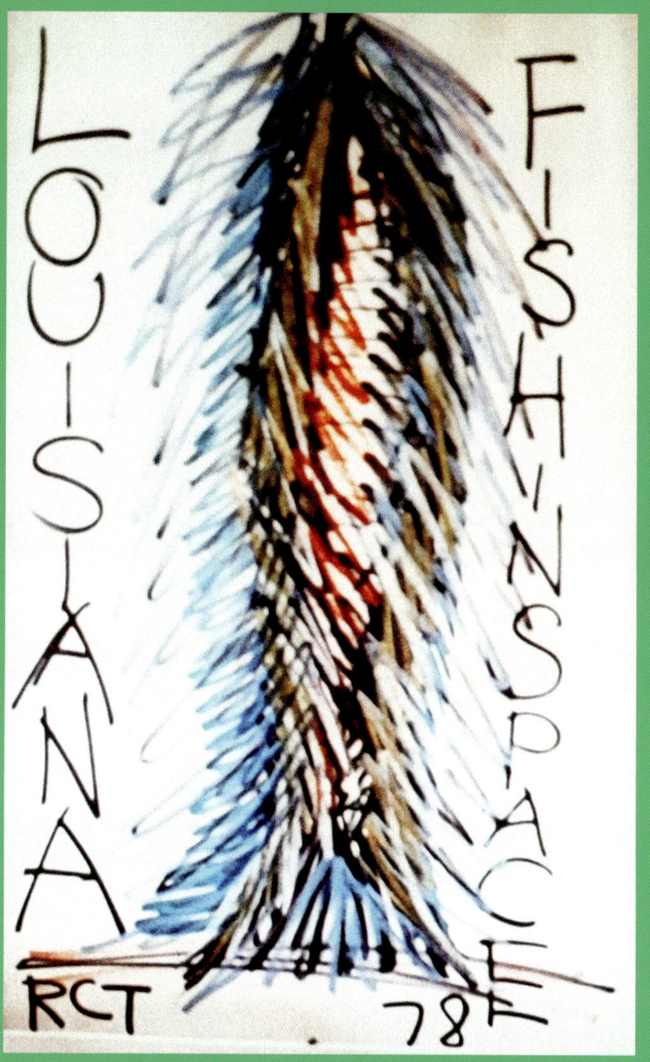

FISH IN SPACE (1978) ROBERT TANNEN

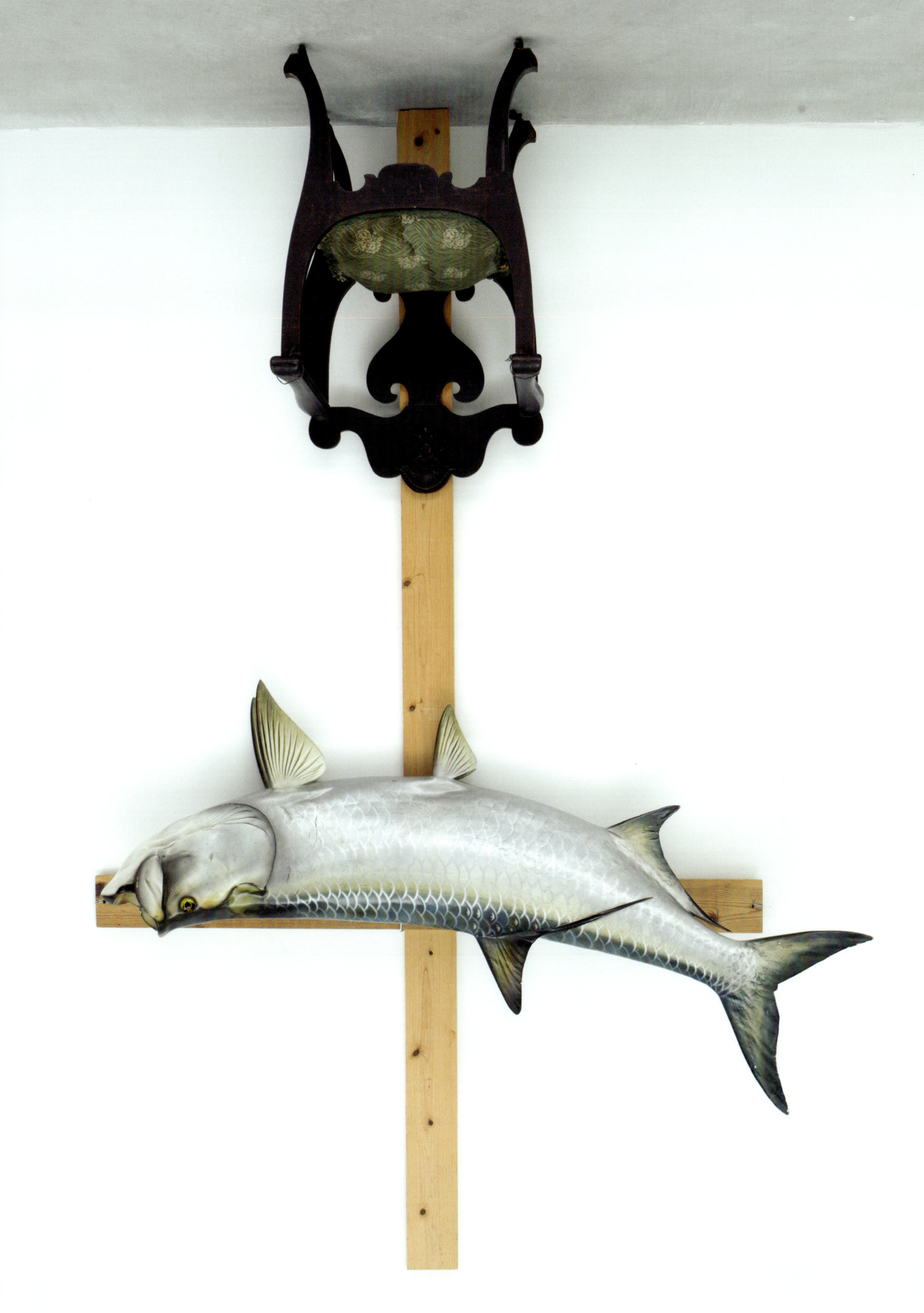

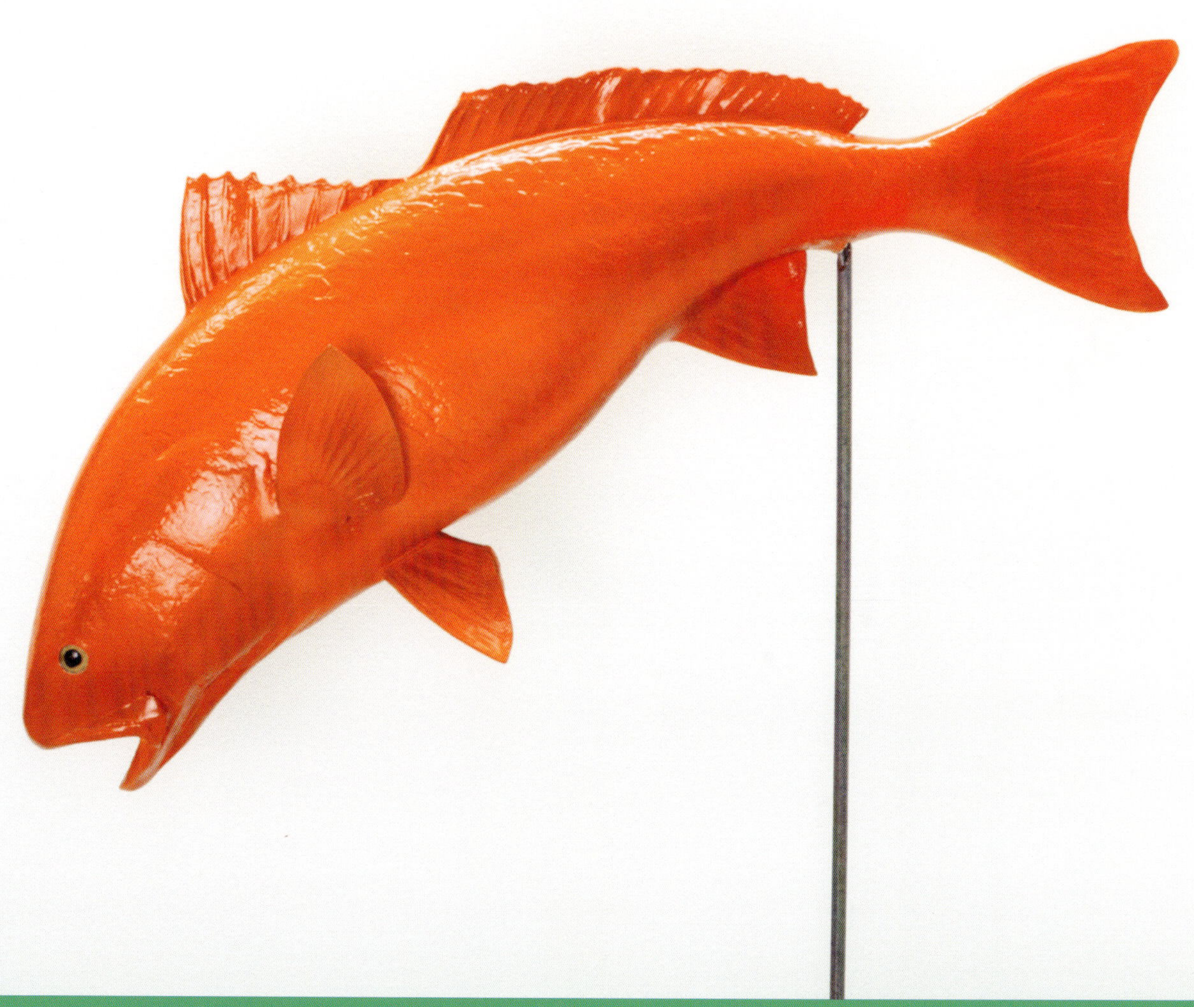

Crucifish (1975)
Robert Tannen

Tarpon is a fish desirable to sports fishermen and women. Here it is nailed to a cross evoking awareness of the importance of saving all life, not just human. Tannen claims that if we only save human life, the planet will die. The wooden cross is attached to a chair designed by a friar, Girolamo Savonarola, who was legendary for his commitment to revive the Christian principles at the heart of Christianity.

Red Fish on a Stick (1976)
Robert Tannen

Red Fish on a Stick and the two accompanying drawings were part of Tannen's 1976 exhibition in the French Quarter titled *Sportsman's Paradise*, consisting of drawings and sculptures primarily of the red fish, which is an iconic symbol of the Louisiana South. Here, he takes these by-products of a regional pastime and pride and recontextualizes them as sculptures and art.

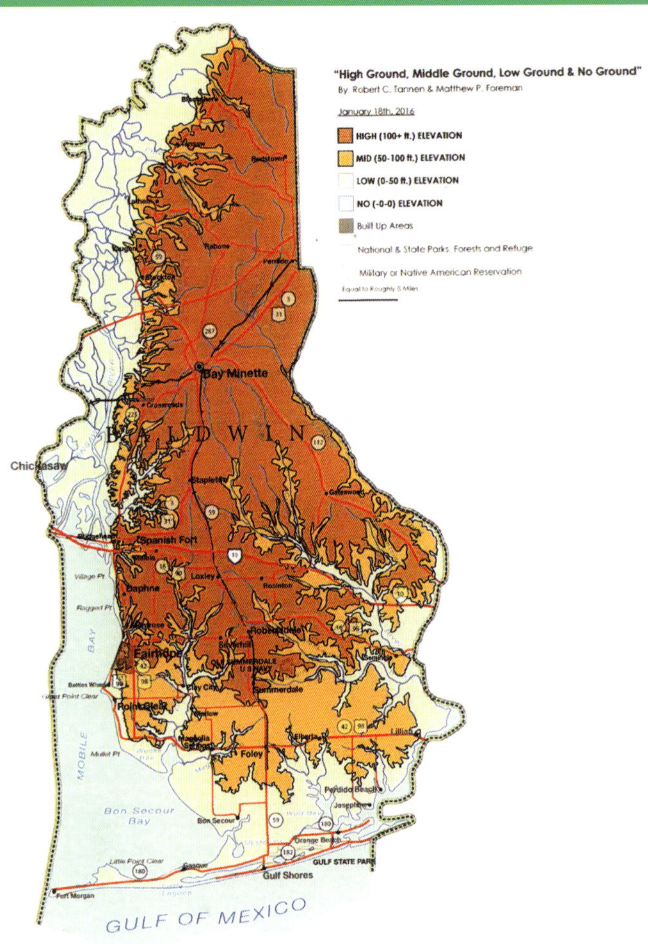

GOM

THE IDEA FOR THIS PROJECT BEGAN IN 1969 FOLLOWING HURRICANE CAMILLE, A CATEGORY #5 STORM WHICH DEVASTATED 3 MISSISSIPPI COASTAL COUNTIES, PLUS THE SECOND TIER OF COUNTIES AND SOME LOW LYING AREAS OF SOUTHEAST LOUISIANA. I WAS THEN A MEMBER OF METASYSTEMS INC. A WATER RESOURCES ANALYSIS AND PLANNING FIRM SELECTED BY THE STATE OF MISSISSIPPI TO STUDY AND PLAN THE RECOVERY AND REDEVELOPMENT OPTIONS FOR THE FUTURE OF COASTAL MISSISSIPPI. A MAJOR RECOMMENDATION OF THAT WORK WAS TO ENCOURAGE MIGRATION NORTH OF THE STORM SURGE AREA ALONG INTERSTATE HIGHWAY #10 THEN UNDER CONSTRUCTION, IN 1969 THERE WAS LITTLE PUBLIC CONSIDERATION, THOUGH, ORGANIC MIGRATION OCCURS. (1)

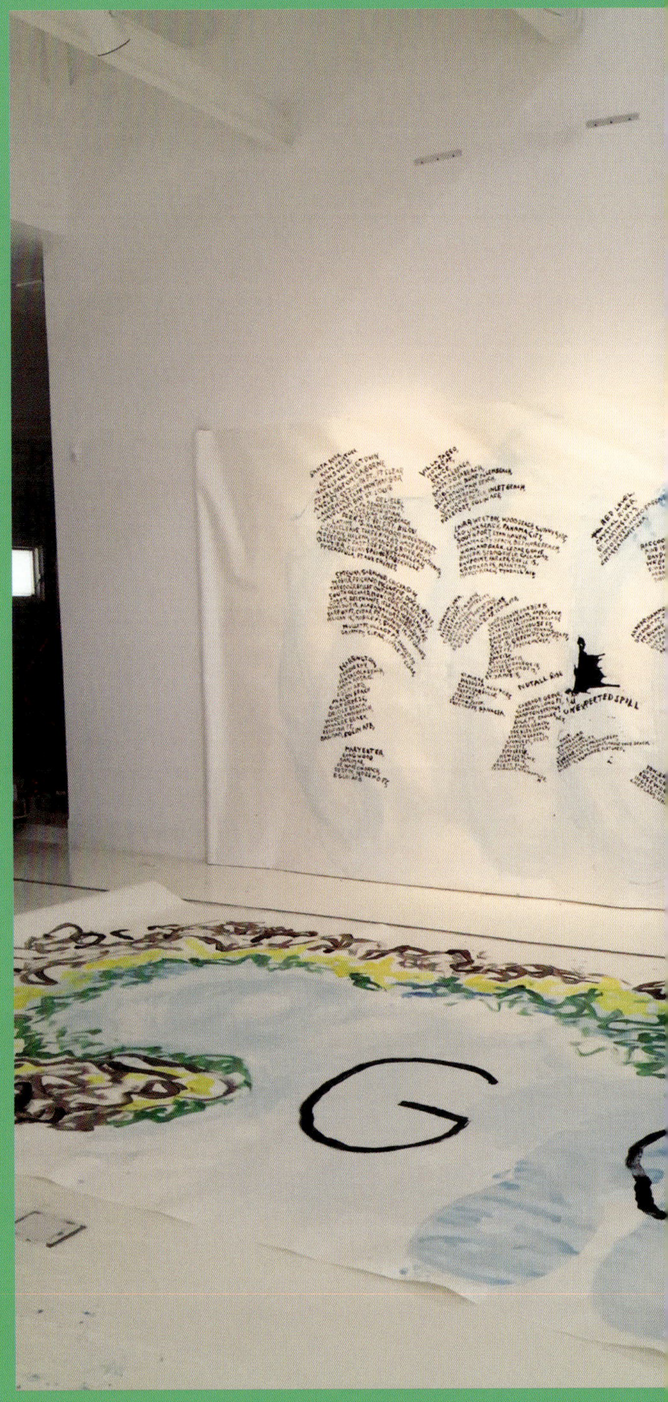

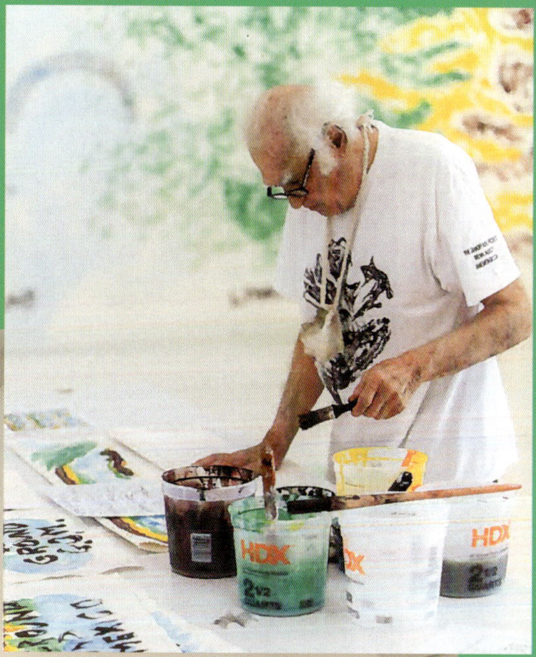

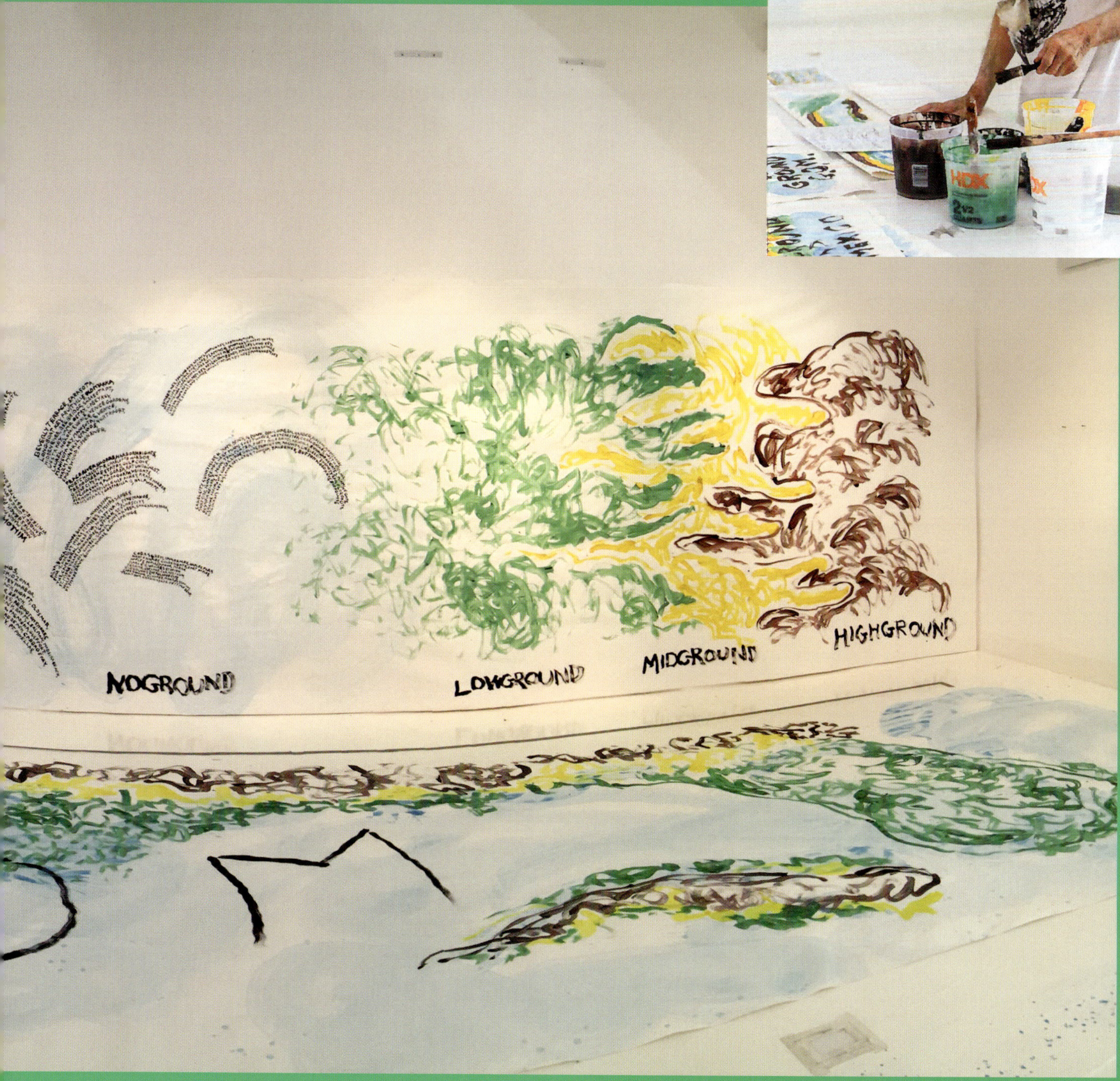

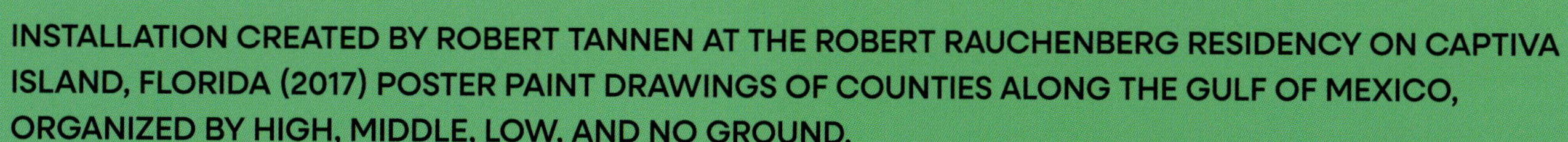

INSTALLATION CREATED BY ROBERT TANNEN AT THE ROBERT RAUCHENBERG RESIDENCY ON CAPTIVA ISLAND, FLORIDA (2017) POSTER PAINT DRAWINGS OF COUNTIES ALONG THE GULF OF MEXICO, ORGANIZED BY HIGH, MIDDLE, LOW, AND NO GROUND.

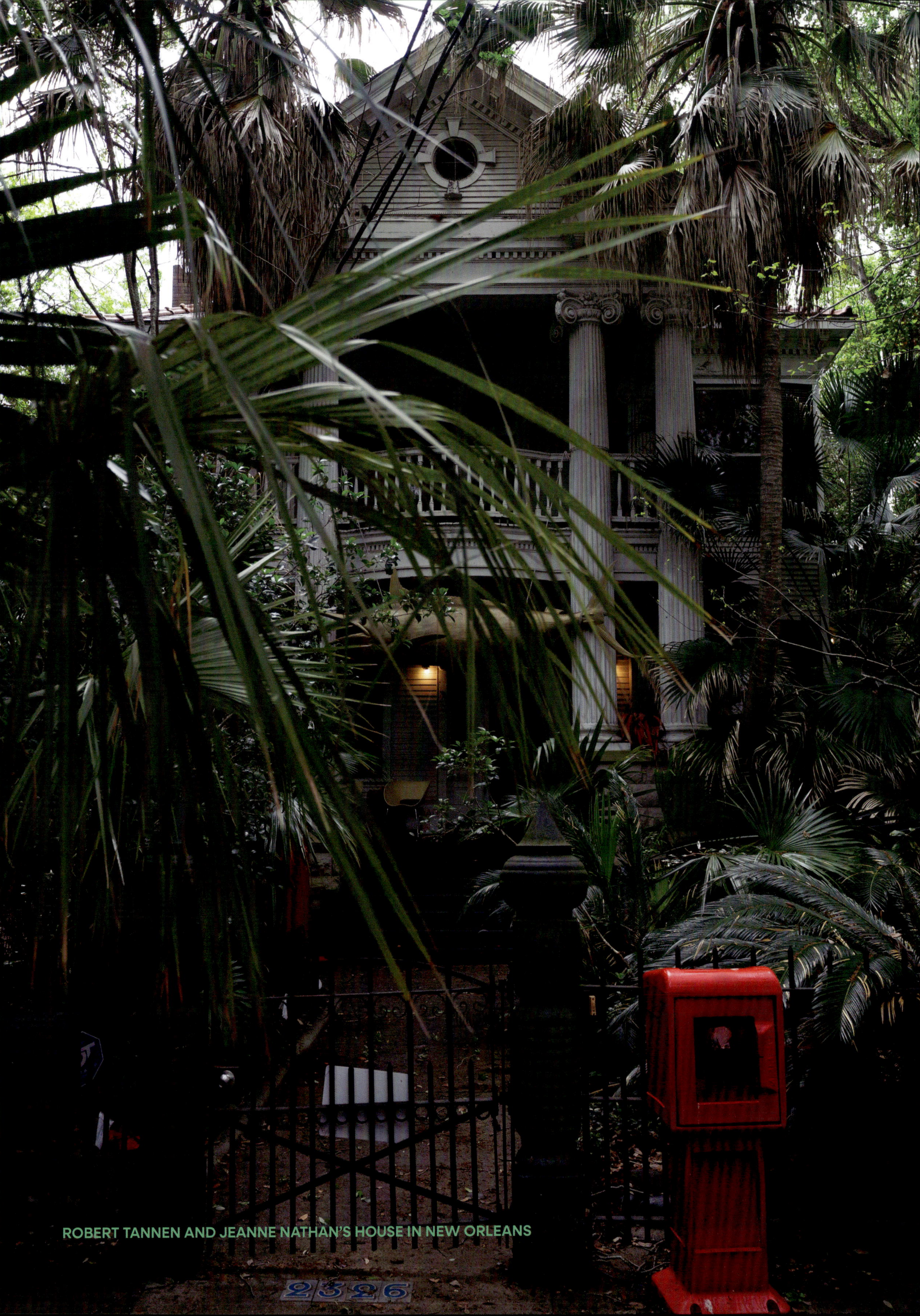

ROBERT TANNEN AND JEANNE NATHAN'S HOUSE IN NEW ORLEANS

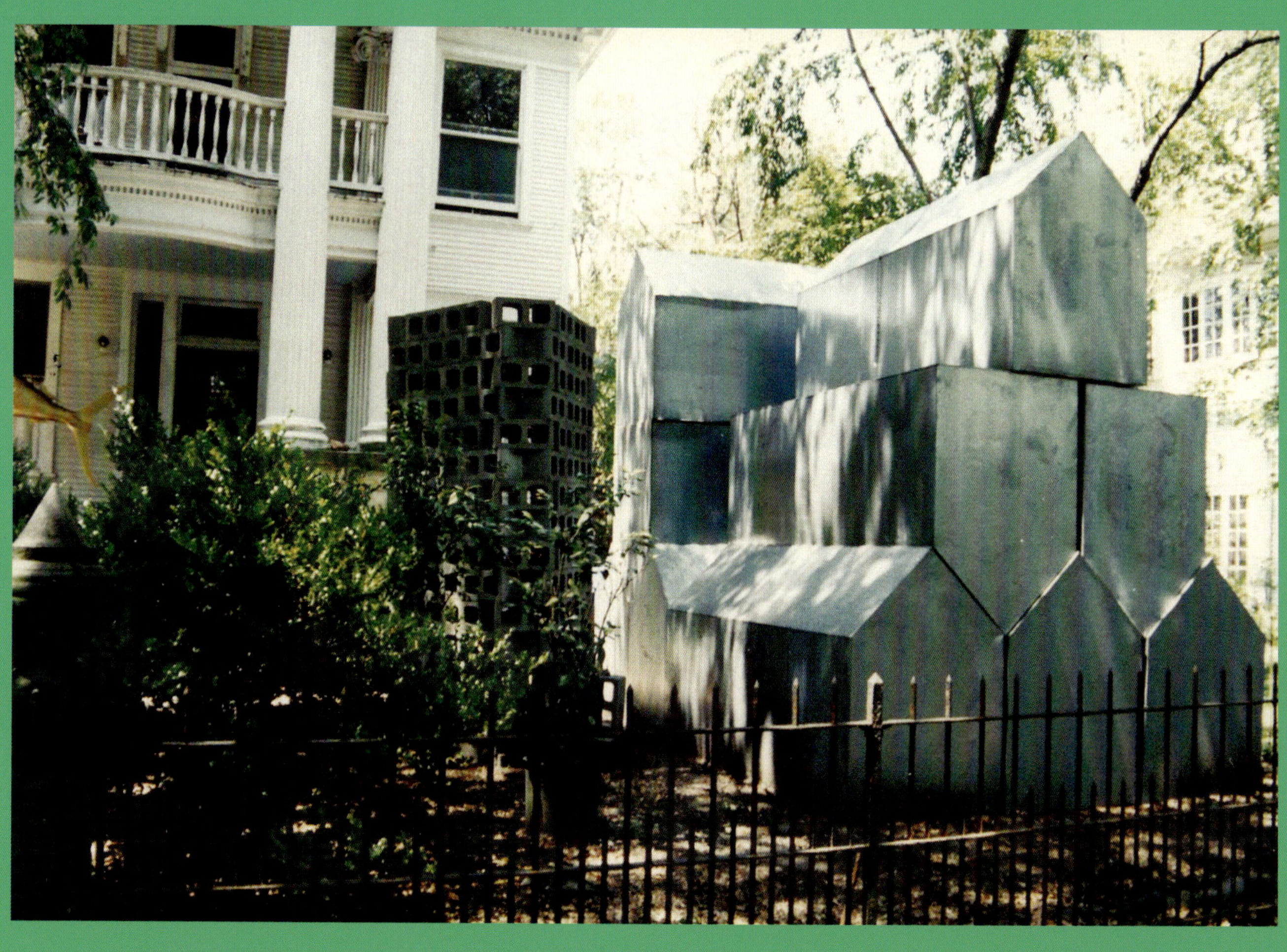

"People are often looking over their shoulders worried about their place in the pecking order, but Tannen doesn't do that," Gehry says. "Approval doesn't seem to be important to him."

TEXT BY KRISTINE MCKENNA | LOS ANGELES TIMES | FEBRUARY 21 , 1993

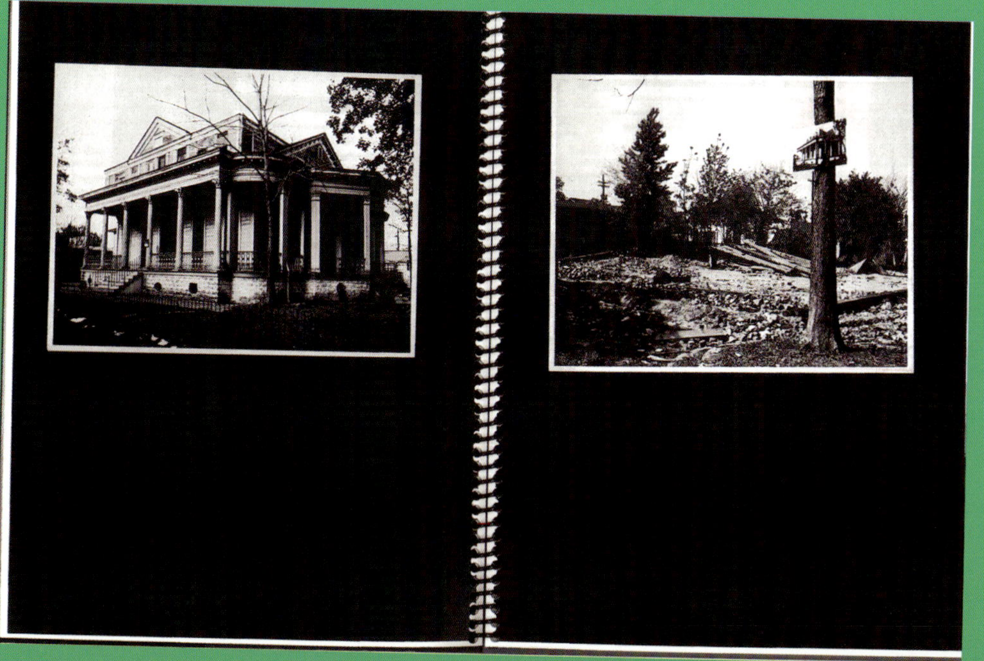

FRANK GEHRY & ROBERT TANNEN

Text by Robert Ivy

TOGETHER

Like an unexpected flash of summer sheet lightning, Jeanne Nathan and Robert Tannen telephoned at *Architectural Record* in Manhattan, and I invited them for a chat at my brownstone on Hicks Street in Brooklyn Heights. Interesting people whom I had not seen in years, always bubbling with ideas, they had a notion to float. After trundling up to the third floor and sharing the requisite Brooklyn and New Orleans stories, they broached the topic: Biloxi, Mississippi was going to build a museum for George Ohr, the consummate American potter, and wouldn't Frank Gehry be the perfect choice as architect?

He would be perfect. Yet Gehry's star had risen, in part thanks to the Guggenheim Museum in Bilbao, Spain. The digitally fueled, gritty yet sculptural project changed the course of three-dimensional design and launched new museums as pilgrimage sites. In fact, Gehry kept a small, crumpled tissue-like vase by Ohr near his desk in Santa Monica, an impossibly fragile object among his hundreds of cardboard, paper, and metal models, nearby. A physical link from the hands of the potter to another like-minded spirit in Louisiana, Robert Tannen.

The small object memorialized a friendship. According to Gehry, the two had met in the late 1970s in New Orleans, when Gehry had been approached to reenvision Lafayette Square, a downtown urban park near the upcoming World's Fair site. Each saw kinship in the other and remained friends.

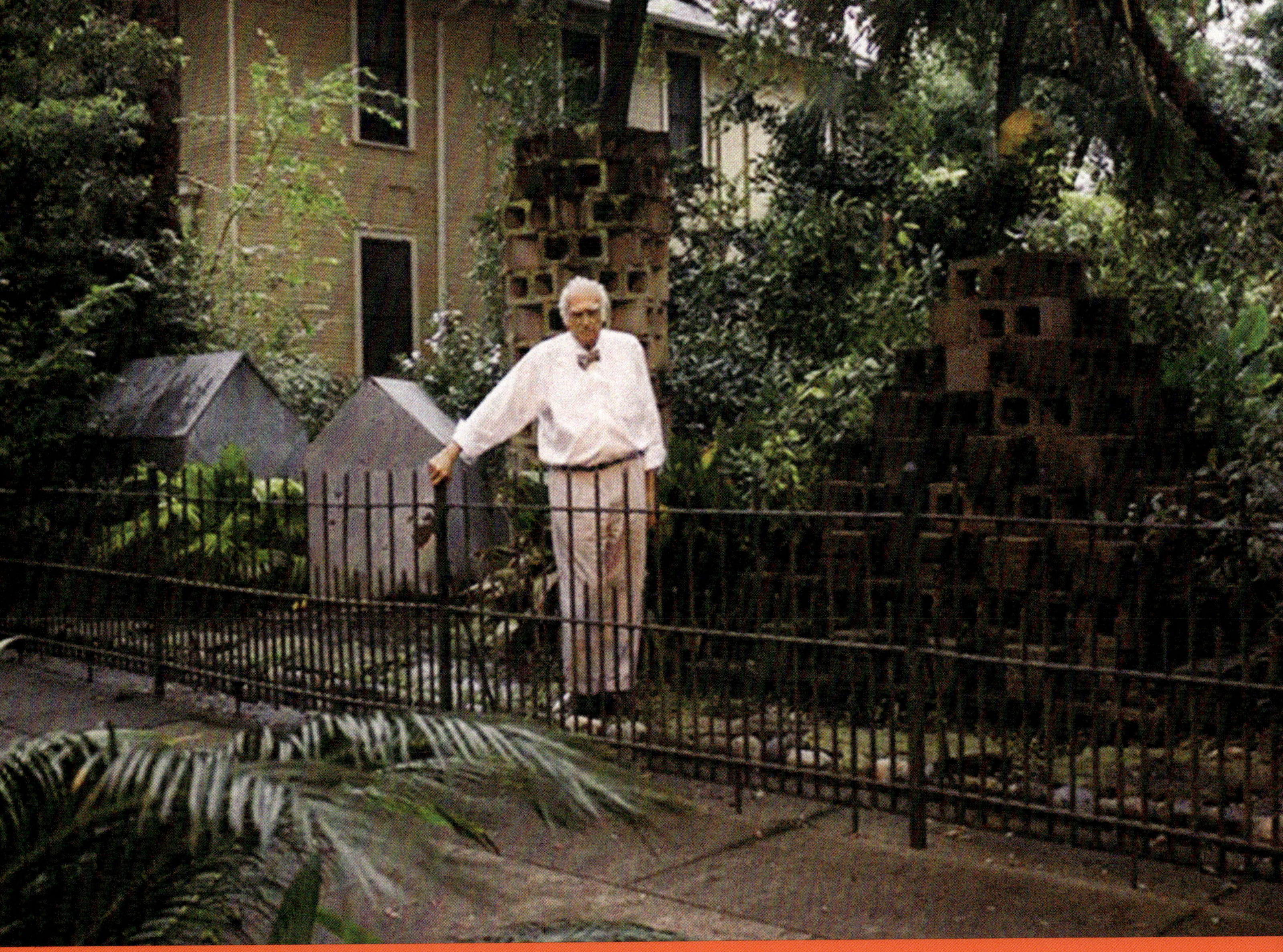

And what did they recognize? Two artists, both iconoclasts. Iconoclasts in the sense that they refused to accept institutional norms. They constantly observe the world and challenge expectations of artists in the translation of their ideas into material objects that represent larger truths as they understand them. One, an architect, ultimately creating sculptural forms that cradle experience; the other, an artist and urban planner, creating cities that enhance experience.

The tactile arts continually serve as repositories of their thinking and dreaming. Each has been drawn to what others might consider the ordinary, reinterpreted. Tannen has taken telephones, wrapped them in their own cords and painted them red. Who would expect that? Both Gehry and Tannen have reinterpreted fish. Tannen's modus operandi has sometimes been to literally upend the familiar, such as his sculpture of shotgun houses, stacked on his lawn on Esplanade Avenue. No one can foresee their next acts.

(LEFT) ROBERT TANNEN IN HIS SCULPTURE GARDEN BEFORE HURRICANE KATRINA (2005)

(BOTTOM) FRANK GEHRY AT THE OPENING OF THE OHR-O'KEEFE MUSEUM OF ART

Their hungry minds and their interests wander from the maquette to the drone's-eye view. Both are scale-shifters, from the immediacy of the sculptural to entire cities. Gehry devised a plan for Los Angeles, and Tannen has counseled cities from the neighborhoods and movement systems of his chosen New Orleans home to international urban centers. Together, they worked on a reinterpretation of a familiar house type, the New Orleans shotgun, as a potential replicable housing solution after Hurricane Katrina.

Gehry ultimately accepted the commission for what became the Ohr-O'Keefe Museum, a brilliant choice for the Mad Potter of Biloxi. Despite having been destroyed in Hurricane Katrina by an errant casino barge that crashed into the initial buildings in 2005, today the individual pavilions representing Gehry's homage to Ohr's genius dot the parkland housing the museum. Tannen and Gehry's ongoing dialogue floats around the site, wondering what's next.

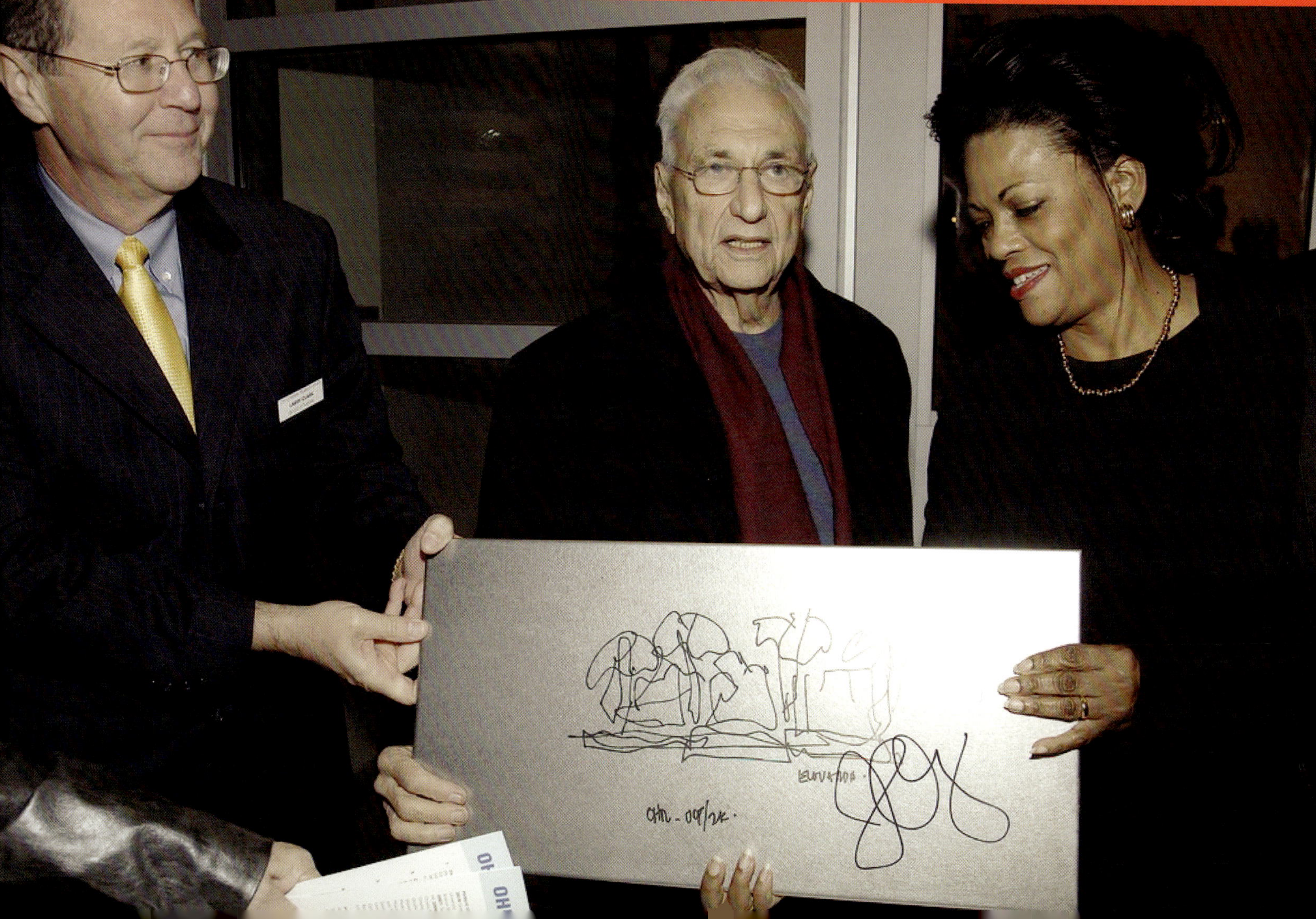

ARCHITECTURAL RECORD | JULY 15, 2009 | TEXT BY SHAWN KENNEDY

It appears that Frank Gehry, FAIA, is finding fertile ground in New Orleans

In addition to designing a duplex for Brad Pitt's "Make It Right" project, Gehry has teamed with urban planner and artist, Robert Tannen, to create a modular shotgun house that they say will be affordable, sustainable, and compatible with the city's historic housing types.

The duo's concept, dubbed Mod Gun, is an expansion of a one-room, emergency-housing prototype that Tannen designed in 2006 as an alternative to the typical FEMA trailer. (The structure was displayed at the Ogden Museum of Southern Art but it was never reproduced.)

The new one- and two-bedroom models—1,000 and 1,200 square feet, respectively—are designed to fit the long, narrow lots common throughout New Orleans. But the Mod Guns will not share the room-into-room-into-room floor plan of the shotgun house. Instead, a screened-in porch will separate the living/dining/kitchen space from the bedroom-and-bathroom suites.

Aspects of the Gehry-Tannen design are still being refined, but a signature feature is fourteen-by-fourteen-foot modular rooms that can be put together to form larger rooms. Many elements like doors, windows, and interior doorways will be consistent in size. "This is part of the economy of the house," says Tannen. "This will also offer the most flexibility for the buyer to configure rooms to suit their needs."

While the final number depends on demand, the developer, New Orleans-based Fortune Development, is expected to build between five and ten houses. The first dwellings will be infill housing on empty lots in Treme, a historic neighborhood bordering the French Quarter that was settled in the early 1800s by free people of color.

New Orleans architect Ray Manning, AIA, of Manning Architects, will be responsible for the final design services.

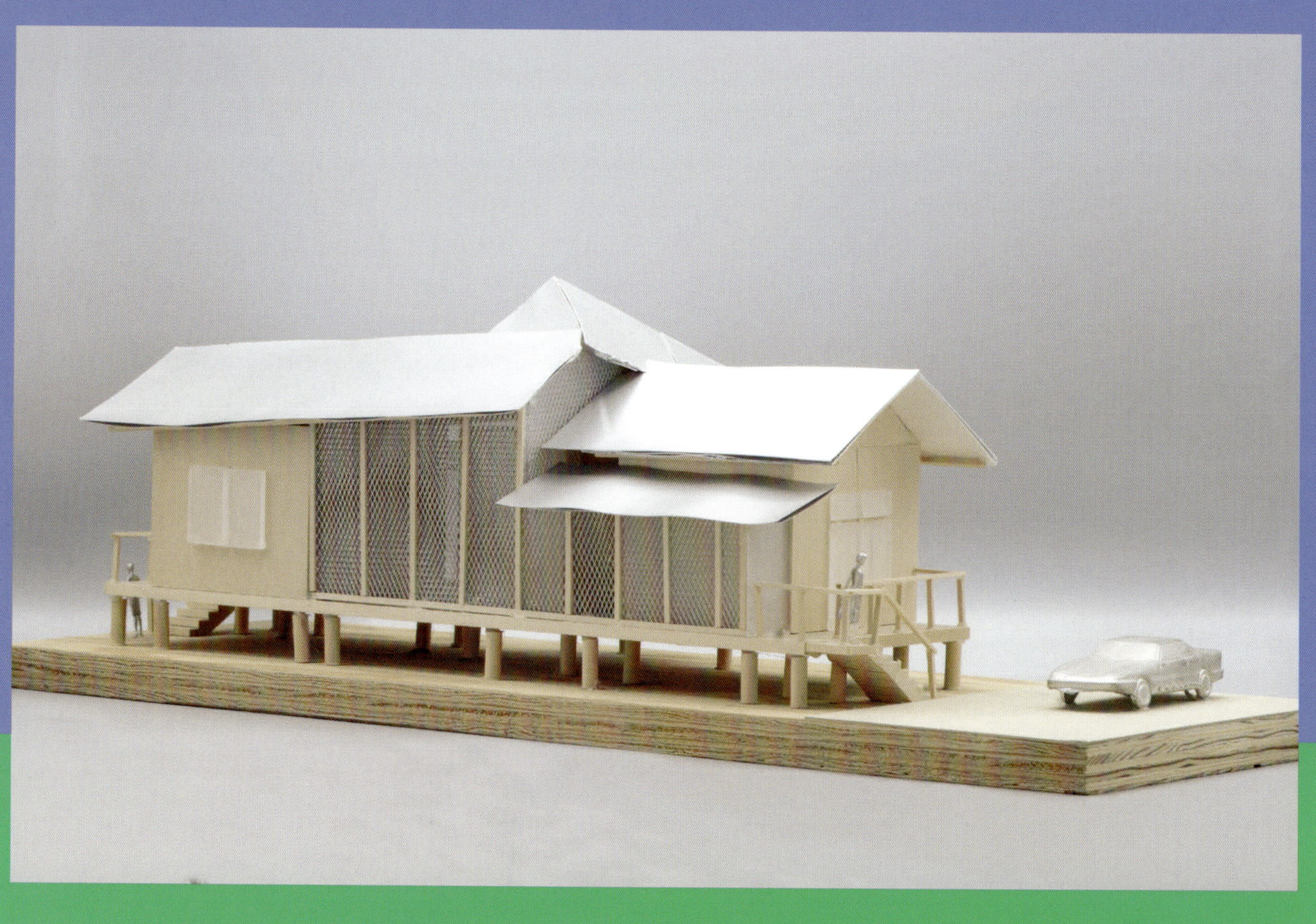

ModGun House
2023 (built)
Pass Christian, Mississippi

Robert Tannen and Frank Gehry's design for a modular shot-gun house, called "ModGun," or "Gehry Gun," was the first experiment using modular technology and the shotgun-style, common to New Orleans and the Gulf Coast. Their goal was to create a modular house that was affordable, sustainable, and compatible with the city's historic housing types. In this coastal variation, the house is separated in the center by a screened-in porch. The duo's concept is an expansion of a one-room, emergency-housing prototype that Tannen designed in 2006 as an alternative to the typical FEMA trailer.

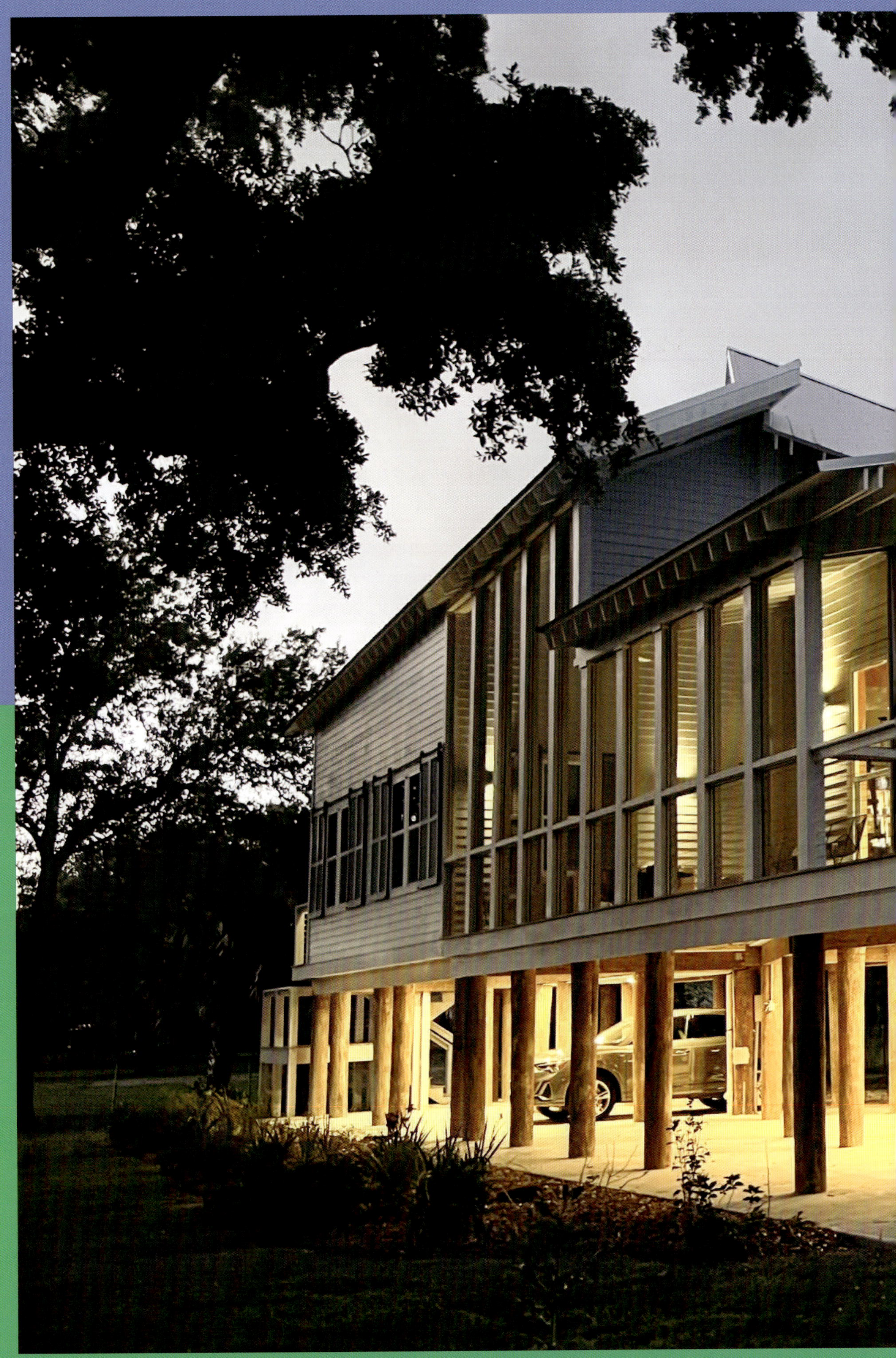

MODGUN HOUSE, 2023 (BUILT), PASS CHRISTIAN, MISSISSIPPI

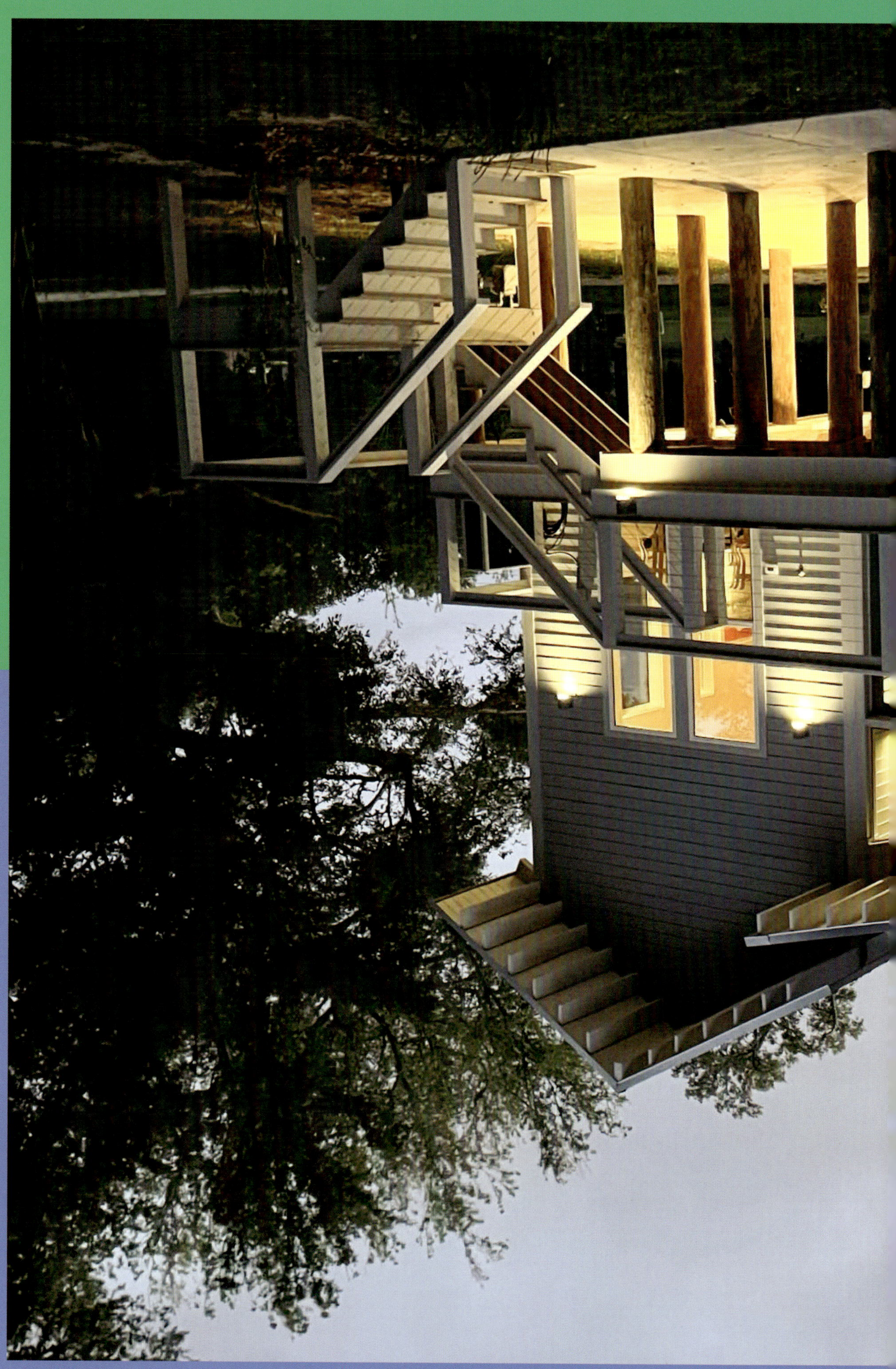

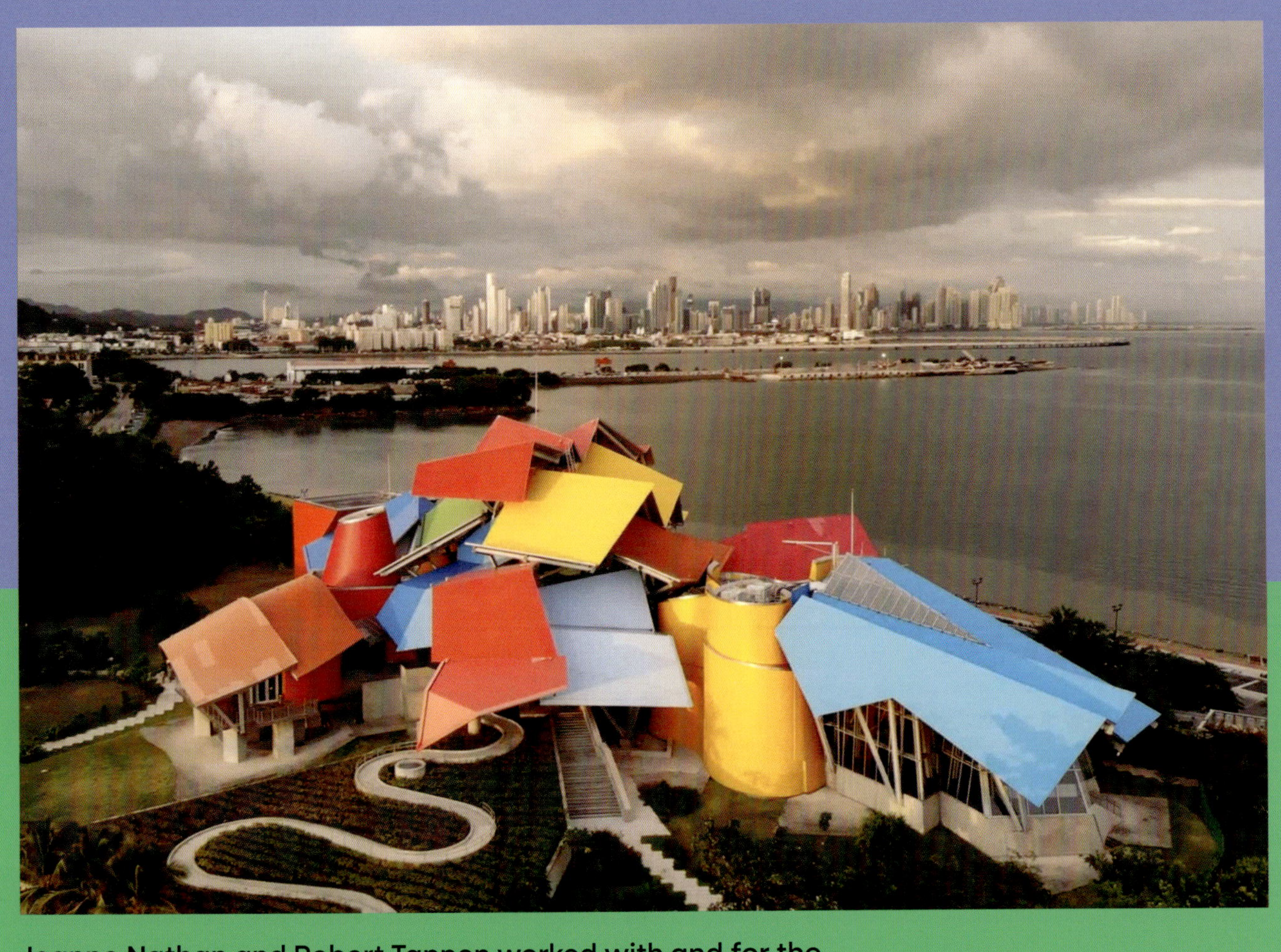

Jeanne Nathan and Robert Tannen worked with and for the Gehry organization to plan the Gehry-designed Biomuseo in Panama City, Panama.

"We're both interested in a multiplicity of ideas and moving forward as opposed to repetition."

—Robert Tannen

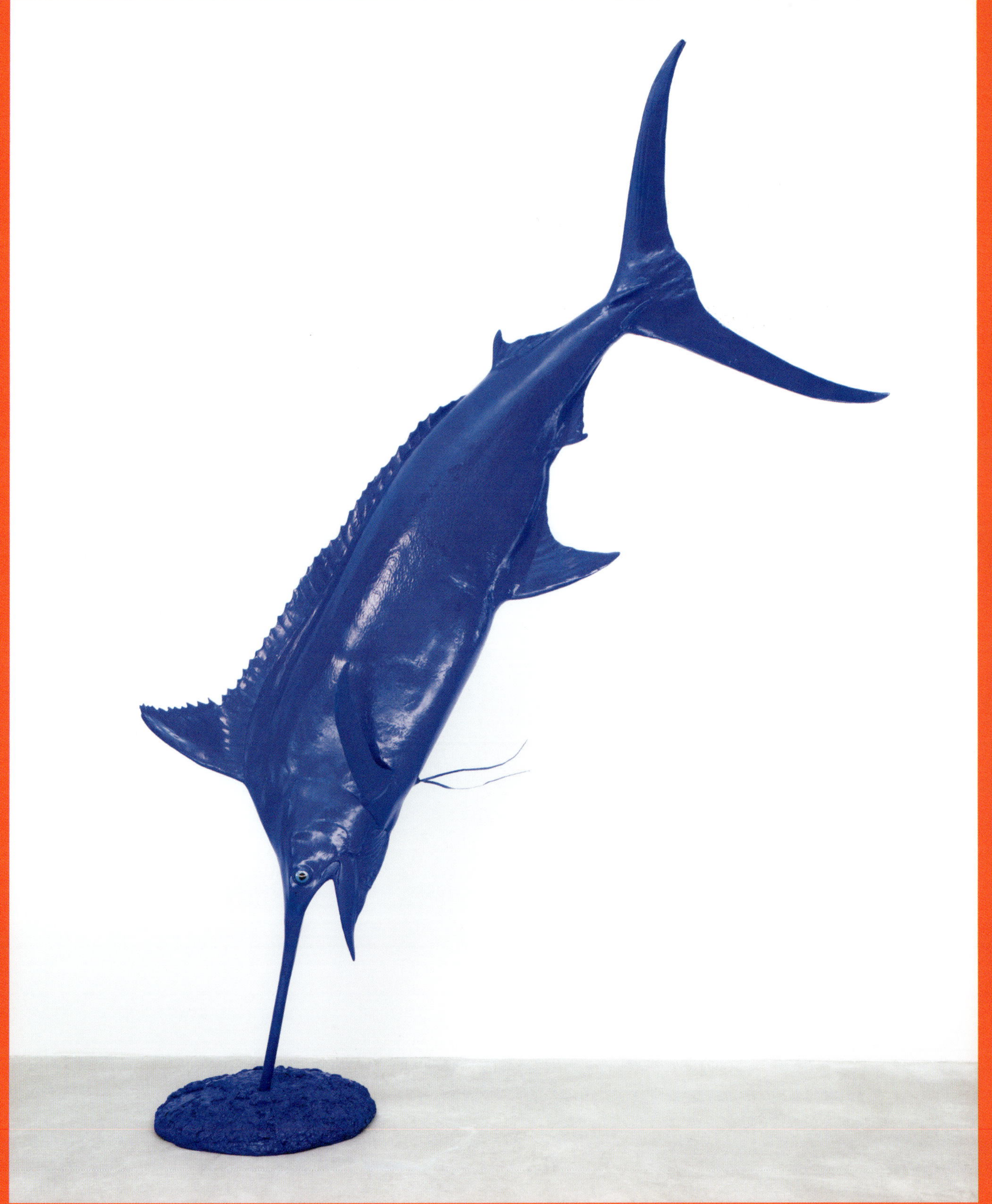

ROBERT TANNEN

←